About Island Press

Since 1984, the nonprofit organization Island Press has been stim-
ulating, shaping, and communicating ideas that are essential for
solving environmental problems worldwide. With more than 1,000
titles in print and some 30 new releases each year, we are the
nation's leading publisher on environmental issues. We identify
innovative thinkers and emerging trends in the environmental
field. We work with world-renowned experts and authors to
develop cross-disciplinary solutions to environmental challenges.

Island Press designs and executes educational campaigns, in
conjunction with our authors, to communicate their critical mes-
sages in print, in person, and online using the latest technologies,
innovative programs, and the media. Our goal is to reach targeted
audiences—scientists, policy makers, environmental advocates,
urban planners, the media, and concerned citizens—with information that can be used to create the framework for long-term
ecological health and human well-being.

Island Press gratefully acknowledges major support from The
Bobolink Foundation, Caldera Foundation, The Curtis and Edith
Munson Foundation, The Forrest C. and Frances H. Lattner Foundation,
The JPB Foundation, The Kresge Foundation, The Summit Charitable
Foundation, Inc., and many other generous organizations and indi-
viduals.

The opinions expressed in this book are those of the author(s)
and do not necessarily reflect the views of our supporters.

No Farms, No Food

No Farms, No Food

UNITING FARMERS AND ENVIRONMENTALISTS
TO TRANSFORM AMERICAN AGRICULTURE

Don Stuart

ISLANDPRESS | Washington | Covelo

Library of Congress Control Number: 2021942243

No Farms No Food® is a registered trademark of American Farmland Trust.

Manufactured in the United States of America
10 9 8 7 6 5 4 3 2 1

Keywords: Agricultural Conservation Easement Program (ACEP), agricultural easement, American Farmland Trust, Conservation Reserve Program (CRP), Douglas Wheeler, Farm Bill, farm debt, farm economic development, farm policy, farm subsidies, John Piotti, land conservation, land trust, land use planning, local food, PACE programs, Peggy Rockefeller, Ralph Grossi, soil conservation, sustainable farming

Give me a place to stand, and I shall move the world.
—Archimedes

Contents

Foreword

America has a uniquely large endowment of productive farmland and forestland. Americans are also uniquely accepting of development that involves the conversion or loss of even the most fertile agriculture. In periods of rapid economic growth and a high rate of home building, great swaths of exurban land and their crops fall to the bulldozer. As a result, vast acreages of serene and often beautiful countryside become re-envisioned as housing developments, streets, malls, and sprawl. The process has been viewed as progress for so long that attempts to understand the dynamic driving it—and raise questions about whether to embrace public policies to impose some order on it—are relatively recent.

The vision animating the creation of the American Farmland Trust (AFT) was largely that of Mrs. David Rockefeller—Peggy. She raised, bought, and sold cattle, and was an active participant and trader at cattle auctions in the West. She had observed with concern the transformation of pastures, green fields, forests, and open space, and it pained her to see changes in the scenic places familiar to her. And she considered herself a cattle farmer. I recall one balmy evening having dinner outdoors with her and her husband when she became distracted by a bellowing steer she took to be in distress. Peggy excused herself to check up on her animals.

With her inspiration, we filed articles of incorporation and began to assemble a board and staff. I was involved at the outset, owing to my interest and training in land use planning. I served at the time as president and CEO of the Conservation Foundation, which spearheaded this effort until AFT was organized as its own nonprofit. And then I served on AFT's board.

Like others concerned about agriculture and the environment, I found AFT's mission both ambitious and inspiring. Could we arrest some of the thoughtless discarding of the agriculture endowment under way throughout the more populous and growing regions of the country?

An important characteristic of American Farmland Trust, one recognized and respected by its first president, Douglas Wheeler, was collaboration. AFT embodied a passionate ambition that could be called environmental, but its drive was never animated by anger. Nor did it look to litigate over the loss of ecosystems. AFT established itself early on as a friend to the farmer and landowner. Some initial suspicion of yet another environmental crusader with an agenda adverse to farmers and obstructive of their freedom to sell or develop the family farm was alleviated as AFT began to offer its services, including its legal and tax counsel, to farmers who were concerned that estate taxes would make it impossible to keep the next generation on the farm.

AFT understood the dynamics of family farms and worked to accommodate the financial reality that land was often the principal or only asset capable of being monetized and supporting retirement. And so restrictive covenants and easements entailing permanent limitations on development rewarded with large savings in taxes became a familiar instrument of AFT's early work.

Today, thousands of completed deals catalyzed by AFT's work in all parts of the country are helping to stabilize land and natural systems.

Yet more than forty years since the founding of AFT, the challenges in dealing with farmers remain daunting. The farm population is aging, and the hurdles confronting younger cohorts interested in farming are formidable. We face continuing water quality impacts from the runoff of fertilizers and pesticides, which can lead to toxic algae blooms, as we saw in Lake Erie and continue to see in the Gulf of Mexico. Perhaps most challenging is the onset of climate change, upending weather patterns, bringing extreme weather events, droughts, flooding, wildfires, new pests and pathogens, and more. Planting and harvesting are obviously affected by the foregoing.

As I write this, farmers in Iowa are dealing with significant damage to corn and soy crops from a derecho with winds that swept through the Midwest at upwards of a hundred miles an hour. An estimated fourteen million acres have been affected, and the economic impacts are still being tallied.

As Robert Bonnie's research at Duke University has shown, rural Americans care deeply about where they live and their responsibility for land stewardship—and they are aware that climate change is under way. Yet rural residents are often mistrustful of mandates from Washington, as well as pronouncements from environmentalists. As we pursue climate-smart agriculture, policymakers, nongovernmental organizations (NGOs), and others must keep in mind not only ways to engage and work productively and cooperatively with these landowners and operators, but also the undeniable importance of the business model, the finances, that enable farmers and ranchers to continue providing food and fiber.

In other words, the current class of climate activists could learn a lesson or two from how AFT has approached its work over the years.

What do we need in this new era? Among the most important priorities is to build the resiliency of farms and ranches and forestlands in light of changing weather patterns, changing water patterns, wildfires, and comparable threats. As the owner of an Illinois grain farm, I can also say that there is an important task for a reinvigorated United States Department of Agriculture that advises on resilience and incorporates new knowledge and technology to protect and increase nutrients, conserve and improve soils. The movement toward regenerative agriculture advanced by AFT is both welcome and necessary.

In recent years, influential advocates of climate policies have pushed for forest management that entails the preservation of trees with no cutting. Such a policy ignores the fact that most American forestlands are privately owned. And it also ignores what we in California have learned through vast fires fueled by forests long allowed to accumulate saplings and dead trees. Forests need to be managed. When they are, as in the southeastern United States, they add annually to biomass.

Likewise, many advocates for climate policies have long mischaracterized the potential role of agriculture in climate change, seeing farmers only as generators of planet-warming emissions. But, due in part to the efforts of AFT, there is a growing appreciation of how regenerative farming practices can capture atmospheric carbon in the soil, offsetting greenhouse gas emissions. These beneficial practices range from use of cover crops to active rotations to intermixing trees with crops or pasture. Some draw on new research and technology, while others are traditional techniques that represent a return to the past.

I recall the hedgerows that in my boyhood served as the buffers to high winds. They had been planted to block a repeat of the Dust Bowl, when vast clouds of soil were blown away. They also were home to foxes, pheasants, and songbirds. Yet most of the old hedgerows are now gone, removed because they were seen as barriers to larger equipment, greater efficiency.

We need to plant more trees—just as the Trillion Trees initiative envisions. Trees are good for soil health, water resources, wildlife, the potential for new crops, shade for farm animals, and more.

We must also maintain and improve wetlands and buffer strips along waterways to benefit water quality and other ecological resources. In many states, as much as 90 percent of wetlands have been filled in and those that survive are doubly precious.

We need to learn about and take advantage of emerging crop species that offer benefits to water and soil management, to plant growth and nutrition, to protection against pathogens.

And we must continue to stem the loss of productive lands, the founding mission of AFT—and to support farmers and ranchers with the tools they need to steward their lands well, as AFT has worked to do for decades.

A tall agenda, for sure, and one, as noted, that must respect the financial viability of our farms and ranches. Meanwhile, the country is struggling to contain a pandemic and rebuild the economy. It will take the best efforts of all of us—political leaders, government at all levels, land grant universities and research institutions, NGOs, and, of course, landowners. Progress will take investments, grant and loan programs, innovative payment programs drawing on the insights and experiences of the natural capital movement.

I remain encouraged, even optimistic, for I see in our country's history a drive toward innovation, progress, success.

AFT's focus on farmland, farming practices, and farmers is essential. At stake is no less than our food and water security in the face of dramatic, potentially catastrophic weather patterns. We can and must rise to the occasion—as agriculture and its transformation must be central to America's future.

As it has for forty-plus years now, the American Farmland Trust has an outsized role to play in driving this transformation.

William K. Reilly—former US EPA administrator and president of the World Wildlife Fund; longtime AFT board member and past board chair
San Francisco, California
Fall 2020

CHAPTER 1
A Quiet Revolutionary

Not every big idea changes the world.

Seventy percent of small business start-ups are gone within a decade.[1] Of the ten million patents registered at the US Patent and Trademark Office, a vast majority have never been used.[2] For every book accepted in the United States by commercial publishers, perhaps a thousand are rejected.[3] Of the hundred thousand legislative bills introduced annually, under 4 percent become law.[4]

New nonprofits fare no better. Well over half are gone after five years.[5] And almost never does one go on to broadly influence the national debate.

No one knew those odds better than Peggy Rockefeller.

By 1980, Margaret McGrath Rockefeller had been active in national public affairs for most of her adult life.[6] Peggy was the wife of the legendary David Rockefeller, a global banker and highly visible public figure who was widely seen as the very embodiment of wealth and power in America. She was also a committed philanthropist and a member of several nonprofit and charitable foundation boards, including one created by the Rockefeller family itself. So when she first proposed a new national nonprofit organization to save the nation's farmland, she surely understood the challenges it would face.

In the years leading up to 1980, Peggy had acquired a deep appreciation for agriculture. The Rockefeller family owned working farms in New York, California, Massachusetts, and Maine—serious commercial enterprises all. Peggy could frequently be found at one of these farms, delivering calves, driving a tractor, or building fences. "She could muck out a barn with the best of them," said a family staffer. She was sufficiently involved in farming that she took time out from an incredibly busy schedule to complete a course at the University of Pennsylvania's School of Veterinary Medicine on how to artificially inseminate cattle.[7]

The Rockefeller family's farms, especially those in New York's Hudson Valley, were in areas often highly vulnerable to suburban development, where sprawl from nearby population centers was pricing the land well out of reach for most working farm businesses. It was increasingly evident to Mrs. Rockefeller and to her farming neighbors that, when the next local farm sold, it would probably end up in development. Like it or not, everywhere you looked, farms were becoming strip malls, factories, apartments, and housing developments.

Of course, the Rockefellers could protect their own properties from that fate by donating and recording conservation easements that prevented their future development. And they did. They placed agricultural conservation easements on some 2,500 acres of their family's land, easements also specifying that these farms were to be environmentally responsible and would be managed under conservation practices approved by the USDA Soil Conservation Service.[8]

Yet few if any other working farmers were in a financial position to donate an easement—doing so would significantly reduce the value of their property. Many of these farmers had substantial debt. Even if they had built up enough equity so the bank would allow them to donate such an easement, and even if their farms were currently profitable, agriculture was a risky business. Who knew what the next season might bring? Their farms represented most of what they owned: their life savings and their only source of retirement income. How could they afford to give up so much?

Peggy Rockefeller knew these people. They had long histories on their land and a powerful sense of place. Their identities were inexorably tied to their farms and to the communities where they lived. They'd spent their lives laboring to develop farm businesses by understanding everything there was to know about their specific pieces of land. Selling to a developer would mark the end of what was often several generations of commitment by their forebears. For them to watch that heritage farm be converted into a strip mall or suburban estates was nothing short of a personal and family tragedy.

But for many of them, that outcome was unavoidable. While the approaching suburban sprawl was unwelcome, it offered their only realistic endgame. With their entire savings tied up in their farms, selling was their only real path to retirement. Even if they stuck it out and kept the land, could they count on (or should they even ask) their children to maintain the farm? These were kids who'd often moved away to the city, perhaps even at the urging of their parents, who themselves saw little future in farming. Selling felt like selling out, but what choice did they have?

They needed an alternative.

Beneath the sheen of the Rockefeller name, Peggy was a quiet advocate. Ever humble, she advanced her cause with calm, reasoning with her opponents rather than trying to defeat them. She had robust, well-considered opinions tempered by common sense and political wisdom. It was a mix that made her very effective.

In a 1994 American Farmland Trust board meeting, for example, a discussion was under way about the Walt Disney Company's plans to build a huge theme park on historic farmland in Northern Virginia. Peggy Rockefeller, then seventy-nine years old, had, thus far in the conversation, said nothing. But she had obviously been listening. Finally, when the room momentarily fell silent, this aging envoy from high society spoke: "I'll go out there myself and picket, if necessary," she said.

This was the woman who proposed creating American Farmland Trust (AFT).

The Early Vision

It's hard to know exactly what she or any of AFT's early founders truly anticipated for the future of their new organization at its inception. Obviously, it was to be a national farmland trust. And they certainly knew it would work in federal public policy. Given the influence of the nation's agriculture industry, the only conceivable path to policy success would have to be through coalitions with farm groups.

The new organization's ultimate environmental mission was murkier. Environmental activists were already changing the world of agriculture— very often by working counter to the nation's farmers.[9] But given AFT's early goals, while Peggy Rockefeller may have seen the need for farmer–environmentalist mediation, it seems unlikely that she and the rest of the founders fully appreciated how vital that role would become in the years ahead.

As they saw it, American Farmland Trust would be a national land trust focused on protecting agricultural lands. It would hold agricultural easements, particularly in the many regions not then served by land trusts with knowledge of farmland—which, in 1980, was most of the country. It would support and encourage state and local government programs that purchased agricultural easements. And it would pursue federal policies that supported the protection of farmland. Soil conservation certainly seems also to have been an early objective.

But a role in helping farmers protect the broader environment was considerably less clear. And building bridges between farmers and environmentalists on land use and environmental issues may not have been considered at all.

An Unlikely Mission

If finding common ground between farmers and environmentalists had been anticipated as a central objective, it seems highly unlikely that American Farmland Trust would ever have been formed.

For one thing, the obstacles to farmer–environmentalist reconciliation were enormous. Success would require that the new organization scrupulously till the center of the political field. It would have to cultivate partners on both sides of the farm–environmental divide and both sides of the political spectrum. It would need to value consensus and avoid conflict.

The often-blistering confrontation between the nation's farm and environmental communities was driven by disagreements about key issues such as land use planning, water quality, soil erosion, wildlife habitat, and toxic chemicals. Farmers managed over half the total American land base, and farming profoundly affected that land in ways that made environmental impacts inevitable. Meanwhile, the farm owners struggled to earn a living in one of the most precarious, stressful,[10] and competitive enterprises on the planet. The farm–environmental debate crossed cultural chasms between urban and rural, professional and entrepreneurial, liberal and conservative. And it fed on fundamental differences in human values like respect for the past versus concern for the future, free choice versus social responsibility, science versus life experience, the intellectual versus the emotional.

Overcoming these divides was made ever thornier by the practical realities of funding an advocacy organization. It was common understanding in 1980, as today, that the way to raise money for nonprofit policy advocacy is to fuel our worst fears and arouse our deepest biases.

If I'm an environmentalist and I am told that socially irresponsible farmers who care nothing about the environment are polluting our rivers, destroying habitat, endangering wildlife, fueling climate change, and placing the future of our planet at risk, of course I'll chip in to make them stop. If I'm a farmer and I'm told that environmentalists who care nothing about agriculture and know nothing about the way I farm are demanding ridiculous rules that will drive me and my neighbors out of business, putting at risk the struggling farm started by my great-grandfather, which I hope to pass down to my children—all to solve problems that either don't exist or were caused by others—of course I'll do everything I can to resist them.

These are clearly vast oversimplifications. But who would donate to an organization that claimed to bring these two hopelessly alienated groups *together*? Had Peggy Rockefeller recognized how central consensus building would become to ATF's success, she might have had second thoughts.

Instead, she launched a more-than-forty-year endeavor that has turned a small, little-known group of center-of-the-field activists into a national force on agriculture and the environment.

CHAPTER 2
A Changing Landscape

The year was 1980. With the Vietnam War over, the Cold War sputtering to a close, and the Gulf War still a decade away, America was struggling to redefine itself. On the heels of historic inflation, an unprecedented embargo that produced a huge global spike in the price of oil, Soviet aggression in Afghanistan, and a humiliating hostage crisis in Iran, Americans turned the US Senate over to Republicans for the first time since 1954. And they awarded the presidency to an elderly, well-spoken, comfortably conservative cowboy movie star by the name of Ronald Reagan.

So it was a time of peace but also a time of unsettling public events and shifting politics. In the midst of that upheaval, even a close political observer might have overlooked agriculture as a defining issue. Peggy Rockefeller and the small group she'd enlisted to her cause did not. She and her fellow founders sensed the need to transform the way the country farmed.

That change had already begun with an amazing body of environmental law that had passed the US Congress over the previous decade. In the aftermath of the 1960s and in the wake of the first Earth Day in 1970, Congress and the Nixon presidency created the Environmental

Protection Agency. They then followed up with a decade of environmental legislation the likes of which had never occurred before and has not been repeated since. New legislation passed dealing with water quality, air quality, endangered species, marine mammals, toxic substances, and a host of other environmental threats.[1]

With farmers owning and managing half the nation's land, it seemed obvious that they would be affected by these new laws. And it was inevitable that they would worry about the threat these laws seemed to pose to the already-risky business of agriculture.

Emerging Land Use and Property Rights Movements

While all this was happening, a new "smart growth" movement was also emerging.[2] Its proponents aimed to make cities more efficient and livable and to protect their surrounding environment by concentrating development. The economy was booming, cities were growing, and land in the path of urban growth was, of course, quickly increasing in market value. Much of that land—especially that which was flat, accessible, and easily developed—was agricultural.

The farmers who owned that land mostly wanted to continue farming. But they were unlikely to object when, for whatever reasons, their land increased in value. Predictably, farmers feared new zoning laws that might dramatically devalue their property by restricting future opportunities to develop it, however speculative those prospects might be.

One might think that was greedy of them. But Peggy Rockefeller and her colleagues knew that the net worth of nearly all those farmers (and their families) was tied up in the value of their land. They were often also in debt that had been extended, in part, based on the land's value.[3] And their success often depended on future lending.[4] Newly proposed zoning laws could suddenly place that value at risk.

The idea of growth management was relatively new in spacious, sprawling America. It was only natural that farmers would resist it and that, in response, a vigorous new, mostly rural, property rights movement would also take root, a movement that aimed to protect private lands and insisted on compensation for reductions in property value resulting from "regulatory takings."[5]

The Law of Conservation Easements

Closely linked to the new smart growth and environmental movements, another, less public, development was taking place in 1980: a change in the law of conservation easements.[6] In most places in the country, landowners were allowed to use long-standing real property easement law to set aside a limited ownership interest in their land, an interest that would protect from future destruction certain environmental and other public benefits provided by their land. These were called conservation easements. Land under a conservation easement remained in private ownership. But through such an easement, the owner could convey certain specific property rights to another party in a way that would, in effect, extinguish those rights. By this means, one could prevent future development and protect natural values provided by that undeveloped land—values like wildlife habitat, water quality, or open space. Or, in the case of an agricultural easement, one could protect the land for farming. The easement interest would then be held by some secure agency or institution organized for the purpose of making sure it was honored. Very often that agent would be a land trust.

In 1980, however, conservation easement law was not well settled. It differed from state to state. Such transactions were often uncertain. Generally, conservation easements were used to protect in perpetuity, environmental values like wild streams, wetlands, forests, and wildlife. Securing protection nearly always required that the landowner make a gift of the easement as a donation to a government entity or, more commonly, a nonprofit land trust that would hold it in the public interest. At that time, these gifts were not eligible for a charitable deduction under the rules of the Internal Revenue Service. And there were few appropriate land trusts to receive and hold them.

Not surprisingly, conservation easements were rare.[7]

In 1979, however, the national Uniform Law Commission (ULC) had begun work on a proposed uniform state law that could regularize the law of conservation easements. The ULC proposal was offered publicly in 1981, and at about that same time, the IRS adopted rules allowing the charitable deduction. Ultimately, some twenty-five states adopted the ULC proposal.[8]

Evolution of Land Trusts

Following the new ULC-inspired state laws, and with congressional action in 1980 and an ensuing IRS ruling approving the deductibility of conservation easements,[9] they exploded across the country. There was a matching explosion of private land trusts.[10]

Land trusts had existed for generations. But in 1980, those organizations were relatively rare. Today there are more than 1,400 land trusts operating in every state in the country. As of 2015, some fifty-six million acres of land had been protected by land trusts alone in what is surely one of the ongoing environmental revolutions of our day.[11]

Yet, at the time of American Farmland Trust's formation, there were far fewer land trusts and only a handful with any interest or experience in agriculture.

Sadly, the protection of agricultural lands with conservation easements was *not* included in the IRS-approved charitable deduction. Even if a farmer had the wherewithal and desire to make such a contribution, there was no federal tax incentive to do so. Few land trusts were interested in holding such an easement. And how many farm families could afford to make such a donation, in any case?

A few local communities were beginning to experiment with buying agricultural conservation easements from willing farmers at market value.[12] But the idea was new and largely untested. Mostly, the only way to prevent development of vulnerable farmland that was increasingly within reach of urban commuters was to restrict its subdivision through zoning ordinances. The financial cost came entirely out of the farmer-landowner's pocket. It was an appealing solution to farmland loss—but one that understandably, made many farm landowners very nervous.

A Globalizing Marketplace

All these changes came on the heels of a dramatic expansion in markets for American farm products. After World War II, new methods of food processing, packaging, refrigeration, and shipping overhauled the food system. By 1950, more than 80 percent of American farms and more than 90 percent of urban homes had a refrigerator.[13] People could now buy and keep food that was processed, refrigerated, or even frozen, and for long periods of time. Meanwhile, the invention of the modern standardized shipping container allowed the seamless transfer of cargo between ship and truck and railcar.[14] By 1970, shipping giant SeaLand had thirty-six container ships and twenty-seven thousand containers serving upwards of thirty American ports, and that was only the start.[15]

By the time of AFT's birth, a decade later, container shipping and refrigeration were dramatically increasing international trade.[16] Combine this with the post–World War II economic boom and adoption of the new General Agreement on Tariffs and Trade,[17] and it is clear that American farmers of the early 1980s needed to operate very differently from even twenty or thirty years earlier. They faced what was becoming a truly global marketplace for nearly every farm product.

A Relentless Reliance on Credit

It was during this time that it became commonplace to hear the refrain: "American farmers feed the world."[18] But consider what had made that possible.

With the postwar transformation in international trade, American farmers were now in direct competition with international agribusiness everywhere. This competition now affected nearly every farm product—not solely the traditional dry bulk commodities like corn, wheat, soy, cotton, and sugar.

In this new international marketplace, Americans faced some big disadvantages. Farm labor was costly in America. There arose a heavy dependence on migrants, a workforce that, because of our country's sometimes equivocal perspective on immigration law, was not always consistently available.

American farmers were also blessed with some very big advantages. They had easy access to advanced farming technology, which could replace hand labor. They had an educated workforce, costly but useful for the operation, maintenance, and application of all that technology. They were also able to draw upon the products and infrastructure supporting the increasingly widespread use of chemical pesticides,[19] which could be costly but drove dramatic increases in farm productivity.[20] A new, federally funded, interstate highway transportation system was making it easier for farmers to get their crops to market.[21]

And, of course, there was lots of highly productive farmland.

Perhaps as important as anything else: our farmers lived in a democratic country. Their government provided the political stability needed for a sound, dependable economy and offered a secure legal framework for business and lending. They had, therefore, relatively easy access to inexpensive capital, a critical consideration given their need for technology and its ever-rising price tag.

Unsurprisingly, farm debt in the United States was spiking,[22] a situation that would, by the mid-1980s, lead to an all-time historic collapse in the American farm economy.[23]

Disappearing Land and Farmers

As late as 1900, farmers represented 40 percent of the US population.[24] A mere eighty years later, that had fallen to under 3 percent.[25] In 1945, there were about seven million farms in the United States. By 1982, there were only about two million.[26] Some of this change represented business consolidation. Much of it was the result of increasing productivity. We were seeing a new American agriculture that was bigger, highly efficient, highly technical, much more specialized and industrial. And heavily dependent on credit.

Farm debt is almost always secured by farmland; a debt crisis is also a land crisis. It seems natural that national concerns about the environment and urban sprawl, and the apparent threat of regulatory approaches to addressing these concerns, would be met by the farm community with grave skepticism. In 1980, much of that anxiety was driven by a disruption in the permanence of the land and in the security of our connections to it.

All these far-reaching developments were no laughing matter for American farmers. The sweeping federal "conservation cost share" incentives programs that we know today did not exist. For the most part, it looked as though farmers might end up being required, by regulation, to adopt costly new management practices, build expensive new farm infrastructure that would enhance the environment, and address huge nationwide land use problems for which they were, at most, only partly responsible. There was little real prospect of financial help.

In the midst of shifts in the legal, environmental, economic, cultural, and agricultural landscapes and the political turmoil they produced, people like Peggy Rockefeller and AFT's other early founders started looking for answers in the "middle ground."[27]

CHAPTER 3
An Idea Whose Time Had Come

In 1974, James M. Jeffords was a newly elected Republican member of the US House of Representatives from Vermont. The charismatic Jim Jeffords was one of those "moderates" who are so difficult to find in politics today; he later left the Republican Party and became an Independent.[1] Representative Jeffords came up through the public schools but was also a Yale graduate and Harvard-educated lawyer. And he was a creative thinker, a man willing to step beyond party and tradition in the search for workable solutions to public problems.

One of those problems was farmland loss. And one of his solutions turned out to be public programs to protect that land by purchasing its development rights. These would later come to be known as PDR programs or purchase of agricultural conservation easement (PACE) programs.[2]

The Oil Embargo

It all may have started with the infamous 1973 Arab oil embargo.[3] One of the miscellaneous side effects of the embargo was that, in some places in the country, regular food supplies were interrupted by the scarcity of diesel to fuel delivery trucks. Some of the areas hardest hit were in New England, which lay at one of the tail ends of the national food supply network.

People were worried. Supermarket shelves in parts of the Northeast were only half full. People were asking themselves how their communities, often ones with deep historic agricultural roots, could have lost their food self-sufficiency. This all coincided with the loss of historic New England landscapes to a rapidly accelerating urban and suburban sprawl that seemed to be creeping northward from massive urban centers in New York and Massachusetts.

Soon after taking federal office in 1975, Representative Jeffords proposed a creative new way to address this problem. He suggested a new federal program to help local communities around the country purchase, at market value from willing farmers, agricultural conservation easements that would reimburse these farmers for extinguishing their development rights. This would enable farmers to cash out much of the value of their farmland without actually selling it—thus keeping the land in private hands and in working agriculture.[4]

It was a groundbreaking idea. Conservation easements, generally, were in very limited use at the time. And few people had even heard of *agricultural* conservation easements. Jeffords was, no doubt, aware of a similar county-level program that had been proposed in 1974 for Suffolk County, New York, by a Republican county executive by the name of John Klein. Suffolk County, out on eastern Long Island, was a rural agricultural area under major threat from New York City's sprawl.[5] And it wouldn't be long before other local government easement programs would begin emerging in places as far apart as Lancaster County, Pennsylvania,[6] and King County in Washington State;[7] the first private farmland trusts would appear, such as the Marin Agricultural Land Trust in Northern California;[8] and the first state program would start up in nearby Massachusetts.[9]

A Policy Struggle

Jeffords's bill struggled in Congress. But Jeffords himself was in this fight for the long haul. In 1979, Peggy Rockefeller, who wanted to replicate the Suffolk County proposal asked Thomas Wahman, a program manager at the Rockefeller Brothers Fund (RBF), to investigate what else could be done to address farmland loss. Among Wahman's recommendations was that RBF consider making a grant to a private organization that could study this issue and that, specifically, could provide public education to encourage passage of the Jeffords bill in Congress.[10]

At Peggy Rockefeller's urging, RBF did make such a grant. It went to the National Association of County Officials (NACO), whose president was none other than John Klein from Suffolk County, New York, the moderate Republican who had advanced a new county-level agricultural easement purchase program.

NACO set up a separate organization called the NACO Research Foundation, which accepted and managed the RBF grant for its intended research and public education purposes.

A young environmental activist lawyer by the name of Edward Thompson was hired to manage the project.[11] Ed assembled the research, developed and published public education materials, solicited media, and held public information seminars around the country to support and advance the Jeffords legislation. Thompson worked with a Jeffords staffer, Robert Gray, to coordinate his efforts and to build a political coalition to pass the bill.

The National Agricultural Lands Study

Meanwhile, Representative Jeffords had other tricks up his sleeve. Earlier, he had also convinced the United States Department of Agriculture and the President's Council on Environmental Quality to undertake a national study of farmland loss—what would become the National Agricultural Lands Study (NALS). The study would be headed up by Bob Gray,[12] the same Jeffords's aide who was coordinating with Ed Thompson over at NACO.

The official NALS study later reached a startling conclusion: some three million acres of American farmland were being converted, every year, to nonagricultural uses, a land use conversion that was, in the words of the study, "for all practical purposes . . . irreversible."[13]

The NALS may have been bipartisan, but some came to view the entire study as a part of the "liberal environmental agenda" of the Democratic Carter administration. President Carter, himself a farmer, might have been perceived to have a special interest in the matter. When Ronald Reagan was elected in November of 1980, there were grave concerns that the upcoming report would be buried once he came into office on January 20, 1981. Bob Gray pulled out the stops to get it published in January 1981, just prior to President Reagan's inauguration.

CHAPTER 4
The Big Ask

Patrick Noonan had a problem.

He was president and CEO of the Nature Conservancy (TNC) and had led an astounding spurt in growth over the previous seven years, making TNC one of the preeminent environmental organizations in America.[1] The very last thing he wanted was to place all of that at risk.

But in 1979, a key member of Noonan's board of directors approached him with an unusual request.[2] The member in question was the hugely influential Peggy Rockefeller, someone of inestimable value to his organization. What she wanted was for TNC to take on a whole new area of responsibility: to protect and conserve America's working farmland. Probably the second-to-last thing Noonan would have wanted was to disappoint Peggy Rockefeller. But he didn't see how he could avoid it.

Noonan's formula for TNC's success had been to make the organization less opportunistic and give it a laser focus on protecting biodiversity and endangered wildlife. He wanted TNC protecting the most threatened, environmentally complex, and productive natural places on earth, what they would later come to call "the last great places."

To now begin protecting less pristine properties like active working farms would badly dilute that focus. And that wasn't the only problem.

Protecting private farms would inevitably require working with both the agriculture industry and the growing smart growth community. That alone was a daunting challenge. But even more worrisome was how it might be seen by TNC's existing members and funders.

Many members, and the charitable foundations that supported the organization's work, contributed to TNC largely because they expected TNC to fight the good fight for the environment. Many of them saw farms and farmers as a part of "the problem." How would those members react when they learned that TNC was suddenly collaborating with the very same people who had been their bitter opponents?

It didn't end there. TNC was an environmental group. Its board and staff were environmental leaders and professionals. The proposed new direction would demand acquiring an entirely new expertise in agriculture. They'd need to hire new staff with different backgrounds and priorities, with the expertise and inclination to appreciate the needs of farmers, as well as the credibility to work with the organizations that represent them, groups like the Farm Bureau. Given TNC's environmental roots, would farmers ever come to trust the organization and be willing to work with it? Peggy Rockefeller's proposal might also require new leaders on TNC's board, people with strong backgrounds in agriculture who could provide the needed leadership and guidance. They'd need to develop new funders, new members, and a new network of coalition partners who cared about this work.

And there was also the deep uncertainty over whether collaboration between farmers and smart growth activists was even vaguely possible.

It was a very big ask. In the end, it was just too big for Noonan or his TNC board members to accept.

A Search for Alternatives

What Peggy Rockefeller wanted to accomplish made a lot of sense, however. Noonan was convinced that it was an important step. So he offered his personal help, and she took him up on it. Among other things, Noonan suggested that they might canvass other national organizations to find one that might be more able to take it on. Together, the pair made a formidable team. Undeterred by TNC's denial, Rockefeller and Noonan turned for help to William Dietel, the executive vice president of the Rockefeller Brothers Fund; Tom Wahman, the RBF program officer; and Doug Wheeler, executive director of the National Trust for Historic Preservation.

Noonan, Dietel, Wahman, and Wheeler made extensive inquiries nationwide. Despite a concerted effort, they were unable to come up with a likely and willing group. Whether a group's current focus was on agriculture or environmental issues, none could take on this new role without disrupting current programs and priorities and unsettling a good part of its present membership and funder base.

In the end, the only reasonable approach to the problem was to form an entirely new organization, a group whose sole mission would be preserving agriculture and protecting agricultural lands. Peggy Rockefeller, Pat Noonan, Bill Dietel, and Doug Wheeler ultimately teamed up to do just that.

Out of this collaboration was born American Farmland Trust.

CHAPTER 5
Beginning the Journey

In looking at the people who joined the American Farmland Trust effort and committed themselves in a lasting way, it's worth asking what drew them to the cause and kept them involved. Much of the answer has to do with AFT's mission and the critical need to protect farmland.

The first major challenge facing AFT's initial founders (Rockefeller, Noonan, Dietel, and Wheeler) was to enlist a board of directors. They needed people with impressive credentials in agriculture, land protection, and farm conservation management. They needed people with the experience and wisdom to quickly launch the new group on solid financial and political ground. But more than any of that, they needed people who would be personally committed to the organization's long-term success. A tall order.

Identifying and then persuading such candidates depended on the significance of the organization's goals. For AFT, it all began with the name: American Farmland Trust. The initial concept was that AFT would serve as a national agricultural land trust—a "Nature Conservancy for agriculture," as Peggy Rockefeller sometimes referred to it.[1]

This was only logical. A national farmland trust could find and hold agricultural easements in places where local land trusts were unavailable or uninterested; at the time, that was almost everywhere.

Given the founders' concerns about sprawling development and the sweeping findings of the National Agricultural Lands Study, they also saw an inevitable role for AFT in public policy, federally as well as locally.[2] Rep. Jim Jeffords's bill in Congress featured significantly in their worldview. And that bill was specifically designed to provide federal financial support for local purchase of agricultural conservation easement (PACE) programs all around the country. AFT could also support local farmland conservation efforts by providing technical assistance and policy help to local land trusts, farmland protection groups, and government programs protecting farmland. Certainly, they saw all that work as achievable only through collaboration with farm groups and nonfarm interest groups.[3] This would require working in the middle ground.

That was the extent of the initial AFT vision. Protection for the farmer and the farm business might have seemed an implicit goal. But even a year later, in 1981, Doug Wheeler mentioned only in passing that the farmer was essential to the existence of farmland. He said nothing specific, however, about a role for AFT in making farming more economically viable. While he referred to the preservation of farm natural resources (presumably productive soil, irrigation water, and the like), he never discussed the broader environment or how AFT might help agriculture become more sustainable.

All of that would come later.

Building an Initial Board

Armed with their mission, the founders' next question was: Who would help advance it? Doug Wheeler became the first staff hire: president and CEO. The participation of Peggy Rockefeller, the driving force behind the whole effort, was, of course, a given.

The organization also needed a strong board. One of the first people the group approached was Frederic Winthrop, Commissioner of the Massachusetts Department of Food and Agriculture. In the early 1970s, as a private citizen, Fred had led a Massachusetts grassroots political effort that produced one of the nation's earliest "current use taxation" programs for agriculture.[4] That public campaign brought him to the attention of the Massachusetts governor, who appointed Winthrop as agriculture commissioner. From that position, Winthrop then led a further campaign that produced the nation's first state-level purchase of development rights program in 1977.[5]

Winthrop was a friend of Pat Noonan's and well known to Peggy Rockefeller. He was also a respected Massachusetts farmer who had grown up on his family's multigenerational dairy. A direct descendant of John Winthrop, leader of the Puritan pioneers who founded the Massachusetts Bay Colony in 1630, Fred had a deep family connection to the land. And, given his position, background, progressive leanings, and political experience, he was a natural choice for AFT's founding board. He became its second official board member after Peggy Rockefeller.

In making their earlier canvass of potentially interested nonprofit groups, Doug Wheeler, Tom Wahman, and Bill Dietel had identified local organizations throughout the country that were engaged in work related to farmland protection. That research now helped them identify potential members for the new AFT board. One of the groups they'd found in their canvass was the newly formed Marin Agricultural Land Trust (MALT),[6] located in California, north of San Francisco. MALT had a young, charismatic leader, a progressive dairy farmer by the name of Ralph Grossi.[7]

It helped that Grossi was already active in protecting agricultural lands at the local level. Another plus: he was a westerner and from the state of California, a serious heavyweight in American agriculture. But the founders also recognized something else. They knew how important

it was that Grossi was a genuine commercial farmer, a member and former elected president of his local Farm Bureau, and a man respected
by his farmer peers. As Fred Winthrop, himself a farmer, expressed it,
the new board needed more "real farmers—and preferably not from
the Northeast."[8] Grossi became the third founding member of the
AFT board.

The next board member was Father A. J. McKnight, a respected civil
rights activist with the Southern Cooperative Development Fund, who
was deeply concerned about the overwhelming barriers to Black farm
ownership in the South. AFT's initial work may have disappointed
Father McKnight; he left after less than a year. But his invitation to
join the board suggests a hopeful breadth to the founders' vision. Father
McKnight's concerns about limited Black farm ownership are as relevant today as they were then.[9]

Another key addition was William Reilly, a former staffer at the President's Council on Environmental Quality who would later serve as
administrator of the US Environmental Protection Agency (1989–93).
At the time, Bill was president of the Conservation Foundation.[10]

AFT's board soon added Robert Chinn, a former Ford Motor Company executive who was by then a senior vice president with Control
Data Corporation, a tech firm, and was working in the Caribbean on
international small business development, which included small farms.

The new board also included Mrs. William Hewitt: Patricia was a
long-distance horse rider and jumping trainer, photographer, philanthropist, and direct descendant of the legendary John Deere. Patricia's
husband was CEO of John Deere Corporation.

Although Pat Noonan did not join the initial AFT board, he agreed
to chair an influential AFT Advisory Committee that included Thomas
McCall, a former governor of the state of Oregon and the leading force
behind the passage of Oregon's revolutionary statewide Land Use Management Law.[11] This committee also later included Norm Berg, a former

chief of the US Soil Conservation Service who would ultimately become a pivotal employee of the new organization.

With their initial board, AFT's founders had done well. But it was the members' lasting engagement that allowed the organization to develop strength and influence. No fewer than fifty of the ninety-four AFT board members who have worked with the organization since 1980 served for at least eight years. That's an unusual record of stability for any nonprofit.

That stability derives in part from the nature of agriculture itself; farming is, after all, an occupation that closely binds farmers, both practically and emotionally, to the land and to their community. AFT is all about protecting that land. Its board members' participation undoubtedly reflects that deep connection to the land. Their AFT affiliation is closely linked to their role as its stewards.

CHAPTER 6
A New Voice in American Farm Policy

Over the half century that followed the Dust Bowl and the economic catastrophe of the 1930s, federal farm policy had been taken firmly in hand by the farm industry itself. The US farm bill had mostly become a vehicle for delivering public support to the farm industry, largely in the form of huge farm subsidies. Congressional debate was driven by a powerful farm lobby led by industry trade groups like the Farm Bureau and the trade associations that represented the major commodity crops receiving those subsidies.

When Peggy Rockefeller and American Farmland Trust's early founders first came up with the idea of AFT, what they had in mind was an important but distinctly limited mission.[1] Yet a mere five years later, their tiny new organization had suddenly become a key player in, and the farm bill had become an important instrument of, the nation's environmental policy.

Much of what happened in those first five years was directed by AFT's first president and CEO, Douglas Wheeler. In 1980, Wheeler was executive director of the National Trust for Historic Preservation, a group that preserves the nation's threatened historic places. He had a slew of accomplishments in public advocacy and organization management; he knew the nonprofit world well. And, of course, he'd been closely involved with the formation of American Farmland Trust from the moment of its inception.

Doug Wheeler was then thirty-nine years of age and ready for a new challenge. He strongly believed in AFT's objectives. And he had to be impressed with the energy of Peggy Rockefeller and Pat Noonan. Still, he must also have understood the challenges ahead and realized that the chances were high the whole enterprise could end in failure. Yet he decided to go for it.

Wheeler and his new board knew from the start that protecting America's farms simply couldn't happen without the willing participation of the farmers who owned them. They also knew that if our nation's farms were to be protected, the work could not be done by farmers alone; they'd need help from other interested groups. They'd need support from farm groups, of course. But this work also needed to include the smart growth advocates who wanted to prevent sprawling development, and the environmental groups who could appreciate that farmland provided open space, wildlife habitat, water recharge, and other benefits. Thus, the political conundrum: How could AFT enlist broad, enthusiastic environmental community support for farmland protection while also securing willing and active farmer participation?

When Wheeler submitted the organization's first annual report in 1981, just one year after he took the job, AFT was still mostly a national land trust. But by the time he left in 1985, AFT was orchestrating a coalition that would, soon after, create the nation's first farm bill Conservation title and launch one of the most important environmental programs in the nation's history.[2] The 1985 Farm Bill would move well beyond simple soil conservation. It reshaped the relationship between American agriculture and the broader environment.

The Farmland Protection Toolkit

Wheeler and the founding board understood their options well. If their broad objective was to protect farmland from being lost to development, there was only a short list of ways to go about it—at least directly:[3]

Charitable easement acquisitions. AFT could find, acquire, and hold charitably donated agricultural easements after the fashion of a traditional land trust, albeit one operating at the national level and tailoring easements to work for agriculture. It could also raise charitable money to purchase easements from interested farmers. This work could be advanced by supporting local land trusts that were open to doing the same, and by choosing and publicizing AFT's own land acquisitions as demonstrations of what was possible.

PACE programs. AFT could foster publicly funded purchase of agricultural conservation easement (PACE) programs through local, state, and federal government agencies, along the lines proposed in the Jeffords legislation and in Massachusetts; Suffolk County, New York; and a small sprinkling of other progressive local communities around the country.

Growth management. AFT could enter the robust new smart growth arena, advocating for local zoning and state land use management laws similar to the one that had been recently put in place statewide in Oregon. This straightforward approach could simply prohibit nonagricultural use of critically valuable privately owned farmlands.

Farm economic development. AFT could strengthen farm business profitability so farm owners could more successfully compete in the free market for farmland.

If you scan down this list of options, a few points are worth highlighting: (1) Some of these approaches might be quite appealing to one side in any hoped-for farmer–environmental coalition but hugely unpopular with the other. (2) Some of these approaches, while certainly useful, offer a good deal less sweeping leverage than others; some would provide only minimal help at best, given the massive market forces driving the problem. (3) Of these approaches, the one that seemed most likely to appeal to both sides while offering significant scale were it implemented on a national level was the creation of publicly funded PACE programs—it could be expensive,[4] but it could work. (4) To make publicly funded PACE programs succeed would call for a massive effort in the public policy arena.

The Shift to a Public Policy Agenda

During those first five formative years, Doug Wheeler and his board soon came to appreciate the limits they faced. As a land trust, AFT was committed to undertaking direct land protection projects, usually gifts from committed farmers. These projects were essential to demonstrating what was possible and to engaging the public in the AFT mission. But the board also realized that it needed to do more. Protecting farms one at a time with hard-to-find donated funds or patiently awaiting charitable gifts of land or easements was painfully slow. And strategizing the process was very difficult to boot. AFT could leverage this work by proselytizing, educating, and supporting the broader national land trust community. But it was still hard to see how traditional land trust work could be ramped up quickly and dramatically enough to truly address the grave national scale of the problem.

Given those challenges, it is probably no surprise that AFT was soon directing its attention to goals that could be achieved through public policy.[5] The organization also recognized that the only way to succeed with an ambitious policy agenda was to build the broadest possible political coalition, a coalition that must, inevitably, include the smart growth and environmental communities.

A Different Way of Thinking

A focus on policy collaboration can require a shift in thinking. The political arena seems composed of winners and losers, a field of constant battle. Like good trial lawyers, capable public policy advocates can come to see their job as one of assembling their arguments, mustering their forces, and launching into battle.

Our normal democratic legislative process can encourage this combative way of thinking. It is typically quite easy to stop new legislation and quite difficult to pass it. A bill can be stopped if leadership assigns it to a dead-end committee. It can be stopped by a single committee chair who decides not to hear it. It can be stopped by a vote on referral in any one of several committees through which it must pass. It can be unfavorably scheduled for a floor vote. Or it can lose that vote. Should a bill actually pass one legislative chamber, the process starts all over in the other. Even if it passes both House and Senate, it is still vulnerable to a presidential veto.

To pass a bill, ultimately hundreds of members of a legislative body, each of whom is concerned about electability, must say yes. Yet to kill a bill, often all it takes is a single strategic no.

Given that contentious process, no politician wants to face off against any vested interest that could become a dogged, well-funded opponent in the next election. Thus, in the legislative setting, any determined, well-organized, and reasonably influential interest group (be it agricultural or environmental) can almost always stop action on something it truly doesn't like. If it can produce even a modest outcry from its membership, sometimes only a few dozen angry calls or letters, the bill, whatever it may be, is dead.

But by the same token, a nonpartisan bill with significant backers on both sides of the issue—a bill that doesn't create concerted, credible, or bitter opposition—stands a good chance of passing.

Between the private, nonprofit world of environmental and smart growth groups and the world of groups representing commercial agriculture, collaboration was largely absent. Environmentalists were convinced that the planet was at risk. Farmers were convinced their industry was on the verge of bankruptcy. Neither saw room for compromise.

That placed AFT in a unique position. If it somehow found a way around this impasse, the policy payoff could be impressive. But how does one do that?

Creativity, Compromise, and Trust

There were three keys to coalition building: creative problem solving, a willingness to compromise, and the mutual trust to make the first two work.

Creativity. The first key to building coalitions was to find new solutions that could appeal to everyone. On farmland protection, AFT seemed to have such an answer in its proposed PACE programs.

Purchasing agricultural easements had all sorts of advantages for farmers.[6] Farmers were fully compensated in these transactions, paid at market value. This compensation allowed farmers to extract some of the equity tied up in their farmland without having to sell that land, often freeing funds for some needed farm business investment. And because most farmland protected with an easement sells in the future at a lower price—at its "farmland value" rather than its "development value"—PACE programs were also a way of ensuring that more good farmland would be available in the future at prices farmers could afford. Beyond all this, as these programs were entirely voluntary, no farmer who didn't care for the idea needed to participate.

PACE programs also had advantages for environmentalists. For advocates of growth management, they offered a new means for constraining urban sprawl. They could also be strategic, placing roadblocks in the critical path of urban development. And open, undeveloped, properly managed farmland could provide wildlife habitat, address flooding, aquifer recharge, water quality, and a host of other environmental concerns.

Compromise. The world of public policy also offered possibilities for dealmaking. Therefore, another way to build coalitions was to look for potential compromise.

Farmers felt threatened by new environmental regulation. They were looking for solutions that avoided regulation and might even help insulate them from it. And they were being priced out of the market for farmland; new farmers were unable to enter the business, and existing ones were unable to expand. Would farmers accept some new, carefully constrained environmental or land use restrictions in exchange for protections for their land and economic development support for their farm businesses?

Environmentalists saw an agriculture industry that owned and managed a full half of the nation's land base, lands with amazing prospects for improvement. Many environmentalists also saw farmers as environmentally irresponsible. If they were to support farmland protection, they were going to need assurances that it would be responsibly managed. Perhaps they could help farmers enlist the needed broad public support for farmland protection in exchange for improved conservation programs that helped pay the cost of environmental improvements.

Somewhere within this complex of perspectives there had to be opportunities for compromise.

Trust. Despite these possibilities for a farmer–environmentalist coalition, the critical weak spot was trust.

These two groups had been at odds from the beginning. After a long history of acrimony, who would be willing to trust that proposals from the other side wouldn't come with some hidden agenda? Who would feel sure the other would follow through on a negotiated deal, however appealing? Who would rely on any fact, argument, or supposed scholarly study their counterpart might offer? Who would even express their true underlying concerns, when admissions like that could be used against you?

What the American Farmland Trust offered was a bridge. It could become an advocate for farms *and* the environment, championing the necessity of both, insisting always that neither be sacrificed. And through credible research, it could create factual foundations for collaboration upon which farmers, environmentalists, and policymakers could all confidently rely.

From that position, AFT could become a trusted intermediary.

CHAPTER 7

The 1981 Farm Bill:
An Early Policy Victory

American Farmland Trust would get an early opportunity to test its policy chops. In August of 1980, the ink was barely dry on its articles of incorporation. Doug Wheeler was leasing office space.[1] His new board was holding its first official meeting, adopting bylaws, electing officers. The staff members were just settling into their new jobs.

And the next federal farm bill, an event occurring no more than once every five years, was already under negotiation. The farm bill is among the most comprehensive bodies of legislation considered by the US Congress—just about every issue dealing with agriculture and food assistance is combined into a single omnibus bill. It is also among the most expensive legislation that goes before Congress: the 2018 Farm Bill authorized expenditures of some $867 billion over five years.[2] Unsurprisingly, its periodic reauthorization is an effort that engages a vast array of deeply committed constituent interests, rural and urban, farm and environmental.

What Is the Farm Bill?

In today's increasingly urban existence, most of us seldom meet a farmer. Agriculture employs less than 2 percent of the work force. Despite the public hype about corporate agriculture, today the vast majority of farms are still small, noncorporate, independent operations. Even so, agriculture, collectively, remains one of our nation's largest industries.[3] The food and fiber it produces are among our most valuable exports, helping us maintain our international balance of payments. Agriculture drives the economies of several states. Farmers and ranchers own, manage, or work over half the nation's lands—a startling amount, if you think about it. And agriculture has almost overwhelming political influence in at least a third or more of our states and in perhaps as many of our nation's congressional districts.

It also has massive environmental impacts, some positive and some negative.

American farm policy is mostly embodied in a single, periodic legislative enactment that has been passed under various titles over the decades,[4] but is generally known as the farm bill. At any given time in history, this one bill has reflected the federal government's responses, mostly supportive, to our nation's agriculture—but, over the decades, new matters related to farming have tended to accumulate there.

Today's farm bill is detailed and comprehensive. It contains titles that deal with the following:[5]

- *Commodity Programs*, to provide support for growers of various dry bulk commodities (known as commodity crops);
- *Conservation*, to protect farmland and encourage environmental stewardship;
- *Trade*, to support farm exports and international trade;
- *Nutrition*, to provide food programs for low-income households, traditionally half the total cost of the farm bill;
- *Loans*, to offer credit and loan guarantees to farmers;
- *Economic Development*, to support rural and farm community business development;

- *Research and Extension*, to provide for agricultural research and university extension programs;
- *Forestry*, to support healthy, economically viable forestry;
- *Energy*, to encourage farm and community renewable energy;
- *Horticulture*, to support production of fruits, vegetables, and other non-commodity crops, organic farming, local foods, and the like;
- *Crop Insurance*, to provide risk management through the permanently authorized federal crop insurance program; and,
- *Miscellaneous*, to benefit other programs, including livestock, help for beginning farmers, and so forth.

Although the Conservation title was not added until 1985, and many other programs have been added over the years, even back in 1980, the farm bill was one of the largest and most far-reaching pieces of legislation Congress ever dealt with.

Immediately upon its formation in 1980, AFT entered into the fray of entrenched interests, long-standing alliances, and bitter competitors, each with a stake in this legislation. The initial AFT board had a mix of views about the proper role of the new organization.[6] AFT's involvement in the farm bill, however, was inevitable.

Certainly, AFT's early staff members were experienced in this arena. Doug Wheeler's first hires included Bob Gray—the former staffer for Rep. Jim Jeffords, who led the production of the landmark National Agricultural Lands Study (NALS)—and Norm Berg—who joined AFT in 1982, after stepping down as chief of USDA's Soil Conservation Service, where he had created the National Resources Inventory (NRI), upon which NALS was based. Today the NRI is the nation's principal source of farm natural resource statistics. Notably, while at AFT, Berg was also the Washington, DC, representative of the Soil Conservation Society of America. Both these men had been essentially "let go" by the incoming Reagan administration, a loss for the country but a huge gift to AFT. Ed Thompson also soon joined AFT's staff. He was the committed environmental lawyer-activist who led the NACO campaign to pass Jeffords's farmland easement bill.

The Farmland Protection Policy Act

That early focus on policy produced fruit in AFT's very first year. Late in 1981, Congress incorporated into the farm bill yet another Jim Jeffords proposal: the Farmland Protection Policy Act (FPPA).

Bob Gray's NALS had included a listing of the federal government's programs and activities that were having a negative impact on farmland. The FPPA's logic was straightforward: if NALS was to mean anything at all, it should at least cause the federal government itself to begin managing its own operations in a manner that would protect farmlands. The FPPA identified farmland as a "unique natural resource," in need of protection from being "irrevocably converted" to nonagricultural use. The purpose of the act was clearly stated:

> to minimize the extent to which federal programs contribute to the unnecessary and irreversible conversion of farmland to nonagricultural uses, and to assure that federal programs are administered in a manner that, to the extent practicable, will be compatible with state, unit of local government, and private programs and policies to protect farmland.[7]

While the FPPA relied heavily on voluntary measures and discretionary agency interpretation, for the first time, farmland protection had been officially recognized as a priority for the federal government. The NALS had called for a national statement of policy by the federal government supporting farmland preservation, and there it was. AFT had seen it actually adopted into law. This largely passive declaration of policy would later become quite significant.

Early Limits

At the time, however, FPPA did seem largely symbolic. Ed Thompson, the former Environmental Defense Fund activist lawyer, had a lot of experience with a similar law: the National Environmental Policy Act (NEPA). And he had a different view. NEPA, too, was a law designed to guide policy decisions inside the government. But it allowed citizen lawsuits requiring that officials approving private land projects be guided by processes to protect the environment. Thompson proposed to AFT a much more vigorous take on FPPA. He suggested amendments to it that would have empowered the same kind of private enforcement litigation as was allowed under NEPA. That would have made FPPA a powerful tool for change.

There was, however, no appetite on the AFT board for such an assertive approach. The board's very first resolution was that the organization itself would *not* engage in litigation.[8] From the very start, AFT was headed decisively down the middle of the road. The board knew right then that it was never going to be possible to enlist farmers in policy and other coalitions while, at the same time, either suing them or the government over environmental issues or advancing a land use agenda likely to gravely diminish the market value of their land.[9]

This decision by ATF's founders provided an early indicator for its funders, supporters, initial staff, and especially its potential partners. It defined AFT. The very adoption of FRPP had illustrated the possibilities that might exist when they stepped beyond not just the ordinary land trust role of holding easements but also one-sided environmental or farm industry advocacy. It provided a peek at the first page of a massive volume of possibilities emerging in the policy arena.

At the same time, Thompson never stopped pressing for more direct and aggressive policies. While he wasn't always successful, Thompson played a valuable role in an organization that was willing to entertain internal debate. Ralph Grossi would later refer to Ed Thompson as "AFT's conscience."

Initial Status Report

AFT's *1981 Annual Report* described an organization that was well launched. AFT had some fifteen thousand new members. Its 1981 income was $658,000, of which $156,000 was from new memberships. This growth was a reassuring sign that, while "middle ground" politics might not appeal to everyone, there was at least a significant segment of the public and of the donor community willing to support it.

"A crisis in the making" were the first words in that *1981 Annual Report*, used to describe the yearly loss of some three million acres of agricultural lands in the United States,[10] and words quoted from President Reagan's new secretary of agriculture, John Block, who was already a convert to AFT's cause. By quoting Secretary Block, AFT president Doug Wheeler was tipping his hat to Block and to the new, conservative Reagan administration; he was letting them know that AFT's collaborative approach might offer a constructive political response to the continued upswell of environmental activism across the nation.

Significantly, Wheeler referred to AFT in the report as "a distinctly new kind of organization reflecting the mutual concerns of farmers and conservationists." Careful use of the term conservationists would have been no accident. It had taken but a single year for AFT to start down this new path through the jungle of American environmental politics.

CHAPTER 8

The 1985 Farm Bill:
A Transformation in American
Farm Policy

President Reagan signed the next farm bill into law shortly before Christmas of 1985.[1] That previous fall, Secretary of Agriculture John Block had participated in a reception at USDA Headquarters. In his remarks, Block welcomed a man whose name was not so familiar among the tight political circles of Washington, DC. Some in attendance must have wondered: Who was this obscure dairy farmer from Marin County?

The man in question was Ralph Grossi, and the occasion was Grossi's move to the nation's capital, where he had taken up the reins as president of an almost equally unknown organization: American Farmland Trust. The timing of Block's remarks reveals a great deal about what was happening at that moment, during the run-up to the passage of one of the most historic farm bills to come before Congress.

AFT was five years old. Doug Wheeler, Grossi's predecessor, had stepped down July 1, 1985, just months before the farm bill's passage. The two men were trading coasts: Wheeler had taken a job as executive director for the Sierra Club in San Francisco, a mere hour-and-a-half drive south of Grossi's farm. Grossi, a founding board member, went on to serve as AFT president and CEO for twenty-three years.

Much had already changed at American Farmland Trust during Wheeler's tenure. AFT no longer saw itself solely as a national land trust; it was embracing larger policy and becoming a credible matchmaker between advocacy groups representing farmers and environmentalists. The new farm bill would be AFT's greatest test in coalition building. Grossi's inaugural task was to bring it home.

A Striking New Vision for Soil Conservation

Soil conservation had been part of US farm policy for decades, ever since the first farm bill, the Agricultural Adjustment Act of 1933. That celebrated Depression-era legislation created the original USDA Soil Conservation Service (SCS) in response to the Dust Bowl disaster.

But the early justification for "conserving soil" and some of the tools chosen to accomplish it might not be what one would imagine today: In the 1930s, people believed that unfair foreign competition plagued certain commercial farm crops known as dry bulk commodity crops (such as wheat, corn and other feed crops, rice, soybeans and other oilseeds, peanuts, cotton, sugar). These were at the time (unlike today) the only major farm products that could easily be stored for long periods and, hence, inexpensively shipped long distances. They faced, therefore, significant competition in international markets. These crops happened to be mainstays of US commercial agriculture. There was also the perception that low farm prices and the depressed farm economy were the result of overproduction, and the United States had a "farm surplus."

It is probably best not to overanalyze either rationale. From an economic perspective, neither is perfectly logical; together, they seem inconsistent. Suffice it to say, from that point forward, US farm policy was focused on correcting these "problems." Low prices were addressed by providing American commodity farmers with price support subsidies. And oversupply was addressed (somewhat ironically, if the problem was caused by international competition) by making payments in exchange for the farmers' removing land from production, referred to as soil conservation. Thus American farm policy played the dual role of artificially elevating what farmers were paid for their crops (which would increase their supply and lower the real market price) and artificially taking land out of production (which would decrease supply and raise the real market price).

In the original theory of soil conservation, farmland would be taken out of commercial production and securely planted to unmarketable cover crops. The soil would be protected from erosion and thus "conserved" or "banked" so as to be available for future agricultural use. Various US farm bill programs were grounded in these general theories all the way into the 1980s.

Environmental Activism

In 1985, the prevailing theory of soil conservation changed. Within fifteen years or so, the growing influence of American environmental activism had finally shouldered its way into US farm policy.

The Conservation Reserve Program

The 1985 Farm Bill was the first time agricultural soil conservation was seen as having a purpose other than "banking" soil and thereby protecting the future of agricultural productivity.[2] The federal farm bill was no longer solely concerned with agricultural profitability and productivity; it would soon engage in a much broader public environmental responsibility besides.

The National Agricultural Lands Study had expressed a good deal of concern about the loss of agricultural soils through erosion. It proposed the creation of a national agricultural "reserve," an excellent theoretical basis for conserving the land itself. In response, the 1985

Farm Bill created the Conservation Reserve Program (CRP), which, like its predecessor programs, in effect paid farmers to take land out of production. But unlike previous programs, CRP was specifically designed to conserve those particular lands whose protection would provide the greatest broad environmental benefit. And once conserved, rather than being planted to cover crops, these lands were planted with native species to restore their environmental function.

This was novel territory indeed.

The analysis that made this choice possible drew on data assembled by the National Resources Inventory (NRI), which AFT's staffer, Norm Berg, had instituted when he was the SCS's chief, back in the Carter administration. The new ranking system protected not only highly erodible lands but also those that were particularly sensitive to environmental damage or promised environmental improvements.

The innovative program expanded federal policy, reducing production and conserving soil for future agriculture use while also protecting the environment. After a fifteen-year lapse in land retirement programs,[3] CRP received substantial funding aimed at conserving some 36.4 million acres of agricultural lands.[4]

Wetlands, Highly Erodible Lands, and Conservation Compliance

The emerging environmental thrust in public policy was not limited to CRP. In the 1985 Farm Bill, wetlands would now be protected through a so-called swampbuster program. And highly erodible lands were to be protected by a sodbuster program.[5]

Perhaps more significantly long term than anything else in this farm bill, through a system referred to as conservation compliance, farmers were required to complete and implement a USDA-approved farm conservation plan before drained "swamps" could be farmed or when farming highly erodible lands. Farmers who wished to place lands in CRP were also required to have conservation plans. The on-the-ground significance of this requirement is subtle until you understand that something like half the erosion occurring on agricultural lands was taking place on about 6 percent of the farmland, on marginal lands that needed special protection.[6] These conservation plans could address a multitude of environmental issues, and failure to comply with the plan would be penalized through loss of access to price supports, crop insurance, and other USDA programs—a powerful motivation.[7] These conservation compliance requirements were the beginning of what would ultimately become a major transformation in the thrust and purpose of American farm policy.

Ten years later, the Natural Resources Conservation Service estimated that annual soil erosion in American cropland had dropped from 1982 levels by 1.6 billion tons, a reduction of 42 percent.[8]

A New Conservation Title

The historic significance of these changes in farm bill programs was underlined by including them in a Conservation title, the first such title in farm bill history. This was the most dramatic soil conservation legislation since the 1930s.

The new title had the word *Conservation* in its name. But it would include the various federal programs designed to help farmers both "conserve" soil *and* responsibly manage their land to protect our nation's broader shared environment. For the first time, the direction of US farm policy had been significantly influenced by groups *other* than traditional agriculture.[9]

And no one could mistake the intent. Not since the federal Food Stamp Program (renamed the Supplemental Nutrition Assistance Program, or SNAP, in 2008) was introduced as a farm bill title, back in 1973, had such a politically significant change been incorporated into farm bill politics. At that time, the creation of a farm bill Nutrition title, along with the inclusion of food stamp assistance (later SNAP), compelled two quite disparate social groups—proponents of food assistance for the poor, and advocates of farm support programs—to negotiate together; otherwise, neither of their programs would pass into law.

Now the Conservation title would usher in a groundbreaking era of interplay between farmers and the environmental community, with huge significance for the country.

Mobilizing a Groundswell of Public Support

So, how did it all come together? With a Republican in the White House and a Republican majority in the Senate, why did the US Congress pass a farm bill that, for the first time in history, stepped well beyond the immediate business needs of the agriculture industry, partnered with voices that had never been heard before, and secured the most environmentally responsive policy to date?

Certainly, the American Farmland Trust had a role—before it came on the scene, there had never been a trusted intermediary to build the needed political coalition and give it weight. But it's also worth considering other social, political, and economic stars that had aligned in 1985.

Land Protection and the Environment

The broader environmental community was emboldened by its substantial legislative achievements over the previous fifteen years. With half the nation's land in farming, there was a distinct logic to turning their advocacy toward agriculture. Farmers and ranchers were a significant source of water pollution, habitat loss, and wetland degradation. CRP also had immense appeal; here was a way to protect and restore large tracts of land for wildlife habitat and migration corridors. And a healthy, environmentally responsible agriculture industry could offer a new rationale for limiting urban growth and create a new bulwark against it.

A Robust New Farm Bill Coalition

Never before had nonagricultural groups played such a significant role in farm bill politics.[10] American Farmland Trust organized a coalition that included—on the environmental side—the National Audubon Society, Natural Resources Defense Council, and Sierra Club,[11] together with the American Forestry Association, National Association of Conservation Districts, and the Soil and Water Conservation Society. This conservation coalition was painstakingly constructed leading up to 1985, and it continued in the years to follow.

A National Farm Debt Crisis

As we've seen, in 1985, farmers were facing a historic crisis of debt, low farm prices, high operating costs (aggravated by record-high oil prices), and bankruptcies in farm country.[12] They'd gone some fifteen years without a land set-aside program. Many wanted to return to removing farmland from active crop production as a means to raise farm prices. With agriculture entering the age of environmental regulation, farmers were also nervous about their future. Facing potential regulation that they feared could put them out of business, farmers much preferred programs like CRP, sodbusters, and swampbusters. These were, at least, voluntary and incentive based.

New Activism from Sport and Recreation Interests

Increasingly, hunting and fishing societies were getting engaged in farm politics, motivated by declines in game bird populations and reduced hunting opportunity. Returning land to bird habitat met their needs.[13] They recognized that new habitat for birds and other wildlife represented the only real long-term prospect for renewing depleted game populations. CRP was the perfect tool for conservation-minded hunting and fishing groups.

This historic farm bill passed Congress on December 23, 1985. When Ralph Grossi sat down with his family for Christmas dinner that year, he felt gratified. The first big challenge of his leadership had been met with success. His organization had carved out a powerful new role for itself in protecting farmland and committing it to sound environmental management.

CHAPTER 9

The IRS Finally Acts, and a Land Trust Phenomenon

Close on the heels of the 1985 Farm Bill, a new rule came down from the Internal Revenue Service. Nearly five years after the IRS decided to allow charitable deductions for conservation easements, it now ruled that the donation of *agricultural* conservation easements could be recognized for the charitable deduction as well.[1] The IRS ruling specifically referenced the 1981 Farmland Protection Policy Act (FPPA), so it was unquestionably a by-product of American Farmland Trust's early success in passing the FPPA. Farmland protection was now official policy for all federal government agencies—including the IRS.

But this IRS ruling also resulted from five years of behind-the-scenes agency lobbying by AFT's policy staff. Work of this kind is often extemporaneous. Ed Thompson, by then AFT's policy director, a lawyer, and the author of AFT's initial, much replicated, agricultural conservation easement language, recalls having attended a meeting at the Feathered Pipe Ranch in Montana, in the early 1980s. The event was held to discuss formation of a new Land Trust Exchange (today's Land Trust Alliance, or LTA). At that meeting, Thompson joined a group in a hot tub at the ranch, where he and an IRS lawyer named Steve Small shared a conversation about some of the legal issues associated with recognizing the charitable deductibility of agricultural easement donations. Later, when that IRS ruling appeared in the *Federal Register*, Thompson was both surprised and gratified to note that a good deal of the published argument provided in support of the decision had clearly come directly from that, apparently persuasive, hot tub conversation years earlier.[2]

FPPA had, of course, been AFT's first major federal public policy achievement. The 1985 Farm Bill was a very strong second. Judging from its subsequent impact, Thompson's spontaneous hot tub meeting (along with much other work) and the ensuing 1986 IRS ruling has to be counted as a third.

Just as had happened for environmental conservation easements following the IRS ruling in their favor back in 1981, the February 1986 IRS declaration sparked private landowner interest in protecting their land with the charitable donation of agricultural easements. Unfortunately, landowners in much of the country still had no place to go to find a qualified holder for their easements. In 1985, the dramatic proliferation of land trusts in America that continues today was only getting started. There were still large regions, especially in farm country, not served by any local land trust. And where land trusts did exist, many were neither interested in holding agricultural easements nor knowledgeable enough about farming to do so well. Their founders and leaders often had roots in the environmental movement, and their formative charters frequently focused on protecting environmental values. Holding an easement while allowing, even encouraging, active farming on that land was an alien concept for many.

Yet somehow these new agricultural easements needed to find a home.

AFT could have tried to fill this role itself; it had originally resolved to become the nation's go-to organization for holding agricultural easements. But ultimately, Ralph Grossi and the board decided AFT would do better in a support role. Instead, AFT staff were assigned to regularly participate in the annual LTA Rally,[3] the annual meetings of the national Land Trust Alliance, and they frequently traveled to local land trust events around the country. In those venues, they argued the case for farmland protection. They created partnerships with local land trusts and encouraged them to get involved with agricultural lands. They also sought out partners in federal, state, and local efforts to create publicly funded PACE programs, many of which relied upon (and compensated) local land trusts to actually hold the easements they funded or paid the land trusts for their work in offering the easement to the program for protection. If AFT did not have the capacity to handle what Doug Wheeler had referred to as a "flood" of new interest in "retail" land protection,[4] it would support the people and institutions that did.[5]

In some cases, AFT got involved in creating new local land trusts. It became the fiduciary agent for fledgling groups during their formative stages before they'd received their IRS 501(c)(3) status and offered advice and training for new staff. In effect, AFT was creating its own replacement in those communities.[6] Examples include the Colorado Cattlemen's Agricultural Land Trust and the Texas Agricultural Land Trust.

In 1996, AFT finally succeeded in building on the original Jeffords legislation and secured adoption of its flagship farmland protection program, initially named the federal Farm and Ranchlands Protection Program. For the first time, there was federal money to match local funds in acquiring agricultural easements. Unfortunately, land trusts were not initially eligible to hold easements that received this funding. So, a land trust coalition led by AFT went back to work, and in 2002, land trusts were empowered to tap into this new funding resource as well. The opportunity thus added yet another motivation for them to seek and hold agricultural easements, which doubtless resulted in a good deal of additional farmland under protection in the years that followed.

With these efforts, AFT slowly but steadily worked itself out of the business of direct farmland protection.[7] As land trusts gained their own experience and expertise, AFT's educational role at the LTA Rally and with local land trusts wound down. Rally organizers could turn to their own, engaged members, who had become as conversant in those topics as AFT.[8] AFT disengaged from holding easements to the point that, for over a decade (from about 2005 to 2016), it stopped actively seeking easements and transferred many it already held to land trusts in local communities.[9]

AFT leaders had once believed that protecting more land would entail scaling up their organization. In the end, however, coping with a blossoming interest in land protection required the added participation of the robust land trust movement then expanding throughout the country.[10]

As of 2017, land trusts and PACE programs had protected more than 6.5 million acres of American farm- and ranchland. Publicly funded PACE programs contributed to 3.4 million of those acres, with the balance of 3.1 million acres coming from private donations.[11]

This strategy freed up AFT to focus on its policy goals, like passing the FPPA in 1981, obtaining the IRS ruling on charitable deductibility of agricultural easements in early 1986, helping to secure local PACE programs through the country, and pressing for the federal match funding for easement purchases that propelled PACE and the land trust movement's participation forward.

CHAPTER 10
Power at the Center

In the days following passage of the historic 1985 Farm Bill, American Farmland Trust's new president and his colleagues considered how to further build the conservation coalition that had made that historic legislation possible. Once they'd experienced the power of broad coalitions firsthand, AFT staff and board members began to joke that they were now working the "radical middle."[1]

They asked themselves, how do you occupy that center position without ending up hated by everyone? Ralph Grossi recalls that, in the early days, when the organization was still establishing its credibility, the farm community would inevitably tell him that AFT was far too cozy with environmentalists. The environmental community thought AFT was much too friendly with the farmers. As Grossi kiddingly puts it: "The answer to both was . . . yes!"

Of course, the arguments AFT made to farmers were not the same ones the organization used with environmentalists. The case was presented to each side in a manner that was grounded in that constituency's values, stated in their language, and respectful of their point of view. But both arguments were true. And the goal was, nonetheless, the same for both: a better world for farmers *and* the environment.

Today, as at that time, AFT staff and supporters frequently make their case before mixed audiences that contain hard-core believers on both sides of the farm–environmental divide.[2] It is actually helpful for each side to hear the arguments made to the other firsthand. That is one of the few ways adversaries can begin to understand what motivates their counterparts and to appreciate the moral legitimacy of the other's perspective. It explains the other side's commitment to participating and thus confirms their trustworthiness as a partner-collaborator. And an airing of viewpoints can sometimes highlight the weaknesses of one's own position.[3]

In the course of some thoughtful discussions among themselves, AFT advocates developed some key strategies for building coalitions.

Avoiding Linkage

A typical problem in coalition building is "linkage": when one party tells the other that before they can cooperate on an issue, they must first have agreement on some other matter. Typically, the "linked" issue is an intractable one, so linking the two makes cooperation impossible. Insisting on its solution before dealing with something much simpler and discrete is tantamount to demanding complete surrender before even beginning the conversation.[4] It isn't going to happen.

In reality, reaching agreement on tough problems requires first working together on the easier ones. If parties can agree on a 1985 Conservation Reserve Program, on funding for incentives for conservation practices, or on a program to purchase development rights, the odds greatly improve that, down the road somewhere, they might also reach agreement on a suite of carefully targeted and constrained but critically needed regulations addressing particularly troubling farm management practices. Maybe on some mutual climate solutions. Or, perhaps, even on some modest but effective growth management regimes that would minimally affect land values. Agreements on those kinds of issues is, after all, not unheard of.[5]

Understanding and Respecting Underlying Motives and Points of View

People will seldom open up to an apparent enemy: honesty can be seen as weakness; revelations can later be regretted. A credible intermediary, however, can learn to appreciate and respect each side's point of view.[6] It can be sympathetic to the perspectives of both groups as it comes to understand the real, underlying motives behind a seemingly intransigent position. It can keep confidences and come to be trusted.

Armed with that insight, it can end up identifying an otherwise-invisible path to reaching agreement.

Balancing Practicality with Principle

As one might expect, AFT's centrist approach has sometimes required compromise. AFT has often supported the voluntary over the mandatory: purchase of agricultural easements rather than zoning ordinances; farm bill conservation incentive programs instead of universal farm management practice laws; environmental markets rather than environmental regulation. It has typically left the bitter battles over regulation and zoning to other groups better suited and more inclined to fight them.

This approach does not, however, mean that the more unpleasant possibilities are ever really off the table. They remain always at the back of every participant's mind.

Sometimes dealing with these issues directly has been unavoidable. Examples include AFT's research on sprawl versus compact development in the San Joaquin Valley;[7] AFT opposition to Oregon Ballot Measure 37,[8] and to a similar initiative a few years later in the state of

Washington;[9] creation of the ACRE program in the 2008 Farm Bill; AFT support for cap and trade in the Waxman–Markey bill in Congress;[10] AFT work (with help from Ed Thompson) as a founding partner of Smart Growth America (and Ralph Grossi's service as its first chairman); and in AFT partnerships with groups like the Urban Land Institute and the National Conference of Mayors and in the national Smart Growth Network.[11] Even where AFT has successfully nurtured a PACE program and has convinced the community that it was worth the cost, the zoning alternative has always been part of the conversation and has often played a role in the ultimate solution.[12]

The Political Relief Factor

There is yet another practical political reality here. When disparate, bitterly opposing groups present themselves and their conflicts to elected officials, no politician wants to be the person who decides their fate, who takes the heat from the losing side. Therefore, some matters end up destined to be insoluble.

But on those rare occasions when the two groups actually do come together and end up, almost unbelievably, asking for the same thing at the same time, the resulting awe and disbelief from policymakers, along with the massive sense of collective relief that sometimes results, can open the way for almost anything. It can be an unexpected source of power.

Empowering Courageous Leadership

Sometimes the source of support can be a surprise. Ralph Grossi says that he would occasionally be independently contacted by courageous individuals in leadership positions with groups solidly entrenched on one side or the other of a farm–environmental dispute—people, he says, who were willing to "go out of their way to give us the opportunity to make our case." As Grossi explains it: "They'd call us in so we could say things to their group that they couldn't say themselves." They were willing to take a risk, saying, "We've got to work with these people."

AFT was there to take advantage of what Grossi calls "a nuance of AFT's work"—the ability to find ways to help progressive leaders within groups accustomed to fighting to consider collaborative alternatives instead. "Very often," Grossi says, "I would go speak to a group and say things that their leadership couldn't say to them. That's a nuanced role that is not always easy for people to understand about what we do."

Grossi says he has, for example, "always admired some of the really good leaders in the Farm Bureau that will go out of their way to bring their own membership along, knowing that their grassroots members weren't really quite ready yet." Unfortunately, these people are seldom recognized or rewarded for facing internal political risks to take their organization where they know it ought to go.[13]

But where they succeed, there is huge power and an opportunity for constructive change.

The Hidden Power in Administrative Follow-Up

It is for good reason that lawmaking is often likened to making sausage. In the rush and flurry of writing new policy, mistakes are made, there are unanticipated consequences, details are omitted. Major new policy measures almost inevitably require future course correction. Thus, complex legislation, of political and practical necessity, often expresses broad concepts rather than details; it frequently leaves large areas to subsequent administrative interpretation and rulemaking.

Those later refinements and course changes seldom garner the intense public interest and engagement that surrounded the original legislation. Earlier participants often lose interest and move on to other priorities.

AFT was not immune to this. Ralph Grossi recalls that AFT would receive funding from foundations to work on the farm bill, and then, when it passed, those funders would typically say, "So long. We'll see you when the next farm bill comes up." They never really understood what AFT was doing in the meantime, behind the scenes. "What we really needed," says Grossi, "was continued funding for all the work we did in these behind-the-scenes administrative processes." But how can you explain all of that in a compelling way in a grant application?

Nonetheless, AFT participated in the administrative rule-making process that followed adoption of the 1985 Farm Bill and each of the farm bills that followed. Those rule-making processes were often just as important (or more important) than the passage of the original legislation.[14] While public interest in the administrative phase of legislation was often minimal, AFT's known role as an objective source of information in the original debate gave it credibility when offering suggestions for later administrative action. Agency personnel who conduct those processes tend to scrupulously avoid taking sides in unresolved disputes—they leave those difficult choices to the politicians. But a mainstream suggestion from a centrist group that might resolve such a dispute is always welcome.

Those later administrative processes also responded well to people with special expertise. Grossi recalls that AFT benefited dramatically from the participation of Norm Berg in the rule-making process following the 1985 Farm Bill. As former chief of the Soil Conservation Service and someone who had been involved in these issues for his whole career, Berg understood the administrative process better than most of the people running it. And he was hugely credible.

Ed Thompson recalls walking into Norm Berg's office to discuss one issue or another and saying, "Hey, Norm, I've got this great idea." After Thompson explained his thinking, Berg would reach into his desk or a filing cabinet and pull out some article or report and say something like,

"Oh yeah, you mean something like this." It might be a document from twenty years earlier, when they'd tried exactly the same thing.

"It could be very discouraging," Thompson says with a fond laugh.

Norm Berg knew all the players. According to Grossi, he worked "very quietly" but had enormous impact on an outcome.[15]

A Case in Point: The Gang of Five

Over the years, these operating principles came together for AFT in the creation of pivotal policy coalitions on many occasions. At least one example of this deserves mention here. It was creation of the so-called Gang of Five.

In 2009, Congress was undertaking its first serious effort to deal with climate change. This came in the form of the Waxman–Markey bill. Included within this bill was a comprehensive cap-and-trade measure that would have funded dramatic new conservation measures throughout agriculture—providing an economic shot in the arm for farmers and kick-starting their participation in helping the rest of us deal with the climate crisis.

At the time, several national agriculture trade groups, led by the American Farm Bureau Federation, were coalescing in a united "anti-climate" political action front to oppose legislation designed to address climate change. A more constructive, proactive agriculture coalition was badly needed. AFT stepped in and assembled a new political action coalition on Waxman–Markey that soon became known as the Gang of Five.[16]

The new group included the National Association of Wheat Growers, the National Corn Growers Association, the National Milk Producers Federation, the National Farmers Union, and, of course, American Farmland Trust.

These five groups reflected only a minority of agricultural interests. But it was a significant minority. They represented producers of some of the most valuable farm products in American commercial agriculture. These were highly regarded national organizations with first-rate professional public policy staff, well known and respected in Congress. They wielded considerable influence. Together, they represented an important agriculture counterweight against the anti-climate action perspective.

With AFT encouragement, the Gang of Five collaborated on research, policy development, and education. They produced joint documents laying out legislative principles, top-priority policies, and policy options that would affirmatively engage agriculture in combating climate change. Their participation made it possible for AFT to interact with and make presentations to their respective boards and leadership committees and to take input and secure buy-in on potential agriculture-friendly climate-change legislation.

And they produced foundational research showing the specific advantages for agriculture in the Waxman–Markey bill's proposed cap-and-trade provisions. Working together, this group conducted economic analyses and commissioned studies that were able to combat misinformation from the Fertilizer Institute and the American Farm Bureau Federation[17]—studies for which AFT was asked to help secure funding.

This group made a pivotal difference in the passage of Waxman–Markey through the House. And, while the bill later died in the US Senate, the Gang of Five ultimately made it possible for farmers to work with other, nonfarm policy efforts such as 25x25, the Clark Group, the Bipartisan Policy Center, Clean Energy Works, and researchers at the University of Tennessee, as well as with environmental organizations like the Environmental Defense Fund and the National Wildlife Federation.

This was precisely the kind of effort that was made for American Farmland Trust. The resulting coalition has also had a lasting impact[18] and created a promising precedent, which will almost certainly help drive constructive agricultural and climate policy going forward.

CHAPTER 11

Helping Farmers Protect the Environment:
An Emerging AFT Mission

During American Farmland Trust's early years, founding board member and first chair Fred Winthrop got the chance to visit Ralph Grossi's dairy farm in Northern California. One of the things he found particularly impressive was the Grossi family's anaerobic digester.[1] Their dairy was one of the first in the nation to have one.

At the time, climate change was not yet a matter of intense national debate. The subsequent national interest in decentralized, sustainable energy was just getting under way and was by no means on a firm footing—not long before, the Reagan administration had unceremoniously removed the thirty-two solar panels that were placed on the White House roof by Jimmy Carter, the previous president.[2] Water quality was thought to be mostly a point-source problem—one that had been decisively addressed in the Clean Water Act of 1977.

Yet here was a progressive dairy farmer producing electricity from livestock waste, preventing methane from escaping into the atmosphere, and capturing potential water pollutants, which might otherwise find their way into the streams and groundwaters of his community.

As his family's anaerobic digester shows, Ralph Grossi's thinking about farm–environmental issues went well beyond just "soil conservation." And many of AFTs projects had environmental protection at their core. In 1991, AFT formed its Center for Agriculture in the Environment, whose central purpose was to focus on projects and research of this kind. In his annual reports, Grossi made frequent references to AFT efforts that supported sustainable agriculture, water quality, wildlife habitat, and wetlands protection.[3] All these goals were reflective of broad, off-farm, community environmental values.

Engaging the Farmers

As Ralph Grossi and his colleagues mapped out their strategy to protect the nation's farmland, they knew their efforts would be useless without broad support from the heart of the agriculture industry.

The Prerequisite Farmer Support

Farmer support with AFT's work was a simple, political necessity. When one went knocking on the door of an elected policymaker with some bright new idea about how to help agriculture, the very first question would always be: "Where are the farmers on all of this?"

AFT could, of course, speak *about* agriculture. But only the industry trade associations themselves could ultimately speak *on behalf of* agriculture.

Getting that ag industry help was difficult. Of course, most individual farmers care about the responsible long-term management of their farms. And many could see the need to protect farmland for agriculture. But that did not easily translate into visible support in the political arena.

Most business trade associations notoriously find themselves fighting hardest for what they see as survival tomorrow. That can mean resisting labor, workplace, product safety, or environmental regulations that could increase their operating cost or even, perhaps, put them out of business. The allies they make in these efforts and the positions they take are very different from the ones they'd need if they were to address longer-term issues like a healthy environment or a broadly positive public image. Focusing on long-term environmental or social issues can easily alienate the well-established coalition partners and many of the elected legislators they'll need to get past the next imminent threat.

Thankfully, early in AFT's existence, the Pennsylvania Farm Bureau had itself become active in supporting one of the local PACE programs under consideration in Lancaster County. Lancaster was one of the most productive agricultural counties in the country. AFT and the Farm Bureau partnered up to advance that county program and also to launch a successful PACE policy effort at the state level. That early relationship paid off as the American Farm Bureau Federation became aware of AFT as a new organization that seemed to be interested in protecting the farm enterprise. It was also an early illustration of how bridging the divide between farmers and environmentalists could be effective in the policy arena.

The Language of Environmentalism

In the aftermath of the environmental revolution of the 1970s and the ensuing property-rights movement, much of the day-to-day language of environmental protection had become taboo in conservative agriculture circles. One simply didn't throw around terms like *sustainable agriculture*, or *wildlife habitat*. Even the word *environment* was suspect. It was fine, in farm communities, to discuss "conservation." Farmers understood that to mean soil conservation, typically referring to efforts to prevent erosion that could cost them valuable topsoil. But references to "the environment" could be tricky.

That obligatory reticence when using the language of environmental responsibility is not much of a factor when dealing with today's farmers.

It took an ongoing organizational effort over several years to finally shift the dialogue. As AFT's fifth president, John Piotti, said some years later, "AFT made it possible for other groups to eventually see agriculture and the environment as AFT did, as totally interconnected, as two sides of the same coin."

Over the years, AFT learned how to talk about these issues in a way that allowed farmers to discuss them in accepted parlance without putting their teeth on edge. AFT accomplished that by respecting the farmers' point of view and trusting that, given relevant and accurate information (sans the polemics), farmers would make the practical and logical choices. Agriculture is, after all, a cold, hard, rational enterprise that obeys the laws of biology, business, and community. Farmers deal in practical realities. AFT merely needed to explain, in language that made practical sense, how environmentally responsible farm management was one of those realities.

Engaging the Environmentalists

As important as it was for AFT to secure farmer support, it would also need the active, enthusiastic support of the environmental community.

A Necessary Alliance

Environmentalists were disinclined to help save a farm if they believed that it might, soon after, be mismanaged in a way that would turn it into an environmental millstone. The passion of advocates for smart growth, fish and wildlife habitat, water quality, flood detention, and (more recently) climate protection would be critical if AFT's efforts were ever to achieve the scale necessary to save the nation's farmland. Since farmland protection required the help of environmentalists, support for environmentally responsible farming would, inevitably, be a part of the deal.

Thankfully, this support was entirely possible for farmers to provide.

First of all, there was already in place a nationwide infrastructure of local government agencies capable of undertaking the work—local conservation districts[4] and USDA/NRCS state and local offices. And there were already federal farm bill programs falling in place designed to help them do that: the conservation cost-share programs pioneered in the 1985 Farm Bill. The public had already shown a willingness to support widespread, voluntary use of well-considered conservation practices that promised substantial benefits for the environment.

Second, there was dramatic leverage to be had. As Ralph Grossi often pointed out: there was enormous potential for environmental benefits on private land if one could "ignite" landowner interest by showing that the public would share the cost of voluntary conservation practices. Meet the landowner halfway, and you'd gain a huge advantage.

A Persuasive Case

For all their recent successes, the environmental community had run up against a significant barrier in their confrontations with agriculture. Farming had a political advantage as a major industry, which assured them a solid block of loyal congressional votes. Farmers, then as now, were held in high esteem by the public at large, at least in general terms.[5] Environmental advocates had learned to exercise care that they *not* be seen as unduly targeting the nation's farmers.

There was also a diversity of opinion about farming within the environmental community, driven in part by the emerging "local food" movement. Farmers markets were springing up all across the country. With more consumers interacting with farmers and realizing that most were hardworking people who cared deeply about the land, public attitudes began to change—at least in some circles.

It was often no longer politically productive to treat local farmers as "the enemy." There was reason to at least consider alternative, negotiated solutions. And if you drove a farmer out of business, given the pressures of sprawl and development, that land's subsequent use would likely be a good deal less friendly for the environment than the farm that had been lost.

A Dual Mission

Thus was born what was, for some time afterward, referred to as AFT's "dual mission" of protecting farmland and supporting farm practices that led to a healthy environment. AFT at times thought of this as protecting farmland both "by the acre" and "by the inch." But that dual mission was—from the beginning—always about much more than saving farmland, preventing erosion, and improving soil health.

It was also about everything that properly managed farmland could do for the broader environment and how—for that reason—retaining the underlying land resource was essential.

CHAPTER 12
Launching a New Farm Policy Vision

Sometime in the run-up to the 1990 Farm Bill, American Farmland Trust staffers Bob Wagner and Ed Thompson made a road trip north to Vermont. They'd arranged to get together with a few committed, local farmland protection advocates from the Vermont Land Trust and the Vermont Housing and Conservation Board.

Thompson, the former activist lawyer who'd spearheaded the Jeffords PACE bill campaign, was now heading up AFT's public policy efforts. Wagner, a former Jim Jeffords congressional aide, was a political strategist and AFT's man on the ground in New England.

Holed up in a room at an old municipal building in Brattleboro, they sat down with local activists and strategized the first decisive steps toward making farmland protection a federal priority.

Thompson and Wagner helped craft what was called the Farms for the Future program. Borrowing heavily from the original Jeffords bill, their draft was sent along to Sen. Patrick Leahy of Vermont, whom they knew wanted to tackle this issue in the current farm bill. Leahy ended up having to lower his sights to a limited pilot applicable only to Vermont. But he got that done, setting a critical precedent. Seven years later, in 1996, that work led to the USDA's Farm and Ranchlands Protection Program

(FRPP). This program ultimately became the powerhouse federal driver for farmland protection. It provided funding to purchase agricultural conservation easements, money used in concert with matched funds from state and local programs.

A Long-Term Strategy for Change

Altering the course of the ship of state is a massive undertaking and can be excruciatingly slow. For that reason, the 1985 Farm Bill was important not just for the specific policy changes written into law that year but also because the coalition created to secure them remained largely intact for a good many years to follow.[1] AFT and its coalition partners would go on to slowly but inexorably build upon what they'd done, effecting long-term change in federal farm policy.

Those evolutionary changes typically took three forms:

First, a small but creative new program would appear. Often, it would be limited or underfunded initially, but it might offer real promise. Senator Leahy's Farms for the Future bill was a perfect example: some years later, it became the Federal Farm and Ranchlands Protection Program and then today's Agricultural Conservation Easement Program (ACEP).

Second, a simple basic theory or approach to helping agriculture in one program might be later widely adopted for many other programs and purposes. The early Wetlands Reserve Program (WRP) and the Agricultural Water Quality Protection (AWQP) program worked so nicely that their conservation cost share approach spawned today's hugely effective and much more comprehensive Environmental Quality Incentives Program (EQIP), among others.

Third, an existing program originally designed to address one perceived problem could be reimagined and redesigned to address another. It could thereby retain an earlier supportive constituency while also drawing support from a new group focused on the newly identified concern. The Conservation Reserve Program (CRP) exemplified this; it gave soil conservation a new and broader environmental and recreational purpose—*and* constituency.

These were the policy goalposts that AFT and the Conservation Coalition kept in sight as the years passed. By following this pattern, the federal farm bill was changed dramatically over time. Programs originally designed as outright market subsidies now help farmers manage and insure against their hugely challenging business risks. And programs originally intended to take land out of farm production in order to drive up farm prices while conserving the soil for future farm use now help farmers (and their communities) address critical environmental challenges like wildlife habitat, water pollution, and climate change.

A Farm Policy Evolution

Consider the historical context for today's overarching established tenets of farm policy and note how their evolution can so often (and so tellingly) be tracked back over time:

Conserving Vulnerable Topsoil while Protecting and Restoring Habitat and Water Quality

The name of the new federal agency created in the 1930s to deal with the Dust Bowl disaster, the Soil Conservation Service (SCS),[2] explains much about the politics that drove the early farm bills. *Soil conservation* generally refers to keeping soil healthy and present for future farm use. But it was also used as a rationale for market manipulation, as setting land aside in "land banks" (or, more cynically, paying farmers "not to grow crops") became a tool for reducing our supposed "farm surplus" and artificially driving up farm prices.

That history underscores the revolutionary nature of the 1985 Conservation Reserve Program. While still conserving topsoil for potential future agriculture, its explicit purpose and operating design were, for the first time, specifically targeted to protect such broader environmental values as wildlife habitat and water quality. CRP may be the single most popular farm bill conservation program in history, in part because it meets the needs of an extremely diverse public constituency. In 1990, it further expanded target enrollment to forty million acres, and it has been expanded and improved in nearly every farm bill since.[3]

Cost-Share Assistance in Implementing Conservation Practices

USDA's current suite of programs that share with farmers the cost of implementing sound conservation management practices also evolved from the 1930s Dust Bowl and desperation to protect the natural resources needed to sustain the nation's agriculture.

The swampbuster and sodbuster programs introduced in 1985 were a huge departure in that they aimed to protect broader environmental values beyond the farm itself. The same was true in 1990, with WRP (said to be a CRP for wetlands), the AWQP program (helping farmers improve water quality), and an Integrated Farm Management Program (help with certain combined conservation practices).

These programs were forerunners of the 1996 EQIP, which would ultimately become a "gorilla" of the farm bill Conservation title, of the Wildlife Habitat Incentives Program, which helped farmers address new listings under the Endangered Species Act, and in 2002, of the fledgling Conservation Security Program.

Conservation Compliance

In 1985, it was a revolutionary notion that farmers who take advantage of other farm bill programs (price subsidies, for example) should be required to use conservation management practices on vulnerable lands.

But once that provision was in place, the concept was expanded in 1990 when additional farm bill programs were included in this requirement and as new categories of vulnerable lands were added to the list requiring compliance. New funding was also added to help farmers comply.[4]

Conservation compliance thus became a key tenet of American farm–environmental policy and has been continued or expanded in farm bills since.

Purchasing Agricultural Conservation Easements

Rep. Jim Jeffords's 1979 concept of a federal program to financially support local farmland easement efforts would ultimately stick. Thanks to Senator Leahy, and even though it was limited, the Farms for the Future pilot passed.

That, in turn, produced a 1996 nationwide Farm and Ranchlands Protection Program, which saw a dramatic increase in its funding authorization in 2002, along with creation of a new Grasslands Reserve Program to protect important rangelands. Finally, in 2008, the unfulfilled FRPP funding authorization was turned into actual appropriations, a huge success. These programs were later rolled into today's much more comprehensive ACEP which was continued, improved, and even better funded in 2018.[5]

In fact, 2018 was a year in which both congressional and Trump administration leaders had predicted a "status quo" farm bill. Nonetheless, AFT led a group of farmland protection advocates in a successful fight to expand annual ACEP funding from $250 million to $450 million for the next ten years—an increase of $2 billion for this program.

Farm Risk Management

Along with soil conservation, the other historic foundation of the US farm bill was farm price subsidies. By 1996, public support for those subsidies was becoming strained. Then as now, the public broadly supported agriculture.[6] But its view of farm subsidies was largely negative, depending greatly on how and why they were provided.[7] US farm subsidies had also come under attack in the World Trade Organization, as farmers elsewhere became increasingly frustrated with the artificially low market prices driven down by competition from subsidized US farmers.

Pure subsidies were increasingly at risk. Members of Congress had begun looking for ways to improve or pare down or rethink some of agriculture's least defensible subsidies.

To this end, the 1996 Farm Bill simplified some existing subsidy programs and created a direct payments program, which would compensate farmers based on their history of crop production. The direct payments program was originally intended as a temporary measure that would, over time, allow Congress to wean farmers off such support.[8] It took until 2014, but Congress did finally eliminate the direct payments program.

Meanwhile, AFT's development of the Average Crop Revenue Election (ACRE) program and its adoption in 2008 heralded a new approach designed to help farmers insure themselves against all major agricultural risks, rather than just those associated with unpredictable prices.

With this highly popular precedent, the 2014 Farm Bill was reimagined under a new farm risk management or business insurance theory. ACRE became the Agricultural Risk Coverage program. Previous price support programs became the Price Loss Coverage program.[9] These programs subsidized premiums, but the implicit public benefit rationale of insurance was much clearer and more popular: we were now protecting our farmers from unmanageable agricultural risk in one of the most unpredictable industries on the planet.

What Does It All Mean?

When you look at it today, the broad environmental reach of current US farm policy feels as though it all evolved naturally, as a predictable response to new needs as they became apparent. But these changes were not inevitable. Instead, today's federal farm policy emerged from a new way of thinking about conservation agriculture. And that new way of thinking was led by American Farmland Trust.

Almost immediately following the birth of AFT, a new farm–environmental coalition emerged in the farm bill debate. Through AFT, reliable research became available. Nontraditional answers to traditional problems began receiving serious consideration.

A system of agricultural conservation incentives emerged, addressing public environmental and growth management needs rather than solely agricultural business needs and soil conservation. A new national network of local land trusts, local and state farmland-protection programs, and local farmland advocacy organizations began seeking and receiving federal support and acquired a voice in federal farm policy. PACE programs added an essential new tool to our nation's growth management toolkit.

Propelled by the AFT-led Conservation Coalition, farm politics came to be driven by broader constituencies that aimed to address the public's interest rather than the interests of industry alone. These changes in perspective helped empower the nation's farmers to demonstrate a key, perhaps even critically important new role in *solving* environmental problems rather than merely causing them.

CHAPTER 13

The 2008 Farm Bill: Strategic Research

In 1992, when Dr. Ann Sorensen accepted a position as American Farmland Trust's first assistant vice president for Research, building the groundwork for the organization's political efforts was to be a big part of the job. An insect researcher with a PhD in entomology and special experience in integrated pest management (IPM), Sorensen would be heading up AFT's new Center for Agriculture in the Environment (CAE). The whole enterprise was aimed at preparing AFT for coming battles in the policy arena, including the farm bill.

Sorensen's Center for Agriculture in the Environment wasn't called that by accident. Its name reflected her vision of an agriculture industry that depends upon but also contributes to the natural wealth of our shared environment.

CAE's work encompassed all three of the ways in which a farm can contribute to the environment: (1) through the environmental benefits it provides simply through its existence—benefits that are hopelessly lost should the farm fail and its land be sold and developed; (2) by using conservation management practices to deal with whatever environmental threats its farming activities themselves might pose, thus making itself fully environmentally sustainable; and (3) by generating precious *new* environmental benefits resulting from the dramatic, additive environmental gains that can be achieved on working, productive agricultural lands: such positive overall environmental improvements as positive regeneration of the soil, creation of new wildlife habitat, restoration of lost wetlands, recharging the ground water that lies beneath it and filtering and improving the quality of the surface water that flows across it, detaining floods, and the like.

Sorensen came to the AFT job with experience in IPM from the Texas Department of Agriculture and as member of an advisory committee for the US Environmental Protection Agency. She also spent six years with the Natural and Environmental Resources Division for the American Farm Bureau Federation. She was at home in the worlds of public policy, business, academia, and agriculture. Sorensen and CAE would play an enormous role in AFT's many policy successes.

The story of the 2008 Farm Bill deserves particular attention. Sorensen and AFT wanted to see a federal farm policy that not only helped farmers but at the same time also improved the environment. But getting there would depend on the legislative interplay between law and appropriations and, like all politics, on the kind of personal relationships that flourish with collaboration and mutual respect.

Critical Beginnings in 2002

The 2008 Farm Bill was grounded in the farm bill that had passed six years earlier.

The 2002 Farm Bill was itself a huge milestone in the growth of the Conservation title first enacted in 1985.[1] There were improvements in and increased funding for major voluntary conservation cost-share programs. The Conservation Coalition remained engaged and was instrumental in creating all these programs, and in 2002, it saw further improvements.

In particular, there were big things in the wind for the Farm and Ranchlands Protection Program (FRPP), for which funding had thus far been minimal. In 2002, among other things, Congress finally adopted a funding *authorization* for FRPP of $1 billion: $200 million a year over five years. This new money greatly broadened the potential impact of existing agricultural conservation easement programs, since FRPP customarily provided matching money for those programs. And it was also enough to seriously motivate wavering states and counties around the country that were considering adoption of local PACE programs. Land trusts were made eligible to participate in holding FRPP-funded easements, thus greatly increasing their interest and participation.

By 2002, Grossi and AFT had, for some years, already been making the case that there must be approaches to farm support that went beyond the traditional commodity subsidies (at the time, primarily price supports and direct payments for the dry bulk commodity crops). The justifications being offered for price supports had originated in the 1930s and were increasingly nonsensical in the modern era of containerized international trade and refrigerated transport. Trade had come to be governed by the modern General Agreement on Tariffs and Trade and then its successor, the World Trade Organization (WTO), with rules that hadn't existed in the 1930s. More environmentally responsible approaches were needed, ones friendlier to international trade and more popular with the public—that last being essential for politically sustainability.

Back in 1996, when Congress adopted a "temporary" direct payment program, the plan had been to find ways to wean farmers off these subsidies. However, when 2002 rolled around, no one was any closer to a solution than before. So, despite well-known, widespread general public dissatisfaction with farm subsidy programs, Congress felt compelled to renew them yet again. The potential environmental gains on the table as congressional leaders closed in on the 2002 Farm Bill doubtless played a role in the final deal.

AFT had been a key critic of those subsidy programs—arguing that while the financial support was definitely needed in agriculture, it could be much more effectively used and more broadly helpful for farmers if spent in other ways. When price supports and direct payments came up in negotiations alongside conservation improvements, AFT made a significant commitment: it promised these key players and members of Congress that it would, over the next five years, search for a better answer for commodity farmers, an answer that would step back from traditional price supports and help make commodity programs more politically sustainable, acceptable to the WTO, and environmentally sound.

Strategic Preparations

In stepping into the commodity program arena, AFT was now working with ag-connected groups like the American Farm Bureau Federation, the National Corn Growers Association, the Wheat Growers Association, and the National Association of Conservation Districts, as well as with major environmental groups like the National Audubon Society, Natural Resources Defense Council, Environmental Working Group, Environmental Defense Fund, and Sierra Club.

So, in 2008, these major farm bill players, along with members of Congress, were going to be looking to AFT to deliver on its 2002 commitment. As the farm bill drew closer, it became increasingly clear that 2008 marked a critical moment in AFT's history—and in the history of the farm bill.

AFT's strategic weapon of choice would be sound research. And deploying that strategy was the task presented to the organization's head of research, Dr. Ann Sorensen.

Sorensen knew the first priority was to understand the needs of the people most directly affected by the problem: the nation's farmers.

Step one was to undertake a series of farm industry listening sessions throughout the country. These sessions would inform whatever AFT might ultimately propose. And they would also help identify and motivate a constituency of grassroots ag industry leaders who might support whatever ended up on the table.

Next, Sorensen tapped into her deep well of professional contacts in the academic community. These were the thinkers, writers, and teachers of farm policy. They were the analysts, critics, and historians who studied these issues, published articles in academic journals, and were, upon occasion, called upon to testify before Congress.

The proposal that emerged was a completely new farm program.[2] Simply put, the program would insure participating farmers' anticipated gross crop revenue. That meant the participating farmer would be protected if, for whatever reason, the price suddenly collapsed or if there was some unanticipated loss or damage to the crop. If some unpredictable natural event (flood, fire, hail, wind, pest infestation, drought, or just an especially bad year) should diminish crop yield, or if some unpredictable economic event produced a collapse in the market price, the farmer would be protected *either way*. The farmer's total anticipated average crop revenue was the asset being insured.

This was revolutionary in several ways:

- By protecting the farmer from risks of both price collapse and crop failure, the program would greatly ameliorate the farm boom-or-bust phenomenon. Previously, if a farmer had a bad crop year, a good price, subsidized or not, was of little consolation. And if the farmer had a very good crop year, the price supports simply provided an occasional windfall.
- Losses (and payments) would be based on *actual* anticipated average crop revenue estimated just before planting, rather than on

some artificial price arbitrarily (and politically) set far in advance by Congress. Here was a genuine insurance program grounded in real-world expectations and losses.

- It would address another massive need: protection from inevitable farm disasters. There was a long history of farmers periodically appealing to Congress for relief from some natural catastrophe: a Midwest drought, flooding on the Mississippi, a hailstorm in Montana, a tornado in Kansas. Inevitably, Congress would feel compelled to write the check. The AFT proposal would protect farmers from those natural disasters and reduce the need for that kind of occasional but expensive and troublesome ad hoc relief.
- It was much more trade-friendly.[3] This was a big deal because at the time, the United States was being "sued" in the WTO for unfair trade practices in the international marketplace. WTO did not look kindly on outright, market-disrupting subsidies targeting some arbitrary price set by politicians without any particular regard to the actual marketplace. It was much more difficult, however, to find fault with a crop revenue insurance program grounded in genuine, real-world advance predictions and actual market prices, a program for which the farmer paid real premiums, even if they might get government help with those premiums.
- By reducing the boom-and-bust phenomenon and basing protection on sound, annual advance crop planning, the new program might reduce the excessive planting of crops on truly marginal, unproductive, environmentally sensitive lands.

This, then, was AFT's 2008 answer to congressional leaders' 2002 challenge that it design a stronger, more publicly understandable, trade-friendly commodity crop support program. Later on, as the 2008 Farm Bill made its way through Congress and AFT's proposal came up for discussion in the Senate Agriculture Committee, the program received the clean, nicely descriptive title of the Average Crop Revenue Election (ACRE) program.

The FRPP Dilemma

Meanwhile, congressional appropriations in the years following the 2002 Farm Bill had not fulfilled the funding authorization promise for one of AFT's signature federal farm policy achievements, the FRPP. Actual funding had never come anywhere near the $200 million per year that was authorized in 2002.

A lot was at stake. By 2008, AFT's work promoting PACE programs was seeing remarkable success. There were at least twenty-seven state-level PACE programs in place around the country. And many more were needed. The organization's several new regional offices were helping to stimulate local and state PACE programs everywhere, successes such as the one in Lexington, Kentucky, where a program AFT helped establish has protected more than thirty-two thousand acres of high-quality farmland. By the end of that decade, AFT had played a leading role in the creation of more than forty local PACE programs.[4]

AFT's energetic education and support of the land trust community had also paid off in an upswelling in local interest by private land trusts in protecting farmland with agricultural easements. These land trusts were generating new local capacity to provide matching funds for whatever federal dollars could be made available.

The long-term success of all that state and local effort now depended on meaningful progress at the federal level. All the years of AFT work seemed to hang by a thread. Those state and local programs, those newly motivated land trusts, they all needed a robust FRPP if they were to survive and flourish.

FRPP money gave confidence to state and local policymakers that PACE programs made financial sense and deserved support. Without federal matching funds, state and local governments would be required to bear the entire cost of PACE programs. And that could mean declining support from hard-won public constituencies and, perversely, from congressional backers as well. Absent federal help, the growing engagement by the nation's land trust movement in farmland protection could falter.

Finding the Money

As is often said, all politics is local. It is also all about personal relationships. Given the importance of the FRPP appropriation, in anticipation of the 2008 Farm Bill, AFT launched a nationwide lobbying effort to *locally* enlist help from members of Congress across the country. One of many such efforts, for example, involved Rep. Rosa DeLauro of Connecticut.

DeLauro was a member of the critical House Appropriations Subcommittee for Agriculture; her help would be needed to fund almost anything in the farm bill. She was also, as it happened, one of a small group of female House members who gathered at one or another of their homes each Thursday evening to cook Italian food and talk politics. The group included Rep. Nancy Pelosi.

Aware that Representative DeLauro was a strong local food advocate, AFT's Northeast regional policy staffer, Cris Coffin, among other steps, helped orchestrate DeLauro's participation in a successful opening day celebration for a popular local farmers market. At that event, after the fashion of major league baseball, Representative DeLauro was asked to throw out the first head of lettuce. That struck the fancy of reporters and earned DeLauro some very positive press.

DeLauro's appreciation probably helped enlist her support when, later that year, the FRPP appropriations came before her committee. As the 2008 Farm Bill approached, various relationships of this kind, throughout the country, had helped to create a climate in which AFT's ambitious FRPP budget appropriations hopes had at least become possible.

Political Chaos and a Faustian Choice

With so much at stake, the 2008 Farm Bill also turned out to be the moment that the nation's environmental groups collectively decided to rebel against the established farm bill order and to strike out on their own.

For upwards of two decades, environmentalists lobbying the farm bill had, along with everybody else, worked their way laboriously through the usual committee process, where they'd dealt with the established congressional power structure and were required to compete (or negotiate or both) with the mainstream agriculture industry. Yet on this cycle, many established environmental groups, seeing an opening to move the needle further, returned to their old habit of portraying agriculture as the problem.

Much of the environmental community decided to bypass all those difficult negotiations and, when the farm bill came up on the House floor for debate, offer a major amendment that would essentially replace the bill that had been produced through the normal committee process. The Kind Amendment, to be presented by Rep. Ron Kind of Wisconsin, would serve as an alternative to the committee work being done on the traditional farm bill. The anticipated amendment received a lot of publicity and garnered considerable support. Supporting it was tempting for AFT. If passed, it would have dramatically altered the course of federal farm policy in favor of much greater environmental protection.

The environmental community was all in. There was a good deal of pressure for AFT to support this floor amendment. And there was a broad sense that it could pass. Some of the major environmental foundations—funders that had substantially supported AFT's work on this farm bill and who were important prospects for future funding—would be expecting AFT to be on board. Joining the effort would, of course, burn a great many bridges built in the preceding years with the mainstream farm community.

The Moment of Truth

It was July 22, 2007, and Ralph Grossi was at home for the evening. The "official" farm bill was before the House Agriculture Committee and would likely go to the House floor for a vote a few days later. At that point, Representative Kind would offer his amendment, which would surely include all sorts of improvements that Grossi would love to see happen. But the proponents were keeping the specifics close to their chest; in the end, Grossi might be forced to decide his position on very short notice and without having much time to assess the contents. Not knowing the details of the Kind Amendment, Grossi had kept AFT focused on working with the committee on more modest improvements in its traditional farm bill.

At the Grossi home, just as his family was sitting down for dinner, the phone rang. On the line was, of all people, Rep. Collin Peterson, chair of the House Agriculture Committee.

"Are you with us on the committee bill?" Peterson asked.

"Will we have the appropriations we've requested for farmland protection?" Grossi responded, referring to FRPP money that was authorized in 2002 but never actually appropriated.

"I will see that you get your funding," the chairman promised.

Grossi made a calculated bet and replied, "We'll be with you on your bill."

After he hung up, he took a deep breath; he now had four days to wait before discovering whether he'd just made the worst mistake of his professional career.

The next day, the House Agriculture Committee passed out their bill. It came up for a vote on the House floor three days later, July 26, 2007. As expected, Representative Kind offered his amendment. The amendment failed by a thoroughly decisive vote, 117–309.

The committee bill passed. And the FRRP funding appropriation was a done deal.

2014 Sequalae: A Commodity Program Revolution

As is so often the case in farm bill politics, the 2008 story didn't end there.

By 2014, public and WTO pressure on commodity subsidies had increased. The nation was still clawing its way out of the worst stock market and economic collapse since 1929. Government subsidies of any kind had become something of a political flashpoint. The direct payment program was still in place. Thankfully, Congress had in hand new, politically viable alternatives. Among these was the increasingly popular ACRE program. And ACRE had provided a road map for a much more robust and publicly acceptable theory for agriculture industry support: a new insurance rationale.

The former ACRE program was reinvented as Agriculture Risk Coverage. The former Counter-Cyclical Payment program would become Price Loss Coverage. The previous direct payment program was eliminated, with some (unfortunately, not all) of its funding redirected into other farm programs.[5]

Farmers paid premiums to participate in these programs. Those premiums were partially subsidized by the government, so one should not jump to the conclusion that taxpayer support for our farmers had come to an end. Nor should it. Our agriculture industry faces a multitude of risks not common to most other business endeavors—and farming is essential to our economy and our national security. Farmers play a critical role in our nation's food self-sufficiency. And they are increasingly being asked to provide a host of environmental services and other broad public benefits—the cost of which could never be made up by raising prices given the highly competitive international marketplace for farm products.

But with passage of the 2008 Farm Bill, farm commodity programs were substantially reformed; critical conservation programs from earlier farm bills were retained and enhanced; and farmland protection, nationwide, went mainstream.

CHAPTER 14

The Power of Research

In public policy advocacy, research can be that rare keystone whose addition or removal will support or collapse an entire edifice of logic. Consider a few examples:

Back in the years before the enactment of the revolutionary Conservation Reserve Program (CRP) in 1985, it was already well documented that cultivation of highly erodible lands in America's farm country was causing serious soil loss and sediment pollution in our nation's vulnerable streams and rivers. Contemporary USDA policies and programs did not seem to be helping; it was believed they might even be making things worse.

It was also well known that environmentalists desperately wanted to reduce cultivation of vulnerable, highly erodible lands in US farm country and to see them restored to wildlife habitat. There were also powerful, increasingly vocal sportsmen's groups wanting to improve habitat for game birds. In farm country, low crop prices were widely believed to be caused by overproduction—farmers were looking for new ways to be compensated for reducing how much they grew.

It quickly became apparent that all those people could get what they wanted if there were just some kind of new federally compensated set-aside program for vulnerable farmland.

But what changes to the law would be needed? How might such a program work? And how much would it cost?

There are rivers throughout America today suffering under assault from worsening nonpoint pollution. This pollution increasingly originates in farm country. And it is very often the product of surface water runoff from reduced flow, damaged riparian vegetation, lost wetlands, and destroyed wildlife habitat.

Environmentalists want those farmers regulated. And they want that streamside environment restored. Farmers, facing hard, inelastic markets for their products, fear the cost of regulation and much prefer voluntary conservation incentives. Meanwhile, EPA, the relevant regulatory agency, fears that these voluntary incentives would be too costly and unworkable:—there wouldn't be enough money provided; therefore, too few farmers would agree to participate. So EPA is loath to rely upon them.

Meanwhile, local industrial point source polluters and wastewater treatment plants on those same rivers are already severely regulated under the Clean Water Act. Unregulated nonpoint pollution simply heightens the point source restrictions they already face and threatens their businesses and the communities they serve. Very often, new high-tech wastewater treatment facilities are seen as the only answer—facilities that can easily cost hundreds of millions of dollars to build and tens of millions annually to maintain.

If the proposed farmer incentives programs worked, however, they could eliminate the need for such massive investments in infrastructure and greatly diminish that point source regulation. They could also fund the restoration of critical riparian vegetation and habitat throughout the watershed. This investment in water quality would also produce extraordinary side benefits for wildlife, carbon sequestration, wetlands, aquifer recharge, and a host of ancillary environmental values.

Meanwhile, those point source polluters would be all in. They'd also be happy to contribute if, as seems likely, the cost would be but a fraction of the direct regulations and new wastewater treatment investments they're now facing.

But how much would it cost? How exactly would the program work? How many farmers would willingly participate?

In growing urban communities across America, there are local food advocates worried that urban sprawl will displace their region's farms. When all their farms are gone, what will become of their much-loved local farmers markets? Where will consumers get their local produce? Very often, local smart growth groups also hope to protect those farms. Farmers worry, however, because many local food and smart growth people seem willing to simply rezone the farms for agriculture. That designation could destroy the farmers' property values and undermine their life savings.

A new local PACE program would often be the perfect answer. But such programs are costly. Meanwhile, many local governments are struggling to adopt and pay for various local climate initiatives, which will already place new burdens on their taxpayers.

If, however, those suburban-edge farm properties are broken up and sold for housing, the added automobile commuter mileage and lost vegetative cover that would result could substantially increase the community's carbon footprint. Protecting those farms with a proposed PACE program could easily prove to be a great deal cheaper than existing initiatives. But what would be the carbon impact? How would the cost for such a PACE program per ton of carbon sequestered or emissions prevented compare with the cost of the current initiatives?

In American Farmland Trust's world, questions much like these come up all the time. And the research required to answer them can often be done at extraordinarily modest cost, considering the importance of the potential policy gain.

Consider what is required (and what is not required) for an advocacy group to be able to take advantage of opportunities like those mentioned above:

Current, active participation. You'd need to be sufficiently active in the policy arena to become aware of these emerging circumstances early enough act on them.

Expertise. Your staff would need the expertise to recognize the opportunity, to conceive of the necessary research, to know what is possible (when it can be done and by whom), to get the research completed, and to credibly translate the results into policy.

Fundraising capacity. You'd need the capacity to identify a potential funder and to then prepare a detailed and compelling application that could successfully secure the money needed to pay for the necessary research.

Communications and public exposure. You'd need the capacity and expertise to assure the research outcome gets appropriate public exposure, so it has the necessary public impact to make the difference.

Coalition building. You'd need the experience and the inclination to work successfully with key players on all sides of the debate and to draw them into the coalition(s) required to push through an agreed action.

Credibility. You'd need the organizational credibility to offer the research results to the public, to constituent and coalition groups, and to appropriate policymakers in a manner that it will be both convincing and decisive for them.

What you do *not* need is a huge organization with hundreds of thousands (or millions) of members, a local office in every community, a well-funded PAC, highly polemic advocacy, and immense political clout.

In fact, AFT's efforts show how much can be accomplished with some key research, whether it's conducted by one organization alone, shared with partner nonprofits and agencies, or supported by outside academic or independent consultants. It would be impossible to try to summarize all of AFT's research efforts. Instead, what follows are a few examples that show exactly how research can be put into practice and used to launch strategic policy initiatives. (Many more examples can be found at AFT's Farmland Information Center and Center for Agriculture in the Environment websites.[1])

Soil Conservation in America

The CRP, first adopted in 1985, has become perhaps the most universally popular farm conservation program in farm bill history. The bedrock upon which it was written was an AFT research report: *Soil Conservation in America: What Do We Have to Lose?*[2]

The study convened a twenty-four-member special advisory panel composed of some of the nation's most respected farmers, ranchers, farm business owners, and conservationists. It reviewed published and unpublished scientific literature, did in-depth interviews with hundreds of farmers, and commissioned twenty-two technical papers by recognized academic professionals. The findings were eye-opening:

The scale of the problem. There was a disturbing gap between the magnitude of soil erosion problems on some 413 million acres of US cropland, and the severely limited soil erosion control afforded through existing government policies and programs and through the efforts of individual farmers.

A strategic opportunity. The first reliable, nationally consistent estimates of soil erosion in the United States, obtained by a USDA survey in 1977, revealed that a very large share of the country's soil erosion was associated with a relatively small proportion of the land.

A failure in existing programs. The highly erodible lands that accounted for much of the erosion problem on US cropland appeared to be eluding most methods of conservation farming, as well as the services of traditional USDA conservation programs.

Potential for solutions. Certain USDA programs, particularly the crop price support programs, could be modified to provide substantial soil conservation benefits, but they tended to subsidize abusive land practices.

Based on those findings, the study reached four startling broad recommendations:

A new farm policy goal. Establish the non-degradation of agricultural resources as a central goal of national farm policy.

A new CRP program. Establish a long-term Conservation Reserve Program for highly erodible cropland under the umbrella of USDA's traditional conservation and commodity programs.

Remove subsidies on vulnerable lands. Eliminate those elements of government policies and programs that subsidize future cultivation of highly erodible lands.

Focus technical assistance on controlling erosion. Focus assistance on cost-effective erosion control methods and on land where soil loss is likely to be causing chronic on-site or off-site damage.

These conclusions resulted in a set of twenty-three specific recommendations, many of which were rolled into the 1985 Farm Bill, where they helped create CRP, led to new conservation compliance provisions, and inspired the first Conservation title in the nation's history.

Cost of Community Services[3]

As frontier settlements moved westward and small towns sprang up everywhere along the way, it was a common view that, given time and local commitment, any of these towns could become the next Chicago.[4] To this day, it is typical for small communities to believe the real solution to their problems lies in encouraging an influx of growth. All those coveted new residents and new activities will surely bring with them wealth in the form of more and better jobs, a richer local economy, and growing tax revenues with which to improve municipal services.

In actual practice, however, all those added people make ever-increasing demands on public services, often more than depleting whatever added tax revenues they provide. The question for local civic leaders is not: How much growth can we attract? Rather it is: What kind of growth will it be, and do we really want it?

Growth means development. And in rural, agricultural communities, especially ones within reach of urban centers, that development all too often manifests as residential sprawl. That sprawl very often converts and destroys the farmland that surrounds the town, land whose agricultural productivity has served for generations as the economic foundation for the town's very existence.

For farmers, nearby development is a mixed bag. On the one hand, those few who sell direct to consumers may find local marketing opportunities in the new growth. Many other farmers might see their property values increase. But for farmers who want to stay in farming, the increased value may be a negative. It can mean an increase in property taxes and hence an increase in the farm's operating costs.[5] Beyond that, a farm located in a high-growth area will often become surrounded by new residents who complain bitterly about the noise and odors of farming and who pressure farmers to constrain their operations. When some farms do fall to development, the local economic infrastructure that supports the remaining farms (equipment dealers, feed and seed stores, farm service providers, and so on) takes a hit. For these and other reasons, the economics of farming generally suffers when this kind of development comes to farm communities.

The financial realities for local governments change as well. For a local civic leader, it would be useful to understand the fiscal and economic consequences of that development. It turns out that the different types of land use that result from growth have distinct tax and fee impacts. And some of those land uses may require considerable upscaling of costly community services—highway maintenance and other transportation services, police departments, fire protection, schools, power, water and sewer, health and safety, and the like. It is therefore vital to pay attention to what land uses will follow from the coveted growth.

In 1986, American Farmland Trust became interested in this conundrum. How did increased density also increase the cost of providing the public infrastructure to support it? The organization's research uncovered a remarkable study in Clarke County, Virginia, that had been completed by the Piedmont Environmental Council (PEC). The study examined the fiscal impacts of three basic land use categories, one of which was farmland and open space.

AFT's Bob Wagner expanded on the PEC approach in a later study in Hebron, Connecticut, and then he teamed up with Cornell Cooperative Extension to further replicate the study. When AFT's new hire, Julia Freedgood, came on board, she further developed and refined the idea. It wasn't long before AFT was offering a new kind of standardized municipal land use study it called a Cost of Community Services (COCS) study.[6]

COCS studies break down land uses into common types, typically three: residential, commercial and industrial, and farms and forests. The study uses public records to ascertain the respective amounts currently being paid in taxes by each land use as compared with the costs being incurred in providing that land use with public services.

Julia Freedgood clarified the foundations for these studies and described a consistent method for accomplishing them.[7] But a part of the effectiveness of Freedgood's methodology was that she made it sufficiently clear and straightforward that, since then, a great many of these studies have now been done by others—universities, private consultants, various nonprofits, and local governments themselves.

That is leverage.

Looking at all these studies collectively, one discovers a range of average costs for community services depending on land use:[8]

- Residential properties cost $1.16 in community services provided to them for every $1 those properties pay in tax revenue.
- Business properties cost: $0.30 in community services for every $1 paid in taxes, and
- Farm and forest properties cost: $0.37 in community services for every $1 paid in taxes.

There's nothing insidious going on here; it just usually works out that residential properties cost more to service than they pay for in taxes. They do have a lot of market value, of course, so what they pay in taxes is substantial. But their public services also cost a good deal more. And that $0.16 deficit represents a very large sum of money, which must be made up by the tax surpluses received from business and agriculture.

Several natural conclusions can flow from these findings:

- If you're going to bring in a bunch of new local residents, you might want to be sure there will be a substantial farm, commercial, and industrial tax base to support them. If those new local residents will actually be commuting to other, more prosperous and business-oriented neighboring communities for their employment and to do much of their shopping, as often is the case in urban-edge farm country, your town's (or county's) public revenues will almost certainly suffer. Communities that can be hit the hardest by growing public service costs are very often ones that may still be largely agricultural but that are located, unfortunately, right next door to an economic powerhouse.

- If you are inviting in new business, you need to consider how many new residents will come in as well to work in them. Where will those new residents live? Their new homes will, almost certainly, draw down any new gains you see from the added business tax revenues you'll receive. If you've offered a bunch of tax incentives to get those businesses to move to your community, that may not turn out to be the great bargain you thought it was.

- Wherever those new residents live or work, if they will be living in homes built on former agricultural lands, they will be driving your local public revenues into the red. If you replace one hundred acres of farmland with, say, four hundred new homes, you will not only have to cover that deficit of $0.16 per $1 you face on every one of those residential properties but also cover your loss of the surplus revenue of $0.63 per $1 over service cost that, until now, you've been receiving from the farmers who previously owned and managed that land.[9]

Those service costs and losses can add up to a lot of money—quite possibly far more than you gain in new revenue.

COCS studies have been done so often and the method is so nicely established that the cost of doing them is now quite minimal. Enthusiasm for one's local community is a good thing. It's hard to fault people trying to boost their local economy. But once they've seen the results of one of these studies, local community ardor for growth and development can cool and become a good deal more intelligent.

Very often, local farmers end up liking these studies because they confirm something the farmers have long suspected: perhaps they're overtaxed. This understanding can encourage them to argue for more of a public services return—funding for conservation incentives, a new local PACE program, local food system improvements, farm economic development assistance, for example.

Farming on the Edge

In 1997, American Farmland Trust's *Farming on the Edge* (FOE) study documented the nation's farmland loss and, for the first time, produced a comprehensive national map showing the areas of the country where the best agricultural lands were most threatened by sprawling development.[10] Its findings were as follows:

Lost farmland. One million two hundred thousand acres of farmland were being lost to development every year; that's more than two acres of farmland permanently lost every minute of every day.

Losses accelerating. The rate of loss was accelerating.

Most productive lands being lost. We were losing the most productive, fertile one-fifth of our farmland at a rate 30 percent higher than average: an outcome to be anticipated, given that our cities most often grew up where the people were. Usually that was where most of the farmers and the best farmlands were as well.

Fruits and vegetables vulnerable. Eighty-six percent of the nation's fruits and vegetables and 63 percent of its dairy production was to be found in areas that were most gravely threatened by development.

Cultural issues driving losses. Much of the problem could be accounted for by wasteful land uses driven by changing public tastes and a desire for each American family to occupy ever larger parcels of land.

Every state hit. Every state was suffering losses, but most of the losses were occurring in the twenty hardest hit.

The 1997 FOE differed from its predecessors in that it made farmland loss local—made it possible for people in the localities affected to begin seeing what was happening to *them*. By listing the twenty hardest-hit communities, it brought the issue home. One could look at their community on a national map that identified the areas of the country where high-value farmland was most threatened. It made the threat personal.

This study was widely distributed, received immense press, and may have had more public impact than any study AFT ever produced. It was used to support farmland protection throughout the country for many years and does so still today.

One example of FOE's widespread impact occurred in Maine, where a small group of farmers and farm supporters reviewed AFT's maps and data—and were propelled into action. In 1999, after collecting more information and organizing initial support, Maine Farmland Trust was founded. The initial board included AFT's Jerry Cosgrove and a farm advocate named John Piotti, who would become AFT's fifth president seventeen years later.

Explained Piotti, "Those of us who worked with farmers knew what was happening to Maine's farmland, but it was hard to convince others of the need to protect this resource before it was too late. *Farming on the Edge* gave us what we needed to make that case."

AFT followed up FOE with subsequent studies and updates every few years. Then, building upon this past body of work yet seeing the need to renew data and incorporate new geographic information system technology, AFT launched an initiative in 2015 called *Farms Under Threat*.[11] This ongoing multiyear, multiphase study constitutes the most comprehensive analysis of US land use and land cover ever undertaken.

Alternatives for Future Urban Growth in California's Central Valley

California's Central Valley produces 250 different commodities worth more than $13 billion a year, making it one of the most valuable agricultural regions in the country. But with a population expected to triple by the year 2040, those incredibly valuable agricultural lands are at serious risk.

In a 1995 study, AFT documented the likely economic and other losses that would occur if the current and anticipated low-density urban sprawl continued, and then compared that outcome with what could be expected given more compact and efficient urban growth.[12] The findings were astounding:

Land loss. Low-density sprawl was projected to consume over one million acres of farmland by 2040, of which 60 percent was either prime farmland or farmland of statewide importance. There was also an expected "zone of conflict" of another 2.5 million acres that would increase costs of doing business and decrease farm productivity. Compact, efficient growth would reduce farmland conversion to 474,000 acres and the zone of conflict to 1.6 million acres.

Economic loss. With compact efficient growth rather than low-density sprawl, the cumulative economic loss by 2040 would be reduced by $72 billion.

Taxpayer loss. The cumulative savings in cost of providing taxpayer supported community services, over that same time, would be some $29 billion.

Shortly after the release of this study, the State of California adopted the initial stages of the California Farmland Conservancy Program, its first statewide farmland protection law.[13] This study and its findings left open the possible methods of addressing farmland loss: regulatory and incentive. The alternative to current sprawl was described by the study as "more compact, efficient growth" in a pattern reasonably achievable in these communities almost certainly only through the use of zoning laws. The California Farmland Conservancy Program that followed, predictably, does include specific direction for growth management to consider farmland loss and the power to address it.

Thus this California study represented one of those occasions when AFT farmland protection advocacy embraced growth management as one solution. Thankfully, there was significant California support for this outcome from agriculture itself, as there has been when AFT has taken this approach elsewhere.[14]

CAE's[15] Work with EPA on Integrated Pest Management Grants

World War II drove forward a new body of knowledge in chemistry. American farmers moved quickly and steadily in the postwar period toward increased use of new highly effective but also often highly toxic pesticides in commercial agriculture.[16] In reaction to this trend, the organic food movement and the federal certification for organic farming were born. That chemical trend ultimately led to the Federal Food Quality Protection Act (FQPA) of 1996, the nation's effort to rein in the accelerating use of toxic pesticides in commercial agriculture.[17]

Pursuant to FQPA, EPA slowly but steadily increased regulatory pressure to cut back on organophosphate pesticides, considered to be especially problematic for human health and the environment. These pesticides can also be very useful in reducing certain insect pests commonly found in agriculture, so they were heavily utilized by farmers. FQPA gave EPA authority to administer grants in the agriculture industry to thoroughly study and document how farmers could reduce their use of these dangerous pesticides or eliminate them entirely, sometimes using replacement products with fewer risks and sometimes using entirely organic alternative strategies. The good news was that they could frequently grow a better crop and save money in the process.

EPA turned to AFT's new Center for Agriculture in the Environment (CAE) to help administer those grants, for obvious reasons. CAE had, of course, been leading research on integrated pest management (IPM) for several years. But equally important, if not more so, was Ann Sorensen's and AFT's credibility on both sides of the farm–environmental divide. EPA obviously needed these studies to be scrupulously done and accepted in the scientific community. But to be effective, the studies also needed to inform and change actual farmer behavior. They needed to be useful and believable within the agriculture industry.

Over the years that followed, AFT's CAE administered these EPA grants in locations all over the country. It oversaw scores of small, independent studies on nearly every conceivable crop and application.

Viewed broadly, these IPM studies sought strategies that could serve as alternatives to intensive use of organophosphate pesticides. Their approach was to find and prove out creative new methods for dealing with agricultural pests, either without pesticides or by dramatically reducing their use. Below are a few examples from among the hundreds of such studies done all across the country:

Washington tree fruit pheromone interruption. Using mating disruption pheromones in the tree fruit industry, some 191 orchards covering 3,500 acres in Washington's fertile Yakima Valley converted away from pesticides and were persuaded by the project's success to move instead to community-wide pheromone disruption.

Wisconsin potatoes, IPM pesticide cost analysis. Eighteen growers representing ten thousand acres participated in the study and were able to document considerable pesticide cost savings through reduced, more strategic use of pesticides.

Georgia cotton. A model for ecologically based cotton production was tested in an effort to eliminate Temik pesticide (aldicarb) in cotton production. A no-till cotton production system was developed using legume cover crops, which eliminated the need for pesticides while increasing farm profits and offering potential for marketing as organic cotton.

Site-specific weather networks. An extensive system of site-specific weather stations established throughout the state of Washington provided farmers with easily accessible and highly precise weather data specific to their own farm, at very low cost. Weather data is critical to predicting the annual emergence of pests, so this new tool allowed farmers to dramatically and confidently reduce their use of pesticides to what was actually needed to protect their crops.

Pesticide risk reduction among Hawaii's new and immigrant farmers. With a large percentage of immigrant farmers in Hawaii having limited English language skills, many were unable to read pesticide labels, and at least 75 percent were overusing pesticides. The project provided extensive training to farmers and to applicators to reduce their excess pesticide use.

There were scores of these studies and projects nationwide. The total collection of projects funded over the years in this program generated a massive body of knowledge, increased use of IPM methods, and helped to usher in a growing organic agriculture and facilitate IPM's acceptance in mainstream commercial agriculture.

Most important, it greatly reduced the use of dangerous pesticides nationwide.

Investing in the Future of Agriculture: The Massachusetts Farmland Protection Program and the Permanence Syndrome

All land, including farmland, has "fair market value," which is the price at which a willing buyer and seller can reach agreement. Usually this is the price that can be afforded by a buyer who intends to put the land to what the real estate industry calls its highest and best use. Whether any given use is actually "highest and best" in noneconomic terms can perhaps be debated. But what Realtors mean by that is quite practical: it is the use that will generate the most monetary value. Usually that turns out to be the most intensive, least environmentally friendly use possible. Unfortunately, farm businesses, which compete in a global marketplace, very often cannot afford to pay enough for land (which for them is a business investment) to compete with those more intensive alternative non-farm uses.

Development-threatened farmland in America, therefore, often has *two* values: a fair market value (a.k.a. development value) and an agricultural business value (a.k.a. farm value). The land's "farm value" is measured by what a willing farm buyer can afford to invest in farmland while still being able to profit from its use in the business of agriculture.

As farmland slowly acquires a fair market value that exceeds its agricultural business value, it also becomes increasingly unrealistic for the farmer-owner to plow new investments into improving that land's farm productivity.

Think about a farmer's dilemma when considering an investment in new farm infrastructure like a new barn, livestock fencing, a dairy waste lagoon, a hop kiln, a more efficient irrigation system, erosion prevention, or long-term improvements in the richness of the soil. Investments like these could improve the future productivity of the farm as an agricultural business. They'd be investments that would naturally be considered by anyone intending to remain in farming in the years ahead.

Suppose, however, that you're this farmer. If you're of average farmer age, you're fifty-nine years old.[18] You will, of course, be entirely aware that your farm has appreciated in value far beyond what any of your farmer neighbors could possibly pay and still continue to farm it. You know, therefore, that when your farm next sells, it will almost certainly sell to someone who intends to put it to a much more intensive use than farming.

Your land is destined for development.

When it next sells, the developer who buys it will have no reason to value all those investments you've made in its ag business value. In fact, your "improvements" will almost certainly *diminish* its value to the most likely buyer. The first things that developer-buyer will do, for example, will be to tear down that now-useless modern barn; rip out that highly efficient irrigation system; coil up and dispose of the cross-fencing you painstaking designed and installed; doze up, sell off, and truck away all that precious farm topsoil you spent a lifetime improving.

From an economic perspective, once farmland has acquired a fair market value that exceeds its agricultural business value, then investing in the land in ways that improve the future profitability of the farm becomes pointless, even foolish. The result is an inevitable "impermanence" in the farm businesses affected by it.

In 1998, AFT decided to document this phenomenon. It did a study of farms that had been protected by the Massachusetts Farmland Protection Program, the oldest state-level PACE program in the country. The study was titled: *Investing in the Future of Agriculture: The Massachusetts Farmland Protection Program and the Permanence Syndrome.*[19] AFT surveyed and interviewed hundreds of Massachusetts farmers whose land had been protected by an agricultural easement. The results were remarkable:

Land remained in agriculture. Eighty percent of the farmers surveyed were farming all or most of their easement-protected land. Fewer than 10 percent said they were farming less than half. These farms included a good deal of land that was in forest, wetlands, or otherwise unfarmable, and in some instances, protection of the land had encouraged the farmer to actually increase land in cultivation by clearing brush; reseeding hayfields; and bringing old, abandoned fields back into production.

Future planned land use. Ninety-three percent were planning to keep their land in agriculture in the years ahead.

More resources available for farm business. Farmers who had purchased or inherited easement-protected land had more resources available to them to devote to farming than those who had not.

Improved opportunity for entry. Younger and highly motivated farmers in the market for farmland were actively seeking land that had been protected by easements. Of those who had purchased such land, 62.5 percent said the program had helped them buy their land.

Greater investment in farm business. Almost 75 percent of the farmers had made new investments in their operations since protecting their land with an agricultural easement. Investments included repairs to farm buildings; adopting new conservation practices; purchasing more land, farm equipment and livestock; and developing new value-added products for the marketplace. Seventy-eight percent of those who made such investments reported that the program had been important to improving their operations. Ninety-five percent believed their new investments were important to the long-term viability of their operations.

Security in land use and ownership. From the personal interviews conducted in the study, it was concluded that the program had created a "permanence syndrome" in the participating farm businesses. Farmers whose land was protected by agricultural easements felt more secure about investing in the long-term future of their farms, and these investments increased the business viability of those farms.

High interest in future participation. Ninety-two percent of the participants said they would participate in a PACE program again.

Reduction in forced sale. Many of the participants also said that, were it not for the program, they would likely not still be farming or would have had to sell their land in order to continue in agriculture elsewhere.

In the years that followed this study, AFT staff used it all around the country when they advocated for proposed new PACE programs, helping to ease misgivings among local farmers.

One shared value among committed farmers is the wish for permanence and predictability. This study directly addressed that core value.

National Assessment of Agricultural Easement Programs

By 2003, some 1.8 million farm acres had been put under agricultural easements purchased by government-funded PACE programs over the roughly twenty-five years since the idea was first attempted locally.[20] It was time for a thorough look at how they were performing.

CAE teamed up with Professor Alvin Sokolow of the University of California, Davis, who, with AFT's Anita Zurbrugg, did a study of forty-six leading PACE programs in fifteen states. Collectively, these programs were responsible for protecting the majority of the farmland then under government-funded easement protection nationwide. Over the next few years, Sokolow issued four detailed reports covering the following: program profiles and maps of protected lands, the criteria programs use in selecting farmland to fund, easements and local planning, and success in protecting farmland.

Below are some of their findings:

Most programs still short of their goals. Though some of the programs were near their target and had protected the desired acreage in their jurisdictions (or soon would), most were still far from their goals and, given the magnitude of the task, would need to focus on more strategic acquisitions.

Some "residential conversions" were still being leased for agriculture. There were some problems with purchasers buying easement-protected farms for residential uses, but many leased the nonresidential portions of the land back to farmers at favorable rates to secure current-use taxation advantages. On balance, these properties were still contributing protected local acreage to agricultural production and helping keep land costs down for local farmers.

Continued loss of local farm business infrastructure. Local farm support service businesses continued their long decline, and overall prices for unprotected farmland continued to rise. This may be because of the limits on available funding, and on the overall balance between protected and unprotected land.

Strategic cooperation with local land use management. Where acquisitions had been made strategically and in cooperation with local land use planning authorities, they had been effective in slowing sprawl and firming up urban growth boundaries, thus protecting non-easement-protected lands as well. Yet this level of strategic cooperation has not been so common as it could have been.

Need for long-term easement stewardship. Many of the programs were still focused on acquisition of easements and had not yet developed strong processes for the long-term stewardship and enforcement of the easements that had already been secured.

Need for greater funding. Overall, the economic and political engine that drives urban sprawl seemed often to overwhelm the limited funding available to purchase adequate easement protection for a sufficient critical mass of farmland in many communities to assure long-term security for local agriculture.

The results of this study helped AFT understand the challenges faced by existing farmland-protection programs and share strategies to make them more effective in the years since.

The Upshot

Over its forty-year history, AFT has completed hundreds of studies and reports of the kinds described in this chapter. Again and again, its research has created critical foundations for policy collaboration between groups. The research has served as a highly leveraged tool in achieving the organization's mission.

CHAPTER 15
Institutional Efforts

At the very start, American Farmland Trust was to be a national organization which would create and hold agricultural easements. That mission inevitably led to nurturing new local PACE programs, strengthening local land trusts interested in protecting farms, and creating new public policy nationally, then locally. These goals, in turn, necessitated protecting the environment in a manner that would assure agriculture's sustainable existence over time. Achieving that objective, required coalitions between disparate interests and affiliated movements dealing with agriculture. And it called for credible research and the generation of creative new solutions.

While these shifts in focus were evolutionary, they were not inevitable. Rather these changes reflected an organization that was unswervingly determined to do whatever was needed to get the job done. The new goals were also not peripheral; they were integral to the core objective of protecting agriculture. In the end, achieving AFT's foundational objective turned out to require tapping the power of agriculture to protect the environment for all of us.

In this context of emerging change, new ideas were often

formalized within the organization. This chapter describes some of those developments.

AFT Research: CAE and the Farmland Information Center (FIC)

The Center for Agriculture in the Environment (CAE) represents one of AFT's earliest efforts to institutionalize the organization's growing expertise, especially on issues related to agriculture's environmental impacts and benefits. Its research projects and reports provide an archive of useful data.

But CAE is only part of that story.

If you've ever worked with AFT, or researched farmland protection or conservation agriculture issues, you've likely also already encountered AFT's Farmland Information Center (FIC) and its website: farmland info.org.

For the past eighteen years, Jennifer Dempsey has been the person most responsible for curating, organizing, and making this body of information readily available to the public.

The groundwork that would later lead to the FIC began with SCS chief Norm Berg.[1] Chief Berg advocated for and helped write the Soil and Water Resources Conservation Act, which created the National Resources Inventory (NRI). Through and because of the NRI, research on agriculture and farm resource issues flourished—work like the subsequent *American Farmland: What Do We Have to Lose* report which was so instrumental in the 1985 Farm Bill. As new research and information accumulated, a central place was needed where it could be collected for public use. The Farmland Protection Policy Act (FPPA) included the initial specific authorization for creation of a national farmland information library. But the Reagan and Bush Sr. administrations shelved that provision. It was not until 1994 that the 1981 FPPA authorization was finally acted upon. USDA and NRCS partnered with AFT in establishing a Farmland Information Library (FIL),[2] which became the FIC.

When the FIL was created in 1994, the volume and complexity of the technical and policy information AFT was accumulating on farmland were already overwhelming. It was not, of course, all AFT's work. Included was a growing body of research reports, technical memos, facts sheets, books, guides, presentations, and scholarly materials from a vast array of sources and on a wide range of topics dealing with farmland loss and protection in America.[3]

By that time, the hoped-for growth in state and local farmland protection programs was already happening all around the country. New local citizen groups were forming everywhere to advocate for such programs. The farmland protection movement was fully under way. And all those newly enthused supporters were desperate for credible, reliable, on-the-point information. The FIC provided cost-effective, comprehensive, easy-to-use access to it. Then and since then, this vast body of shared information has provided a powerful bond of common understanding for the entire farmland protection and conservation agriculture movement.

The FIC website has been modernized several times over the years. Today, it is a go-to resource on farmland, actively used by farmers and ranchers, conservation professionals, urban planners, policymakers, researchers, the media, and, of course, AFT staff.

AFT's National Farmland Protection Conferences

Late in 1980, Ed Thompson was asked to organize AFT's first national conference, to be held in February of 1981.[4] At that point, AFT was a mere four months old, but the National Agricultural Lands Study (NALS) was expected to be completed in January. The new FPPA was about to be passed. Thompson believed a major event for the fledgling farmland protection movement could bring the relevant national leaders together to publicize, discuss, and give these accomplishments impact.

The event was held in Chicago in the midst of a terrible snowstorm. Even so, more than four hundred people attended—which gives one a fair idea of the early interest in farmland loss. Many of them were stranded by the storm. The event included presentations by both the outgoing and the incoming secretaries of agriculture.[5] The recent release of NALS was a substantial draw for the conference. Attendees got their first close look at what the two-year study had concluded and heard what the professionals had to say about it. The event also served as a forum for the first large-scale public announcement of the formation of American Farmland Trust.

In the years which followed, AFT continued to organize national conferences on a regular basis. These events served as one of the ways AFT occupied center stage. Of course, AFT experts would often attend and present at the Land Trust Alliance's annual rally. But AFT's own national conference provided an opportunity to focus on agriculture, and to not only dive far deeper into farmland protection but to also address related and emerging issues, such as a farmland access, farm viability, and environmental sustainability.

What Works

In 1997, AFT was deeply engaged in building its national credibility and establishing itself as an authority on all things related to protecting farmland. At the time, the most natural way to accomplish such a goal was to write a book on the topic.

Julia Freedgood produced a massive volume for AFT titled *Saving American Farmland: What Works*.[6] Freedgood refers to *What Works* as "so 1990s." It truly was a classic pre-internet assembly of knowledge and expertise in book form. It was all printed in studious, no-nonsense black and white and laid out as a comprehensive catalog of strategies, tools, and success stories. Today, we'd almost certainly capture such material electronically and include, at the very least, a color picture or two. The book was designed as a resource that could support a free call-in consulting (answer) service on farmland issues that AFT was offering at the time. Soon enough, this service was also eclipsed by the internet.

What Works turned out to be a key repository of information and expertise on farmland protection. It provided working examples for all the major tools available to the farmland protection practitioner and advocate: easement donations, PACE programs, right to farm laws, current use taxation, land use planning and zoning, farmer-created agriculture districts, estate planning, and more.

Outside of AFT, the book made its way into the hands of many in the growing national cadre of farmland protection planners, land trust managers, government farmland agency directors, and farmland advocates throughout America.

The subsequent explosion of the internet accounts for why *What Works* has not been republished. Much of the material it contains is, however, still relevant. The physical book is available for purchase online at one place or another as well as on AFT's own FIC website, where it can also be downloaded at no cost.

AFT's Fresh Farm Farmers Market

In 1997, AFT also announced the upcoming launch of the Fresh Farm Farmers Market at Dupont Circle in Washington, DC,[7] one of the early major urban farmers markets in modern America. Why would an organization focused on protecting farmland and advancing environmentally sound farming practices want to create and operate a farmers market? Bernie Prince, the AFT staffer who would manage the venture, explained AFT's motivation at the time in this way: "Markets like this one put a face on food by bringing farmers into direct contact with District residents. Fewer and fewer city residents have any understanding of what is involved in food production and the importance of the agricultural resource base in the surrounding area. We believe farmers' markets can help them better understand what's at stake."

At the time, USDA had recently estimated that the number of farmers markets had increased by a startling 40 percent nationwide over just the previous three years. Farmers markets were suddenly becoming a sizable new outlet for farm products, especially those grown in areas threatened by urban development. And that was just the beginning. The opportunity for small, local, modern farmers to earn a decent living selling direct to the public received its first major boost when those farmers were empowered by farmers markets.

As a policy organization, AFT was entirely conscious that the farmers selling at these markets around the country would become a significant source of information about agriculture for the consumer-constituents who shopped there. Farmers markets were a new avenue for public education. The DC Fresh Farm Farmers Market was an effective way for AFT to disseminate knowledge about this rising new trend in direct-market agriculture.

Those farmers market shoppers also belonged to an emerging local-food constituency, an increasingly politically active group. By bringing farmers into direct contact with their urban customers, farmers would themselves become more aware of consumer wishes and expectations concerning how their food was grown, a circumstance that clearly helped push through to completion the final rules for organic certification not long after, in 2002.[8] That same farmer–consumer interaction would drive many direct-market farmers to become certified under one of the several new local environmental responsibility certifications that were springing up around the country.[9]

Doubters also had to be convinced. It turned out that the historic Thomas T. Gaff House, official residence of the Colombian ambassador to the United States, was just nearby. The ambassador believed the farmers market traffic would be inconvenient for his embassy and was dead set against the idea.

Washington, DC, is, of course, our nation's capital. And the views of an ambassador carry weight. AFT and market supporters interceded with the City. The market was scheduled to open on July 4, 1997. As the month began, however, the official permit had not yet been issued. The farmers had been invited and were coming from all across the region to sell their crops. Stalls had been assigned, personnel were on board, publicity had gone out, every preparation had been made. But it was not until two days before, on July 2, that Washington, DC, finally issued its certificate of occupancy, to the massive relief of all concerned.[10]

AFT ultimately stepped away from its operation of the market in 2005, after the venture was fully launched and self-sustaining. By 2015, DC's Fresh Farm Market supported thirteen farmers markets around the DC area and was serving some 415,000 visitors annually.[11]

CHAPTER 16

Local Food, Local Farms, and Local Farm Communities

American Farmland Trust's NO FARMS NO FOOD bumper sticker became the title for this book because it is much more than a slogan. Even in 1997, when AFT was first getting involved in the Fresh Farm Farmers Market at Dupont Circle in DC, its local farms and local food work was already under way.[1]

This work covered complex issues that surround what might otherwise seem a simple matter of people buying and eating locally grown food. For years, AFT had been investigating and advocating on matters like connecting local farmers with large local-food-dependent institutions such as hospitals and schools; assessing local and regional foodsheds for their food security; developing local farm community business plans; and improving health, jobs, and the environment through local food.[2]

At around this time, Americans were seeing a dramatically expanding local food movement emerge. This movement represented another opportunity for AFT. Here was an urban constituency that supported agriculture and was environmentally conscious at the same time. The urban areas where most of these people lived were the very same places where productive farmland faced its greatest threat and where environmental problems like water pollution, flooding, wetland loss, and degradation of wildlife habitat were most egregious. These local food advocates were the political constituents of elected officials who needed to take an interest in addressing severe farmland loss and environmental problems. And they valued their personal relationships with the people who grew their food.

A Rural–Urban Compact

AFT's Julia Freedgood had been passionately working local food and food system issues from early on. She has led AFT efforts on a multitude of food system–related projects, studies, and campaigns. Freedgood came to see the long-term challenge for American agriculture as deeper than just bridging the farmer–environmentalist conflict. For her, the ultimate objective must be nothing less than bridging the much broader cultural divide between America's urban and rural communities.[3]

That will require a transformation in the way many of us, urban and rural, view the role of and our relationship with our sister communities. Rural communities themselves will need to fully embrace agriculture as their economic and cultural mainstay—and be prepared to enlist urban support in the fight to protect it. And urban communities will need to appreciate the fundamental values that agriculture provides—and be prepared to help address the needs of those rural communities.

Quite clearly, *our farms need our cities*. And not solely because those urban dwellers are their marketplace. AFT's overarching mission to conserve agriculture has three tightly interconnected elements. To truly be sustainable, agriculture needs all three: a dependable land base, consistently responsible environmental performance, and sustainable business profitability. All three of those things will require the social, political, and financial help of urbanites. Given the highly competitive realities of agriculture, the overarching demands of the environment, and the pressures of land use, farmers and their rural communities cannot achieve those objectives alone.

Meanwhile, *our cities desperately need our farms*. And not just because farmers provide their food. They also need farmer-provided environmental services, constraints on sprawl, and a quality of life that is enriched by a nearby prosperous agriculture. Securing a viable, responsible agricultural sector requires more than just successful individual farm businesses. It also requires infrastructure, supply chains, and an engaged and supportive community.

Julia Freedgood points to the interconnectedness between those three AFT goals, collectively called conservation agriculture: protecting farmland, creating a sustainable environment, and securing the farm business:

Protecting farmland. Protecting farmland is costly and challenging. Farm profits alone are never going to be sufficient to compete for land in a free economy with unconstrained urban sprawl and land fragmentation. Farming is far too land-extensive. Farmers cannot bear the cost of land alone. They need help from their urban neighbors.[4]

For urbanites to extend that help, they need to see the public benefits. Benefits like the vital urban economy and quality of life that can result from constraints on sprawl. Benefits like easy access to local food, protection for surrounding scenic landscapes, and other environmental values that mitigate for urban development.

Creating a sustainable environment. Agriculture can be either a threat or an opportunity for the environment, just as protecting the environment can be a threat or an opportunity for agriculture.[5] Farmers contribute to some of our nation's most significant environmental problems, such as water pollution, habitat loss, and climate change.[6] But they also offer remarkable opportunities to address those problems, using tools that are prohibitively costly for an individual farm business but quite affordable for the public. Helping that farmer produce those environmental benefits can prove to be a huge bargain for a nearby urban community wishing to secure these benefits, while also providing a valuable new profit center for the farmer.

This mutuality of needs represents an incredible opportunity for farmers to strengthen their farm business while helping the environment.[7] And it represents a chance for the rest of us to achieve environmental gains at relatively modest public cost. If urban communities ignore those opportunities, they may lose them when those farms disappear. If farmers ignore them, they can end up painfully regulated or simply out of business.

Securing the farm business. Farming is risky.[8] Farm business failure is and always will be a continuing concern as it is in other parts of our capitalist economy.[9] But unlike most other businesses, when a farm fails, its land often converts to much more intensive and less environmentally friendly (not to mention less food-friendly) uses.[10] Securing that farmer's help, and the contributions of that land, in addressing food and environmental issues ceases to be an option. Saving a viable farm business is thus an essential part of saving the farmland and, therefore, of protecting local food and the local environment.

All of us, urban and rural, are truly in this struggle together. And each of us must be prepared to help with the other's needs while also being willing to acknowledge, account for, and seek help with our own limitations and weaknesses.

CHAPTER 17
A New Regional Presence

In 1998, American Farmland Trust launched a new national undertaking. It would create regional offices throughout the country in places where farmland seemed most at risk and where the organization could have the greatest impact. Rather than branches directed by a national head, however, these new state and regional offices would be local "mini-AFTs" that could transform local farm–environmental politics in much the same way that the organization was doing in the national arena.[1]

First and foremost, AFT wanted these new offices to inspire new local and state public policy.[2] This was a goal that could not be closely managed from the head office. The new offices would do local research, local public education, local coalition building, and, ultimately, local legislative lobbying. None of that could be managed from afar.

AFT had just completed its *Farming on the Edge* report. It now knew where, nationwide, the best farmland was most vulnerable to development. With that knowledge, it made strategic choices about where to target these new regional efforts. The best way to move the farmland protection needle seemed to be to increase local farmland activism and get PACE programs up and running in these target areas.

Once in place, PACE programs, and their local constituencies, would demand financial help from the federal government and exert local political influence. That would drive Congress to fully fund federal easement programs in upcoming farm bills. Here were multiple new playing fields, all across the country, places where local AFT leaders could explore new opportunities for collaboration between farmers and environmentalists.

There are today some twenty-seven state PACE programs including in the Southeast, in California, in the Pacific Northwest, in Colorado and the Rocky Mountain states, in the upper Midwest, in Texas.[3] All of these were places AFT targeted for state or regional offices.

Local Differences

By early 2000, the new state and regional offices were in place. They were often located in one or another of the smaller agricultural towns in their state or region. Given AFT's carefully nurtured relationships with the agriculture industry, these small towns were considered more appropriate locations than an indistinctive office address in some coldly anonymous urban center. It was a matter of standing humor among the new regional directors that their periodic conference calls, typically on speakerphone, were inevitably interrupted by the whistle and rumble of a passing freight train on tracks close beneath the windows of one or another of these low-budget offices in small farm towns sprinkled around the rural countryside.

In some of these regions, AFT's presence had previously been very limited. So, AFT first conducted feasibility studies. Bob Wagner, the managing director for Regional Programs, or Jill Schwartz, out of the Northampton, Massachusetts, office, would fly out to the proposed region; settle into a hotel for several days; contact and interview leaders in the local agricultural, land trust, environmental, government, and charitable foundation communities; and make an assessment regarding the relevance and likely success of a new local office there. Later on, when the new regional director came aboard, there would be a copy of that feasibility report to help them get their feet on the ground.

The new regional directors sometimes shared a joke about how nice it was to have a boss whose office was several thousand miles away. But they all understood their role as local replicas of the national organization. Each was expected to lead and adapt locally. Each faced unique problems in different local political cultures with different resources and opportunities. In consequence, they all responded in very different ways and developed very different priorities:

California's incredibly productive San Joaquin Valley was struggling to survive competition for its critical and threatened water resources, while also being overrun by development.

In the Pacific Northwest, it quickly became a priority to make agriculture a positive asset in recovering endangered salmon runs. This led to creation of the Pioneers in Conservation program, which provided grants to farmers to improve fish habitat in a manner that also preserved agriculture.[4]

The Central Rockies office fought to control subdivision and sale of fragmented recreational properties that surrounded public lands. Those sales were cutting off critical access to public lands by the region's hugely important cattle industry.

In rapidly growing and poorly protected Texas, the fragmentation of very large rural agricultural parcels was making it ever more difficult for farmers to assemble or retain sufficient contiguous land to make up an economically viable farming or ranching operation.

The Upper Midwest office undertook a broad public education campaign aimed at creating farmland protection programs in an area of the country identified as the third most threatened farming region, an area that, like California's San Joaquin Valley, generated huge economic value for the region.

In the Central Great Lakes, AFT joined with twenty-five other organizations to create a highly strategic and popular "Ultimate Farmland Protection Tour," a five-day, multistate journey that quickly produced more than a thousand graduates among key public officials, nonprofit managers, farmers, and thought leaders of all kinds who were educated on the nature of the farmland loss threat and on the tools available to solve it.

In the Southeast, AFT championed the local food movement and helped create the Black Family Land Trust to stem a dramatic decline in Black farm ownership.[5]

The Northeast office played a major role in organizing the hugely successful New York City Watershed Project protecting the city's drinking water supply by protecting farmland and enlisting farmers to adopt new conservation practices, which then led to establishment of the New York Farmland Protection Program.

And in the Mid-Atlantic, which contained some of the oldest, maturest farmland programs in the country, AFT worked to both improve existing PACE programs and create new ones, while educating farmers on the benefits of participation and helping new farmers enter into agriculture.

Taking the National Strategy Local

The specific local projects these new offices undertook found leverage in the middle-ground strategy that AFT had pioneered nationally. Their local problems and projects were definitely unique. But looking at them today, they all advanced AFT's mission. And more important, they all took advantage of that middle-ground, collaborative strategy, even while doing so in a way that was tailored to their particular region.

What follows is a brief miscellany of representative projects that illustrate how all this came together in practice. These are presented as examples taken from among hundreds of such projects nationwide.

New York City Watershed Project

Suppose you are responsible for water quality for the City of New York. It's 1993, and you have recently learned that the city's drinking water will soon not meet the minimum health standards of the Safe Drinking Water Act.[6]

Most of New York City's water comes from a 1,900-square-mile watershed in the Catskill Mountains of upstate New York where the City owns less than 10 percent of the land.[7] The vast majority of this watershed is owned by some seventy-seven thousand private individuals, rural and summer residents. This includes about 350 farms that cover most of the area and that contribute substantially to the local culture and economy. Because of all that private land ownership, the City of New York doesn't really have much direct control over what goes on there that could be affecting the city's drinking water.

As the city's water manager, your first reaction to this bad news is to investigate the possibility of treating and filtering that water. You are horribly discouraged to learn that a new filtration and treatment facility could cost up to $8 billion to build and several hundred million dollars annually to operate. Even for the City of New York, that is serious money.

You're also well aware of the City's bad reputation in the Catskill community. Though most of the acts that caused that bad reputation occurred decades earlier, the direct acquisitions of some fifty-seven thousand acres of land there, the razing of homes, the use of eminent domain, and even the relocation of entire villages to create new reservoirs had engendered a good deal of bitter distrust among local residents that still lingered. However suspect New York City might be in the rural American West, it may be even more unpopular right next door in upstate New York.

Nonetheless, your second reaction is to propose a set of new, rigorous land management regulations, particularly on the farmers in the region. These rules would have ended up retiring some 35 percent of their land and driving many of the rest of them out of business. The public reaction is both vigorous and startling. Farmers propose, among other things, to blockade New York City with tractors. You're advised that your new rules could collapse the local farm economy with the result that many of those farms could be potentially subdivided and sold for development, thus increasing the population within the watershed and making your problems even worse.

This was the situation faced by officials of the City of New York. And in the end, they sat down around a table with leaders of the Catskill community and instead created what became a model for elsewhere in the country. They formed a new Watershed Agricultural Council, which would oversee a series of mostly incentive-based actions: the purchase of agricultural easements to keep farms out of development and in well-managed farming; the purchase of riparian buffers along streams and rivers that paid farmers the full value of the land plus a signing bonus of up to 150 percent of the cost of installing new restoration and management practices needed to protect the buffer; farm conservation management planning and payments to farmers for the costs of implementing the conservation practices called for in their "whole farm" plan; and marketing support for farmers who wished to sell their crops to restaurants and groceries and at farmers markets and other direct-market venues in New York City.

According to Jerry Cosgrove, then AFT's New York state director, who led AFT's work on this plan, critics often balked when they saw that the Watershed Council would pay the landowner up to 150 percent of the cost of installing restoration management in riparian areas. "Why should you pay them more than it costs?" they would ask.

Cosgrove's answer was simple: "It's a marketplace," he says. "You pay them what it's worth." These farmers were also investing their own uncompensated time and effort in these projects, and they were maintaining the land at their own cost afterward. It was expensive. If they could do it for less than 150 percent of initial installation cost, the council would have paid them less. But whatever the cost, why should farmers be paid less for their efforts than they were actually worth?

As of 2004, the program had enlisted 92 percent participation and was viewed as responsible for reversing the previous decline in the quality of New York City's drinking water. Currently, the Watershed Agricultural Council has protected over thirty thousand acres of farm- and forestland under its easement program. The total cost has turned out to be a small fraction of what would have been spent on a new filtration plant. And the region was enjoying a stable and prosperous agricultural economy, as well as a healthy local environment for all who lived there.[8]

California's San Joaquin Valley Land and Water Strategy[9]

If you ask California's current AFT state director, Kara Heckert, about agriculture in the San Joaquin Valley, she will tell you that it is all about water. "If you're not looking at water quantity in California agriculture, you are not awake," she says.[10]

The San Joaquin Land and Water Strategy was perhaps the first time AFT had focused in a big way on the intersection between land use and water availability in agriculture.

California's San Joaquin Valley has been said to be the most productive agricultural region on the planet.[11] It is also one of the most vulnerable. It faces threats from a changing climate, new regulations, and a growing population. And among the most serious threats it faces is the endangered reliability of its irrigation water.

A recent AFT research study shed some light on the situation:

High quality farmland is water-vulnerable. High-quality farmland with a reliable water source is very limited. Only 9 percent of the roughly six million acres of irrigated farmland in the San Joaquin Valley is high-quality land experiencing low water stress.

Grave threat of conversion to development. By 2050, as many as 323,000 acres in the San Joaquin Valley are projected to be converted into low-density residential uses, mostly around cities. Fifty-five percent of agricultural land that has a high risk of development is high-quality farmland.

Water demand increasing. By mid-century, water demand in the valley could increase by six hundred thousand acre-feet per year.

Availability of allowable water decreasing. Over that same time period, groundwater regulations and proposed streamflow regulations are likely to reduce the amount of water available for farming.

Current overdrafts and natural losses. Thirteen percent of all agricultural water in the valley comes from overdrafted groundwater sources. Owing to increased evapotranspiration, irrigation water may need to be augmented by nearly 8 percent in various parts of the San Joaquin Valley between now and mid-century.

These conclusions portend a "perfect storm" for agriculture at the intersection of struggles over land and water.

Heckert sees this study as a road map for AFT's policy work in California's San Joaquin Valley. She recognizes that a multifaceted approach is required, one that not only protects the land but also conserves water through sound farming practices. There will also need to be thoughtful negotiation between competing interests grounded in a new appreciation for what this agriculturally wealthy state could stand to lose if it doesn't come to grips with these challenges.

California has one of the country's most tightly regulated land use and zoning laws. The 1995 *Alternatives for Future Urban Growth in California's Central Valley* study illustrated a willingness for AFT to boldly approach the land use regulation issue. Ed Thompson, Heckert's predecessor as California state director, built upon that study in a variety of ways, including a demonstration of how urban sprawl versus compact growth would dramatically affect the climate.

Educating Key Leaders about Farmland Loss and Prevention in Georgia

Addressing farmland loss at scale is often all about changing public policy. New public policy is about public education, but also about being strategic. Public education has a lot more impact if you can focus on the specific people who are in a position to make a difference.

AFT's Southeast office made a careful assessment of what groups in the state of Georgia could most likely effect change. Then they set out to provide those targeted groups with information about farmland loss. AFT partnered up with the Association of County Commissioners of Georgia, the National Association of Counties, and the Georgia Agribusiness Council to do a pilot training program in farmland protection. The first two-day workshop in April 2003 put forty key people, including elected county commissioners, county employees, agricultural leaders, university researchers, a nonprofit conservationist, a state planner, and the Chair of Georgia's State Senate Agriculture Committee in the same room to hear the same message.

One month later, in May 2003, Georgia's Oconee County used Georgia Greenspace dollars in a match with federal Farm and Ranchlands Protection Program money and acquired development rights on a model farm. This became the first step toward subsequent adoption of a county PACE program based on an independent local tax. The program is today generally viewed as a model for local programs elsewhere in the country.[12]

The Texas Farm and Ranchlands Conservation Program

In June of 2005, Texas governor Rick Perry signed into law a brand-new state Farm and Ranchlands Conservation Bill. Texas had perhaps the greatest rate of farmland loss anywhere in the country, but it was decidedly not a tax-friendly blue state. How did an agricultural easement purchase program pass?

The answer: by making sure the program squarely addressed the concerns of agriculture.

In March 2003, AFT had teamed up with Texas Cooperative Extension to complete a research report: *Texas Rural Lands: Trends and Conservation Implications for the 21st Century.*[13] Strategically, the report did not focus on sprawling development. Instead, it dealt with the issue of land fragmentation and its impact on Texas agriculture. According to the report, the large farms and ranches so emblematic of Texas were being split up into smaller and smaller pieces. Since 1970, about a thousand "new" farms and ranches had been established in Texas while the total area devoted to agriculture had actually declined by some three million acres. This fragmentation was all in aid of creating new so-called ranchettes that were too small for profitable farming but suited the new landowners, whose interest in owning a place away from the city was largely recreational. These new rural recreational landowners were also often degrading wildlife habitat and depleting scarce water resources.

To yet further advance this ag-friendly take on the farmland loss issue, AFT issued a subsequent summary of the report: *Going, Going, Gone: The Impact of Land Fragmentation on Texas Agriculture and Wildlife*. With this helpful new title, this summary discussed the effect of land fragmentation on Texas citizens, with a focus on the state's wildlife, farming, ranching, and water supplies. It included the following recommendations:

Create a voluntary statewide purchase of development rights program;

Promote agricultural, open space, timber, and wildlife differential property tax valuation;

Provide greater county ability to plan for and manage growth in unincorporated areas;

Promote use and benefits of native grasses rather than introduced grass species;

Enhance the role for land trusts and wildlife cooperatives; and,

Provide state tax relief that would help farmers and ranchers keep their land in agriculture.

With these recommendations, backed up by the study's underlying research, which captured environmental concerns as a farmer-friendly message, conservative Texas became the next state to create a PACE program.

Creating a PACE Program for Washington State

When AFT opened its Pacific Northwest regional office in May 2000, the State of Washington had in place an established program known as the Washington Wildlife and Recreation (WWRP), which prioritized public acquisitions of land through a nonpolitical, citizen-advised process. The program was supported by a highly effective, broadly representative nonprofit advocacy group called the Washington Wildlife and Recreation Coalition (WWRC).

The WWRP did not, however, include farmland protection.

There was already some public awareness of PACE programs because of the one that existed in Washington's most populous county, King County, which includes Seattle. The lobbyist who represented the WWRC in the state legislature, Mike Ryherd, was also a small farmer who had already convinced WWRC to seek to add farmland protection to the state program. The WWRC proposal would set aside roughly $5 million each biennium for purchases of agricultural easements.

Unfortunately, the Washington Farm Bureau stoutly opposed it. WWRC had tried and failed to get it passed over the Farm Bureau's objections. The matter was in stalemate.

The farm industry's opposition was grounded in a conservative mistrust of government and in long-standing opposition to WWRP's public acquisitions of private land, which they believed should remain private. Opposition also arose from misinformation about conservation easements, from an ongoing campaign being conducted by out-of-state property-rights groups, and from contemporary reports critical of the Nature Conservancy.[14]

I was the newly hired Pacific Northwest regional director at that time. I'm convinced my experience was much like that of every single one of the new state and regional AFT directors on the ground at the start of the new century. It illustrates how the AFT middle-ground role worked locally in practice and, at the same time, shows how we all went about our jobs in our own way from region to region.

When I took the position, the arguments for farmland protection had already been assembled through twenty years of AFT's work throughout the country. It was easy to make a case for why a PACE program would be in the interests of our state's agriculture industry. Somehow, I also managed to convince several local environmental funders that I could change the Farm Bureau's mind. Armed with their funding, my first stop was a visit to the State Farm Bureau's headquarters in Olympia, where I sat down with their staff, laid out my case, and explained my intentions.

In that meeting, it was my impression that the Farm Bureau's professional staff were at least marginally convinced by my argument. But they clearly thought my chances of changing their members' minds were dim.

The first test was a "debate" sponsored jointly by AFT, the Washington State Farm Bureau, and the Washington Cattlemen's Association. This was likely the very first time that either of those two farm organizations had ever teamed up with an "environmental group" to do anything. The event was held in Ellensburg, Washington, on our state's agricultural east side. It was AFT (me) versus a young lawyer representing a conservative think tank out of Seattle.

His argument against agricultural easements was, essentially, that easements were permanent and would therefore restrict the free choices of future generations of landowners who should be allowed to make their own decisions about their own private land based on what they thought was the right thing to do at that time.

I pointed out that as "permanent" as an agricultural easement might be, it would never be as permanent as fragmentation and development. Once a hundred-acre parcel has been divided into one hundred separate one-acre parcels owned by a hundred separate landowners, each putting their property to their own desired use, each having invested in their own preferred "improvements"—once that had happened, there was no way that land would *ever* go back to farmland. Nothing short of government condemnation and an absurd amount of money could ever make that even vaguely possible.

Thus, if selling an agricultural easement was "permanent," *not* doing so was ultimately far *more* permanent. And if you were that initial seller, you'd have been fully compensated. If you were a future new owner, the reduced price you'd paid would have been your compensation as well. You'd have had your eyes wide open and would not have lost a dime.

I suggested that what farmers needed to ask themselves was not whether thirty or forty years hence their children or grandchildren would be able to find a small building lot on which to place a home. That was a given. The question was whether, if that grandchild wanted to find a hundred acres (or perhaps a thousand or five thousand acres) of contiguous, high-quality farmland upon which to grow a profitable agricultural crop, would *that* be possible? Because if *that* became impossible, it would truly be a tragedy for all of us. And clearly, *that* was exactly where we were headed.

If farmers were selling out for development, it absolutely wasn't because that was what they wanted to do. It was because they had no realistic choice. A PACE program would give them that choice. It could provide critical capital now, and when they did decide to sell, it would allow them to sell to another farmer who would value that lifetime of improvements they'd made to their privately owned farm property.

After that debate, I took this message around the state and region. I would call up local county-level Farm Bureau presidents and offer to buy them breakfast or coffee or to stop by their farm when they had time. I'd make my case to them, and then to their local county Farm Bureau's regular leadership or membership meeting. At those meetings, along with my pitch, I'd distribute written materials I'd received from AFT or had written myself to adapt to local concerns. These included reports from research studies showing that farmers liked these PACE programs, fact sheets that listed Farm Bureaus from other states across the country that supported their local PACE programs, explanations of all the ways a PACE program could benefit farmers.

At all these local Farm Bureau gatherings, I also told them that their State Farm Bureau opposed these programs. And I handed out a sample internal Farm Bureau resolution form that contained sample draft language they could offer, right there at their local county organization, if they wished, to seek a change in their State Farm Bureau's position on the matter.

It took about three years of traveling all over Washington.[15] But in the 2005 Washington legislature, when the WWRC again proposed amending the WWRP statute to include within it a farmland easement program, the Farm Bureau *took no position*. For the first time it stood aside.

The bill passed with flying colors.[16]

The Ohio River Basin Water Quality Trading Project[17]

Shepherded by AFT's Brian Brandt, the Ohio River basin project illustrates perfectly how AFT's middle-ground, intermediation role could work in each unique local political landscape. Because water quality issues are inherently local, this is the kind of challenge the organization's regional offices faced everywhere, but it is also the kind of project that offers dramatic new opportunities to help agriculture and improve the environment.

The background. In 1972, when the Clean Water Act (CWA) passed, the vast majority of water pollution in America had come from easily identifiable "point sources," like municipal sewage treatment plants, industrial facilities, and other large, known sites. Finding and measuring their pollution was often as simple as taking a sample from an obvious discharge pipe, testing it for pollutants, and measuring the flow. The act turned out to be incredibly effective at bringing those point sources under control.

By 2009, however, a new kind of pollution was increasingly taking the place of these large, direct, easily trackable point sources. The primary source of water quality problems had become nonpoint pollution, to which agriculture represented the leading contributor.[18]

Unlike point source pollution, nonpoint pollution is, almost by definition, difficult to find, pin down, and control. Which among the hundreds of farms up any particular watershed is letting its nitrogen laden topsoil wash into the adjacent creek? Maybe it isn't impossible to figure out, but it also isn't easy. There is no clearly identifiable discharge pipe. Even if you do find a source, they probably won't be able to afford to fix the damage they've done. And they will be far from the only culprit.

AFT involvement. AFT had been working in this water quality arena for many years, helping create programs that made it feasible for farmers to adopt conservation management practices that reduced their nonpoint pollution. AFT's Brian Brandt was one of the pioneers in this effort.

Some of Brandt's work occurred on farms in the Ohio River Basin, where the need for farmer adoption of these practices was clear but where the funding was sorely limited. The only money available was through the farm bill programs championed by AFT, programs like the farm bill's Environmental Quality Incentives Program (EQIP). And that was able to pay for only a small fraction of the need.

Emerging political pressures. Because of growing nonpoint pollution, in many places across the country, point source polluters' legally permissible total maximum daily load allocations (the amount of pollutants that *they* were allowed to emit under CWA) were shrinking. Pollution point sources were being required to invest in water treatment infrastructure paid for by the public through higher taxes and utility rates for water, sewer, and energy.

Naturally, this increased political pressure on agriculture to reduce its water quality impacts. If voluntary incentive-based approaches weren't available, regulation seemed likely to follow.

A hypothetical case in point. Suppose that EPA assigned your small town's wastewater treatment plant a total maximum daily load for, say, the nitrate contributions it makes to the river that runs through your town. Your town is growing, but, because of increased pollution in the river, the allowed pollutant load allocation has been shrinking. The only way your local sewer district could meet the new standard would be by constructing a $200 million treatment plant with an annual operating cost of maybe $20 million, which would, in your small town, be economically crippling.

Meanwhile, local farmers also contribute to the nitrate problem through their collective nonpoint pollution. By adopting certain conservation management practices (vegetative buffers, cover crops, rotational grazing, settling ponds, low tillage, and so forth), they could reduce their nitrate contributions and quite handily bring the river system into water quality compliance.

Their individual cost to do this is greater than any of those individual farmers could afford. But the total *public* cost of helping them do so was a considerable bargain given the alternatives (the new $200 million treatment plant that costs another $20 million per year to operate). If you could enlist those farmers' help and share those costs, you could reduce their nonpoint pollution while also keeping their land out of environmentally harmful development. The cost might be closer to $5 million or $10 million annually, with no initial investment. And it would be more environmentally desirable and sustainable, especially considering that there'd be benefits for improved wildlife habitat, carbon sequestration, flood detention, wetlands, groundwater recharge, and a host of other important environmental values.[19]

Situations just like this were increasingly common across the country.

The Ohio River basin study. It was to seize an opportunity like this that AFT had joined in the Ohio River Basin Water Quality Trading Project.[20] The prospect was possible creation of a water quality trading regime—by which local point source polluters could purchase "water quality credits" from local farmers willing to adopt farming practices that were proven to provide those same reductions.

Brian Brandt enlisted a broad partnership including the Electric Power Research Institute; the Ohio Farm Bureau Federation; the US Environmental Protection Agency; the University of California; and several public water quality and natural resource agencies in Ohio, Kentucky, and Indiana. Their initial project was to study and document the feasibility of such a market driven approach.

That study did as follows:

- demonstrated and quantified water quality benefits from various on-the ground agricultural practices that might be put to use by farmers;
- showed how to manage the uncertainty associated with making improvements in agricultural practices;
- assembled the documentation, modeling, and science needed to assure regulators and the public that *real* water quality improvements would result; and
- established trading ratios to ensure that trades would result in improvements as good as or better than what would be produced by water treatment plant technology.

A few years after this study, the community of Columbus, Ohio, had been confronted with a situation very much like that described in the above hypothetical. The City of Columbus was responsible for drinking water for some one million local residents. Key local businesses, like the Anheuser-Busch Corporation, depended on clean drinking water as well. Unfortunately, that water came from the Scioto River, which was no longer meeting the EPA-required water quality standards. The City of Columbus was looking at installing new ion-exchange water quality technology at a cost of around $40 million. Other users faced similar challenges for a potentially massive collective expense with grave economic impact throughout the community.

These water users and polluters were looking for another way.

AFT's previous Ohio River Basin Water Quality Trading study showed that improved conservation management practices on farms located throughout the upper Scioto River watershed could better address the problem, and at a much lower cost.

Drawing on the results of that study, the Farming for Cleaner Water project was launched in partnership with multiple stakeholders in the upper Scioto River watershed.[21] The project will use funds from downstream water users to help farmers reduce their nitrogen and phosphorus emissions and will avoid the cost of pricey new ion-exchange systems. It will also reduce pollution in the Mississippi and improve water quality as far away as the Gulf of Mexico. And it will very likely benefit wildlife, sequester carbon, and offer many other ancillary environmental benefits as well.

A note on environmental markets, generally. Whatever the environmental challenges we face in the years ahead, we will face dramatic social and economic costs in addressing them—costs very much like those encountered in the City of Columbus.

Environmental markets, like the one under development in the upper Scioto River watershed or like carbon cap-and-trade measures, can allow society to address environmental challenges using the most effective, least expensive solutions. A well-designed ecosystem marketplace can often reduce the cost of addressing the problem and expand the potential scale of the solution.[22]

An arena of controversy. Environmental markets can be controversial.

Environmentalists often find the trading of water quality (and other environmental credits) suspicious. Such schemes seem to allow large polluters to "buy their way" out of compliance. And because the trading of credits doesn't, at first glance, seem to improve the environment, it can appear to merely "move around the deck chairs on a sinking *Titanic*."

Farmers are suspicious as well. They see that a regulatory cap on environmental damage is required before there can be a market for trading the credits needed to meet that cap. The "capped" industry will, sometimes, be one with which the farm industry often partners in political coalitions seeking other, shared legislative or public objectives. And a regulatory cap on the environmental impacts in some other industry (power generation, for example), could end up indirectly visiting increased operating costs on their farm businesses.

There are, however, ways in which environmental markets *can* dramatically improve the environment and greatly help agriculture.[23] Chief among the latter is the fact that farmers are likely to be profitable sellers and providers of such credits. It was for this very reason that AFT was able to enlist significant mainstream farm industry support for the carbon cap-and-trade measures in the Waxman–Markey climate bill back in 2009, when it passed the US House of Representatives. (Sadly, it later failed in the Senate.[24]) Similarly, it was the benefits to upper Scioto River watershed farmers that drove AFT to launch into the study described above.

The environment can benefit for a host of reasons. The first is because, in the simplest terms, by allowing environmental services to be provided by the most effective and lowest-cost producer (in this case, farmers), such a market system reduces the social, economic, and fiscal expense of protecting and improving the environment. And when society can address a problem cost-efficiently, it can often afford to go further, getting results faster and realizing yet greater benefits.

One often hears the assertion that we must fix a given problem "regardless of the cost." But cost is *always* an issue. At any given time, which do we decide *not* to pay for: national defense, public education, pandemic control, police or fire protection, a court system, health care, roads and bridges, protection of abused children or battered women? You get the idea.

And that's when you're talking about the use of government spending, where we all share the cost. Very often, when someone tells you that something must be done "regardless of cost," what they have in mind, instead, is regulation for which others will pay. When farmers hear an environmentalist say that, what they're thinking to themselves is: *Yeah, sure, but what you really mean is: regardless of the cost to me. You're not planning to pay for this yourself at all.* This reaction is particularly acute in agriculture, which faces global competition from farm producers elsewhere who will not be similarly regulated.

That's why fairness also becomes an advantage of environmental markets. While reducing the cost, they can help us fairly allocate responsibility. And fairness *is* an issue. It can be frightfully easy to pick out a social or economic group that is highly visible and simple to regulate but whose responsibility for the problem is remote. When that happens, proponents can face bitter political opposition to a much-needed environmental solution, opposition that might easily have been avoided.

Another environmental advantage to ecosystem markets is that, in a properly designed and managed marketplace, trades will produce considerably more in environmental benefits, on average, than would occur without them. That's partly because highly conservative trading ratios are typically used to guarantee a favorable outcome on each individual trade. The collective average impact of all the trades ends up being positive overall. Beyond that, when we secure one environmental benefit (say, the creation of a vegetated stream buffer to protect water quality), we inevitably also produce other benefits as well (such as carbon sequestration, aquifer recharge, flood detention, wetlands restoration, or improved fish and wildlife habitat), and usually at no additional cost. And finally, with money to spend, there will be many willing sellers. That makes it possible to select for purchase only those credits that will do the most overall strategic good thus greatly enhancing the beneficial impact of your spending.

Farmers benefit as well. Stated simply: while farmers typically cannot afford to produce these valuable environmental credits on their own dime, they are in a remarkably strong position to produce them at a very competitive public cost. Environmental credits can pay for conservation practices a farmer simply couldn't otherwise afford. Credits can also pay for agricultural easements. And by carefully assigning an actual value to environmental services, trading assures that everyone, including the public, is required to more fairly and explicitly allocate across society the costs and burdens of protecting and improving the environment. Farmers thus receive value for their services and are insulated from unfair treatment.

An unexpected irony. In addition to the concerns expressed by farmers and environmentalists, regulatory agencies often also mistrust these markets.

Tracking the discharge from each easily identifiable plant or industrial facility along a river seems much easier than having to oversee dozens or even hundreds of upstream farmers to assure they're properly maintaining their buffers or keeping up their conservation management practices.

But it *is* better. And it is *more certain*, not less. If one or another of those hundreds of participating farmers falls behind in compliance, by the time they're brought back up to speed, little damage will have been done. Yet if something goes wrong at that huge, complex, high-tech treatment plant—if some pump fails, a switch sticks, a pipe bursts, a computer freezes, or any of a thousand other almost inevitable glitches occurs—you could, in an instant, have a massive problem with horrific consequences.

Because both farm *and* environmental groups so often mistrust water quality trading (and other environmental markets), a local project like the one on the Ohio River definitely required a local AFT.

Setbacks

AFT's timing in opening these new state and regional offices couldn't have been worse. In May 2000, just as I was opening the doors of our new Northwest office in Puyallup, Washington, the dot-com bubble was beginning to burst.

Most of AFT's new regional offices lacked a mature independent funding base of local major donors. And these new offices had but a brief history with their respective USDA and National Resources Conservation

Service (NRCS) state offices. NRCS was the most significant—often the only—government funder of projects related to farmland protection and conservation practices. If these new offices were to succeed at raising local money, they needed significant help from their local charitable foundations—most of which were environmental funders.

Very few charitable foundations will part with the serious money needed for direct land purchases, let alone for easements to protect agriculture. They are also seldom interested in funding the research, education, or coalition-building work that might lead to PACE programs. And when it comes to better farming practices, until very recently, few foundations provided support, generally deferring to federal farm bill programs as the source of funds. Charitable foundations with an interest in natural resources often have a very different environmental agenda—not one likely to provide direct support for conservation agriculture.

It was always going to be a struggle to convince foundations that a state-funded easement program to keep farmers in agriculture had serious environmental benefits—or that farmers would eagerly embrace more environmentally sound farming practices. In many cases, they, too, saw farmers as the enemy. And if the foundations were into land use issues, their inclination was to support growth management laws and regulatory zoning, not to pay farmers not to develop their land.

Existential challenges of this kind had always been a part of AFT's daily struggles. But AFT hadn't anticipated the dramatic collapse in the stock market in 2000 and 2001 and the ensuing diminishment of endowment funds available to the nation's charitable foundations. With the economic decline, there was a commensurate increase in social service needs, further stretching thin any remaining funds.

The same impact was seen in government grants and contracts.

By early in 2008, the Upper Midwest, Central Rocky Mountain, and Texas offices were gone. The Central Great Lakes office had been split into Michigan and Ohio state offices.

By early 2009, soon after the 2008 collapse, the only state and regional offices were California, Mid-Atlantic, New England, New York, and the Pacific Northwest. All other states were being handled at large by Bob Wagner out of AFT's Northampton satellite office. In early 2000, AFT had eleven offices located around the country with regional or state program responsibility. By 2009, there were five.

There is also another more systemic reason that AFT's new regional offices were vulnerable to the economic decline. As mini-AFTs, responsible to set their own course, they were not engaged on projects conceived and funded at the national level. Instead, they were doing local work, so they were expected to identify, promote, and fund those projects locally. They were, to some extent, local nonprofit franchisees—start-ups just entering their vulnerable early years in business.

An Interim Report Card

Dr. Al Sokolow's *National Assessment of Agricultural Easement Programs*,[25] mentioned in chapter 14, provided a report card on AFT's local and regional PACE program success at about the time the organization's regional expansion had begun to shrink. The fourth and last volume, published in 2006, attempted to measure the success of forty-six agricultural easement programs in fifteen states.

Sokolow's main concerns were proper easement stewardship, coordination with growth management laws, and whether communities would be prepared to endure considerable program cost over the long haul—all issues that must be addressed on an ongoing basis.

The most troublesome critique was that the geographical scope of these programs so far had been "mostly confined to the Northeastern corner of the nation, two Pacific Coast states and a few Rocky Mountain states." The implementation of PACE programs, Sokolow wrote, "is relatively unknown and unused in the great agricultural heartland of the nation, the Midwest and the South."

Sokolow acknowledged that these programs were still "in their mid-life stages" and "very much a work in progress." But there is more to this as well.

While there is some development pressure on agriculture in every state, in some areas, particularly in the American heartland, one wouldn't necessarily expect to see PACE programs, simply because the argument can legitimately be made that none are needed.[26] There are places where population is actually declining and others where there is no real development pressure. And in a few locations (most notably, Oregon), a rare but rigorous growth management law mostly fills this need. Fragmentation of larger farm parcels is a problem everywhere, but some of these states may avoid the urban-edge problems common elsewhere.

Moreover, there are areas of the country where there *is* a need and where, at the same time, any kind of growth management law is highly unlikely to appear in the foreseeable future. That PACE programs haven't yet appeared in those locales may indicate the difficulty of achieving *anything* in that local political climate. What it may indicate is the grave local *need* for AFT's collaborative voice.

It is still early in the long-term effort to cope with the country's farmland loss problems. When AFT's 1998–2000 regional expansion was under way, AFT scrutinized where the twenty most threatened agricultural areas were located and then sited its new offices to respond to that threat.[27] The expansion looked at where AFT could hope to have the greatest positive impact. In some cases, these were also areas where AFT was invited to open a new office because local citizens had already seen that the need was great. In others, they were areas where AFT saw the need itself and responded to it.

It is not coincidental that the areas where those offices were sited turn out to be the same ones where PACE programs have emerged. Despite their temporary retrenchment, where AFT regional offices did their work, they achieved results.

Even in communities where AFT no longer has a regional office, those impacts persist. In addition to the work completed while the office was open, in many cases, the work AFT started in a new office continued after its departure. For example, AFT's help in creating the Colorado Cattlemen's Agricultural Land Trust left a legacy in that state—resulting in the permanent protection of over 640,000 acres of agricultural land.

A Worthy Inheritance

There has been a public explosion of interest in disappearing farmland. The 1997 release of the *Farming on the Edge* report combined with the growth in AFT's reach and capacity through its regional offices, spread the word of farmland protection to a much larger audience and to a much more locally activist one.

Consider a few of the ways the world has changed since 2000:

There are *new state and local PACE programs* across the country in areas where they would never have been previously possible.

There is an ongoing and *well-funded federal easement program* (ACEP)—greatly aided by AFT's pivotal influence on the 2008 and 2018 Farm Bills which was aided by its local presence.

The *public message* that farmland loss is a problem of both national *and* local concern has reached into local communities all across the country.

There has been a national explosion of *interest in local food*, seen in the growth of farmers markets and local farm advocacy groups that are drawing support for agriculture from urban areas that were previously ignored in the public discussion about agriculture.

There is increasing recognition of the many ways in which farmers are or can be a *solution for society's global environmental problems* rather than their cause—problems like carbon sequestration, surface and groundwater pollution, wetland protection, wildlife habitat, floodwater detention, aquifer recharge, and easing the strain on overtaxed water resources.

Those years of direct, local AFT engagement helped transform our view of farmers. The idea that they can be a solution to our environmental problems rather than a cause has finally gone mainstream.

CHAPTER 18

Individual Land Projects: Getting the Job Done, One Farm at a Time

When Dennis Bidwell took over as American Farmland Trust's director of Land Projects in 1990, the exact role of individual land projects in AFT's work had not yet been settled. Bidwell was convinced that the majority of the sixty-two individual land projects the organization had already undertaken were acquired by "happenstance."[1] The overall accumulation of projects seemed to have had little organizing principle.

He wanted to change that. "AFT was not a traditional land trust," says Bidwell. "It was primarily a policy organization." He believed its land projects needed to reflect that reality, directly supporting its land and environmental public policy objectives. Land protection projects needed to be chosen for their strategic importance, their creativity, or their ability to build local partnerships, develop a critical constituency, or garner media and public support.

What Bidwell was looking for were projects that had leverage. He wanted projects that "demonstrated the power of agricultural easements and showed how they can work."

Making AFT's land projects "strategic" had, in fact, been the organization's goal for some time, but doing so had turned out to be difficult. Bob Wagner, who joined AFT in 1985, recalls spending much of his early work traveling through the Northeast, seeking out just such land deals. He wanted those land deals to be "demonstration" projects that would highlight the many creative ways that farmland could be protected with easements. Even then, the ideal AFT role was to use these easement projects to educate, support, and engage a land trust community, which would ultimately take on the vast bulk of the projects that came available.

Unfortunately, in 1990, there still weren't a great many land trusts around the country for farm landowners to rely upon. AFT helped start several of them, including the Maine Farmland Trust, the Connecticut Farmland Trust, and the Georgia Agricultural Land Trust. When a farmer came to AFT looking for help, especially in areas of the country not served by any land trust interested in farmland, strategic or not, it was hard to turn that project down.

In the early 1980s, AFT's Doug Wheeler had proposed creating and enrolling local land trusts as AFT "affiliates." The affiliation idea never got off the ground back then, but that changed recently. In 2020, AFT crafted formal affiliations with two land trusts: one in Kentucky and one in Georgia. And more recently, AFT has created a new National Agricultural Lands Network to help individuals and organizations working on farmland issues to collaborate more effectively.[2]

A Critical Early Role

By 1990, there were fledgling local and state government PACE programs starting up in Maryland, Massachusetts, Vermont, Pennsylvania, and Washington State,[3] but they were still few and far between. There were also land trusts springing up all across the country, but there were still huge geographical voids in service. And a great many of those that did exist had no interest in protecting working agricultural lands, let alone making it their primary focus.

Land trusts' prospects for making a real difference are limited if they simply wait around for donors to offer their land up for easement protection. In AFT's first year in business, it took an approach that was much more complex and aggressive than that.[4]

Charitable gifts. As of late 1981, AFT was working to finalize charitable gifts of agricultural easements on some forty thousand acres of farmland nationwide, ranging from a "50-acre cornfield in Pennsylvania to a 10,000-acre Wyoming Ranch."[5]

Providing a bridge to public acquisitions. AFT had facilitated the acquisition of two farms by the Massachusetts Farmland Preservation Program by stepping in quickly to acquire important agricultural easements, which could later be resold to the State program once the government funding could be approved. There were similar transactions under negotiation in Maryland, Connecticut, and elsewhere.

Creative financing. AFT had acquired a purchase option on a 340-acre swine operation in Maryland to provide security for a loan and help the family avoid foreclosure. AFT worked with the multiple inheritors of a 600-acre tobacco operation in Kentucky to allow the farm to continue intact rather than be liquidated in the estate.

Agricultural development. On a Georgia farm, AFT enabled a minority farming enterprise to make a start by providing financing for a 660-acre tract in exchange for an agricultural easement. In California's Sacramento Valley, AFT worked to protect the vast majority of a 2,000-acre ranch and to bring dry land into irrigation through financing that would combine the purchase of an easement and the sale of a few carefully selected housing sites.

Tackling the Basics

When AFT formed in 1980, agricultural easements were quite different from other conservation easements already in common use. A typical conservation easement basically restricted all activities that would damage or constrain a natural, undeveloped condition of the land. By contrast, an *agricultural* easement needed to allow the owner to conduct business and do agriculture there, activities that definitely affected the natural conditions on the land.

The issues were complicated: If there was to be active agriculture conducted on the property, structures would need to be built, including fences, irrigation infrastructure, and the like. It might be appropriate to build a farm stand or an on-farm ancillary "value-added" processing capacity. Native vegetation would need to be suppressed and removed to make way for the growing of crops or the grazing of livestock. Soil would need to be cultivated, perhaps plowed, and sometimes even moved in a way that might alter the very contours of the land. Native wildlife would be supplanted and, sometimes, suppressed.[6]

How could one write easement language to account for all these activities, define what should be allowed, and make sure the restrictions would be enforceable? AFT's Ed Thompson took on this challenge and designed easement language that could stand the test of time. It basically prohibited any development or activities on the land that would diminish its usefulness for agriculture in the years to come.[7] Thompson's language was reworked and adapted over time, but it was a starting point for land trusts all across the country.

Making Acquisitions Strategic

To see how these strategies played out, it's instructive to consider a few specific direct land projects.

Upper Elk River Valley and the Colorado Cattlemen's Association

At the time Dennis Bidwell took over management of land projects in about 1990, AFT already held several agricultural easements in

Colorado—valuable acquisitions, but also not necessarily strategic. Shortly after Bidwell came on board, AFT was contacted by Stephen Stranahan,[8] a businessman, philanthropist, and avid conservationist who owned a large ranch property on the upper Elk River valley, north of Steamboat Springs. Stranahan wanted to protect his property with a conservation easement. He had strong contacts with other agricultural landowners in the region and was well respected among the mainstream commercial ranching community there. He was also well known to and respected by the Colorado Cattlemen's Association.

In 1992, the Stranahan family placed an AFT-held conservation easement on 700 acres of their ranchland. Stranahan also introduced AFT to Jay Fetcher, a well-known and respected neighbor. Fetcher's family, shortly after, placed an easement on their 1,259-acre ranch. Then, with AFT assistance, Stranahan and Fetcher went to work convincing their neighbors.

By 1994, their community had come together to develop a comprehensive vision for their valley in what became the Upper Elk River Valley Compact.[9] The compact agreed to protect the open, natural resource productivity of the valley as a basis for both its scenic beauty and its long-term economic viability. This protection included the use of conservation easements to protect the land, the identification of limited reserved homesites necessary to the fulfillment of economic and estate-planning objectives of their owners, and the creation of affordable housing opportunities for residents who live and work in the valley.

The plan encouraged the use of conservation easements and the income tax and estate tax benefits they offered. It proposed ways to fully engage the community in partnership. And it proposed engaging the local county in policy initiatives including passage of right to farm laws,[10] formation of agricultural districts (within which landowners could be offered incentives), and creation of an agricultural lands protection committee.

The compact ended up directly protecting over 8,500 acres in the upper Elk River valley. Stranahan and Fetcher then went on, with help and support from AFT, to encourage the Colorado Cattlemen's Association to create the Colorado Cattlemen's Agricultural Land Trust, which was destined to become a powerhouse that would help protect more than 640,000 acres of threatened agricultural land throughout the state.[11]

The Colorado Cattlemen's Agricultural Land Trust provided instant credibility within the agriculture industry for other agricultural land trusts to form in the Rockies and elsewhere in the country.[12] It also propelled other cattlemen's associations across the country to create their own land trusts. A few years later, when AFT approached the Colorado Governor's Office and the General Assembly for help, it had a built-in infrastructure of local support and a history of successful work in farm country and was greatly aided in creating other statewide and local PACE efforts there.

The portfolio of land projects held by AFT in Colorado prior to its work with Steve Stranahan, while not particularly strategic, probably still helped convince Stranahan that AFT was deserving of his trust. However, the work with Stranahan and Fetcher and their neighbors became hugely strategic and productive in making dramatic changes possible in Colorado and all across the West.

Old Mission Peninsula, Northwest Michigan[13]

By 1989, AFT had become involved in protecting the highly productive and scenic farmland on Northwest Michigan's Old Mission Peninsula by saving over five hundred acres of cherry orchard from development. They followed up in 1992 with the outright purchase of a 156-acre cherry orchard near the tip of the Peninsula.

The peninsula was blessed with excellent soils and growing conditions and had supported a thriving farm industry for over a century. This sixteen-mile-long spit of land near the top of Lake Michigan produced some $7 million in its fruit harvest alone as a part of what is known as Michigan's fruit belt.[14] But population in the adjacent area had grown by some 20 percent over the previous fifteen years to more than sixty-four thousand people. The rural beauty of the place was attracting buyers whose purchases drove the price of farmland out of the reach of local farmers. There were farms for sale all along Center Road, which ran the length of the peninsula.

And those farms were not selling to other farmers.

To recover its investment in the land purchased outright in 1992, AFT worked with township officials and with the recently formed Grand Traverse Regional Conservancy to sell off four building lots, subject to restrictive covenants, none of them impacting agricultural use. That allowed AFT to then sell the larger orchard parcel to farmers at a reduced price, subject to a conservation easement that it still holds and stewards today.

This project received a good deal of media,[15] and became a catalyst for other farmland protection efforts in the Grand Traverse Peninsula Township. A study had demonstrated that, with continued growth, the Township's additional spending on community services would exceed the growth in its tax base and ultimately require an increase in taxes. With this rationale, and counter to national anti-tax sentiment, local voters narrowly approved a current property tax increase that would raise at least $2.6 million (perhaps much more), over the next fifteen years, to be used to preserve farms and orchards in the area. This reflected a willingness by voters to suffer a small hike in taxes now in order to preserve the character of their community and avoid paying higher taxes later, when it would be too late to do anything about them.

This would be the first municipal PDR program in the Midwest. The program remains active and thriving today.

"The Madera Eight" in Madera, California

By the late 1990s, the town of Madera, California (population 46,000), was growing. People who could not afford the staggering cost of land near the California coast were increasingly opting to buy low-cost properties in the middle of California's revered San Joaquin Valley instead. In 2003, the area, which lies between Sacramento and Bakersfield, was occupied by some thirty-eight thousand farms. It included six of the ten most productive agricultural counties in the country. During the decade preceding 2003, the region had grown by some five hundred thousand people.[16] And no one was more conscious of that growing pressure than its farmers.

A local farmer by the name of Denis Prosperi, whose land lay not far west of the town of Madera, needed capital to replant an old vineyard and to replace a well. He decided to sell off twenty-six acres of his land for development, and to make that possible, he applied for it to be annexed to the nearby town. The property had already been designated for annexation, so to Prosperi, the decision to see it develop was perfectly logical.

Prosperi was surprised and chagrined by what followed. He quickly heard from several of his neighbors, who begged him to call off his plans. He received a petition from a dozen neighbors objecting to the annexation. Responding to the wishes of his community, he decided to withdraw his application. "I have known these people all of my life," Prosperi said. The last thing he wanted was to become an outcast in his own community.

Over three years of meetings, Prosperi and his neighbors got together to sort out what could be done. They had a lot to discuss; the problem of sprawling development affected all of them, but the cost of doing something about it was different for each. In the end, AFT helped a group of eight large farm landowners, including Prosperi, reach an agreement to collectively place agricultural easements on some six hundred critically located acres of land adjacent to the town of Madera. In many cases, these owners took a personal financial loss in the value of their land by doing so, but they were committed to making the transaction work.

The group thus created a practical growth barrier, a "farmland security perimeter" that blocked further development and is believed to have indirectly protected some forty thousand additional acres from ultimate sprawling development. It was the perfect example of how, by coordinating with local growth management laws, agricultural easement transactions could dramatically strengthen protections for threatened farmland.

Prosperi and several of the other original Madera Eight landowners still work the land they protected. Their agricultural easements are held today held by AFT.

AFT's Dairy[17]

Before Pennsylvania farmers Anthony and Anya Smith passed away, they had willed that their cherished Cove Mountain Farm be protected and managed for conservation education purposes. AFT was selected in 1996 to operate a New Zealand–style grass-based dairy on the property. The project, which was designed to demonstrate the economic and environmental benefits of this environmentally friendly dairying system, ran from 1996 through about 2005.

AFT leased the farm to the Moyer family of Somerset, Pennsylvania. Glenn; his wife, Evelyn; and their daughter, Greta, moved to Cove Mountain Farm in August 1997 and helped AFT install the needed infrastructure. By 2000, the Moyers were rotationally grazing 120 of their own cows on two hundred acres of land, where the cows remained largely in pasture most of their lives and were provided with small shelters spread across the fields. In New Zealand, they are often milked with mobile equipment that went out to the cows. At Cove Mountain Farm,

AFT and the Moyers built a "herringbone swing" milking parlor that is designed to be very efficient, requiring a minimum of labor.

The system was designed to maximize the use of the land in a way that protected environmental values while also steadily improving its productivity. It required reduced investment in infrastructure and limited the need for labor, thus making it perfect for a small family operation; this was, perhaps, one of the last workable approaches by which a modern dairy farm could remain economically viable without investing in industrial-style facilities with thousands of cows.

In years past, the traditional, environmentally sustainable model for a dairy farm had required a maximum of roughly one cow per acre of grazing land. That meant that a farmer with something over a hundred acres could, in theory, graze perhaps one hundred cows and make the business work while keeping it environmentally sound. When, however, the market value of that land began to skyrocket, its ownership could no longer be sustained by the value of the milk produced by the number of cows that could be sustainably grazed there.

It had become an article of faith, in the dairying industry, that dairy farming could only survive through consolidation. The modern model placed maybe two thousand or more cows on as little as fifty acres, with the cows closely confined to feedlots. Fodder was purchased and trucked in from other sites. Waste was collected in large lagoons and transported away for application to distant fields often owned by other farmers. The number of dairy farms in the United States had been dramatically shrinking.[18] Many in the industry were convinced that small, family-operated dairy farms were a thing of the past.

Cove Mountain Farm showed that a major cause of consolidation was, instead, the rise in the price of land. It demonstrated that the modern industrial model, which was much more costly and less environmentally sustainable, simply wasn't necessary. Instead, with proper land protection to reduce land cost to a price linked to its value for agriculture, and with a more sustainable management model, small, local, family-owned dairy farms could again be possible.

This information was particularly relevant for dairy farming. Because of fresh milk's perishability, the historic model for milk production placed farms close to consumers, near urban centers. Many of the nation's older, traditional dairies were thus located in areas under intense development pressure. Cove Mountain Farm showed how PACE and other land protection programs could change the future for this important industry.

Love Farm

AFT received a charitable donation in 1995: a wonderful farm in Climax, Michigan, owned by Owen and Ellen Love. The gift provided for an annuity payment to Ellen Love for life. When Ellen Love passed away in 2001, AFT sold the farm after protecting it with an agricultural easement and, with the proceeds, created the Owen and Ellen Love Farmland Protection Fund for Michigan.[19]

To date, AFT has used the fund in partnership with Michigan land trusts and PDR programs to complete five farmland easement projects. Matching public funding has greatly extended their impact.

Land Projects and the Bottom Line

There is another challenge to making individual land projects strategic: they can be expensive. The ones that seem most appealing as demonstrations may not be the ones that come through the door with the wherewithal to complete them.

AFT's membership and communications staff often appreciated the organization's land projects because they were so easy to feature in publicity. Promotional brochures, *American Farmland* magazine, newsletters, and other public media often contained pictures of happy farm families and beautiful landscapes that had been protected forever.[20] Potential donors could instantly see how their charitable contributions would have a permanent impact.

Land projects also positioned AFT to receive charitable gifts of land. These could take the form of a charitable gift annuity, which provided the donor with ongoing revenue in exchange for the gift of a farm, a gift that frequently included a charitable donation to the organization.

Or a donor might donate their land but retain a life estate. AFT would protect the land with an agricultural easement and, upon their passing, sell it to a working farmer.

On the downside, however, most land project donations do not add to operating revenue. As generous as it is for a landowner to donate an easement, their gift, in itself, does not support the receiving organization's bottom line, but rather adds expense. There are legal costs and staff time invested. And some projects are risky, as when the organization serves as a bridge buyer to help pass along a farm or easement to a public program.

Once a transaction is completed, if it involves a gifted (or purchased) agricultural conservation easement, AFT takes on a perpetual obligation to steward that easement, including annual site visits. The organization must maintain a relationship with the landowner to make sure they continue to understand their easement obligations. When the property sells, the new owners need to be contacted and advised to ensure they fully understand that the land they've purchased is subject to an easement and what that means. And occasionally, if needed, the easement can require enforcement in court.

Landowners who desire to make a charitable donation of an agricultural easement to protect the future of their property are often surprised to discover that the land trust recipient of this generous gift cannot accept it unless the landowner also makes an additional cash contribution into the land trust's "easement stewardship endowment." These funds are generally invested, and the proceeds used to pay for all those future responsibilities.[21]

Finally, land trust work, generally, can be difficult to fund. Charitable foundations typically lean toward work that seems more strategic than the acquisition of protected land.

Approach/Avoidance

A decade later, AFT stopped accepting new direct land projects as an organizational program. Stewardship of existing easements continued, and a very few strategic or necessary easement acquisitions were accepted. At the same time, the organization began transferring existing easements to other, reputable local land trusts. At peak involvement, AFT held some 197 agricultural easements. By 2016, that number was down to about 100.[22]

There were several reasons for this decision: One was financial. But also, by 2001, the number of local land trusts and government land protection programs around the country had grown dramatically and was continuing to grow. AFT's increasingly appropriate role was to support and encourage those local efforts rather than to compete with them.

There was also a sense that AFT had taken on a considerable responsibility and liability exposure and that its stewardship of those easements needed better attention; it was time to drop back and focus on making absolutely certain those stewardship responsibilities were being fully attended to.[23]

A New Perspective

AFT's new president, John Piotti, came on board in 2016 with a different perspective. Given his former position as president of Maine Farmland Trust, he saw how strategic projects had helped put AFT into the national spotlight. The right choice was not, he believed, to back away from such work but rather to embrace it, while insisting that it be kept strategic. AFT's board agreed.

Piotti moved to reintroduce individual land projects back into the AFT agenda. Shortly after his arrival, he appointed Ben Kurtzman, who had worked in the land protection and farmland information area for several years, to oversee a newly revived land projects division. AFT's new land projects were intended to demonstrate how new public policy advances might be implemented in practice. This began with a comprehensive check to make sure all AFT's policies and practices were up to date, that its easement monitoring and stewardship were sound, and that the organization was properly protected from and prepared for possible litigation costs. At the same time, AFT ramped up its efforts to solicit targeted charitable donations, which would help cover the stewardship and operating expense of the program.

Finally, AFT created policies and criteria to aid the selection of projects.[24] AFT would be looking for individual land projects that had potential for broad educational, coalition building, partnerships, community development, or public policy support that one can see in some of the more impactful of the projects from the organization's past.

A New, More Comprehensive Objective

There was yet another goal of this land project revitalization: to show how land protection could sometimes support the other two key elements of AFT's mission; namely, environmental and economic sustainability.

In the environmental context, for example, in California's Central Valley, where AFT was working on projects that protect the land and water resources, such projects could have special meaning. One objective could include protecting the farm's water for future use in agriculture and protecting farms that have secure water resources. It might also include protecting natural features on the land (streams, wetlands, ponds, riparian buffers, and the like) that might be important to aquifer recharge or surface waterflow as a benefit to the broader public. And it might step beyond water to other environmental values (carbon sequestration, wildlife habitat, water quality, flood detention).[25]

The economic sustainability component of AFT's mission could be addressed with easements as well. Cove Mountain Farm provided one example. Removing development value from the land reduces its cost to its agricultural business value, making it possible for a working farmer to own it over the long term. Making farmland affordable, then, could also become an explicit new goal of the program, appropriate for a demonstration project. This could include encouraging women to enter or remain in the farming business. It could include encouragement for new and minority farmers in need of affordable options.

A demonstration project is pointless unless people know about it, however. If they were to have real impact, these projects would need media publicity and the attention they deserved within the environmental, farming, land use, land trust, and relevant public agency communities.

With this new vision, an individual land project could tie conservation and environmental requirements to farmland protection, and vice versa. A farmland easement that also specifically sequesters carbon, protects wildlife, and prevents pollution, purchased or not, would be one for farmers and environmentalists alike to behold.

CHAPTER 19
Communicating the Message

When intermediating between people who have issues with one another, mastering the complexity of their shared and differing perspectives is essential. Polemic answers are typically also simple ones. But finding solutions that respect diverse human points of view is not simple. Those solutions can be elusive. They can hide in what, at least initially, one might think of as the details.

The complexities of farmland and environmental protection have always been a challenge for American Farmland Trust's communications professionals. It turns out to be extremely difficult to briefly describe what it is that AFT actually does. AFT staff and partners typically tend to be goal focused. Their first priority is generally to solve the problem. Then, later on, to worry about publicity.[1] Unfortunately, that approach can meet headwinds when one needs first to secure political support, and then find the money, before solving the problem.

Publicity became even more difficult as the organization entered the environmental arena and began to find its feet in the "middle ground."[2] When working in the difficult space between environmental and agricultural interests, taking public credit was no longer an easy option.[3]

1997 Farming on the Edge

AFT's communications staff inevitably found that sound research was foundational for AFT's credibility. It could be useful in building coalitions, and, properly structured and presented, taking the credit for it had no particular downsides.

The most successful media campaign AFT ever accomplished was the one that promoted the 1997 version of the *Farming on the Edge* report.[4] Even that got complicated: the 1997 report was in large part a rework and reissuance of a similar report that had come out in 1992. So, in explaining it, one could end up having to differentiate it from the report that had come out five years earlier.

With its big, colorful, nationwide map, AFT's 1997 *Farming on the Edge* report drew the reader in to look up what was happening in their part of the world. It overlaid the nation's highest-quality farmland with the places facing the greatest rate of development. The twenty most threatened regions of the country were then shown on the map in bright red. Readers inevitably looked for their own home and then checked out the list to see how their region stacked up against other parts of the country.

AFT organized public media events to announce the report in multiple locations, targeting areas that rated high on the list of most threatened regions. This targeting encouraged the media to be on hand for their local or regional event so they could hear the big national announcement in person. Local targeting also greatly increased the chance producers and editors would publish a story. AFT also drew on the limited number of local and regional personnel that were then available in the field to help promote the event.

The launch was happening at a time when the local food movement was still just beginning to emerge in the United States. Urban sprawl and farmland loss had, however, begun to penetrate the national consciousness.

AFT's federal policy work was already beginning to spawn farmland protection programs around the country, and many of the nation's land trusts were entering the farmland protection business. So, there was a receptive audience for the tragic story of disappearing farmland.

The outcome was overwhelming. There was mention in national media outlets like the *New York Times*, *Washington Post*, and front-page coverage in *USA Today*. AFT received requests for copies of the report for years afterward. And that interest and attention, which helped AFT recruit new members and secure new funding, contributed to AFT's growth toward the end of the 1990s, which fueled the regional expansion immediately afterward.

American Farmland Magazine

In the spring of 1990, AFT launched *American Farmland* magazine. The magazine provided an opportunity to feature some of the interesting issues the organization faced and describe some of the creative projects in which it was engaged.

In the Winter 2004 issue, for example, AFT's Agricultural Conservation Innovation director, Brian Brandt, described the AFT crop insurance program. The insurance made it possible for a farmer who followed conservation practice recommendations to be protected from any loss in productivity that might result. This project was a trial of what later became a significant factor in reducing pollution.

In the Spring 2006 issue, AFT's Southwest regional director, Gerry Cohn, discussed a project identifying how small, local farmers were finding markets outside the traditional distribution networks. These included farmers markets; consumer subscriptions (now commonly referred to as CSAs or community-supported agriculture); new cooperative facilities for processing local meats, fruits, and vegetables; and sustainability marketing that rewards environmental stewardship.

In the Winter 2008 issue, Ed Thompson, then AFT's California state director, took on the relationship between sprawling development, lost farmland, and greenhouse gas emissions. He discussed an AFT partnership with the Urban Land Institute and the growing evidence that preserving our farms and managing sprawl could significantly reduce the threat of climate change.

In this same issue, the magazine's editor, Kirsten Ferguson, explained other ways in which agriculture could help solve our planet's climate crisis. She discussed how sound environmental management practices could sequester carbon in plants and in the soil and could reduce the rate at which crops or livestock contribute to greenhouse gases.

For most people, including many who worked on agriculture and environmental policy, the opportunity to use agriculture to combat climate change didn't become apparent until the fall of 2018, when the UN's Intergovernmental Panel on Climate Change issued a report confirming that we can never meet the 2015 Paris Climate goals simply by reducing emission; we must also put atmospheric carbon back into the soil.

American Farmland became an award-winning publication precisely because Ferguson made sure its content was thoughtful and challenging and went well beyond the mere promotional material offered in typical nonprofit publications. Each issue was an added value received by AFT's members in exchange for their contributions.

American Farmland magazine ceased publication in 2012 and was replaced by a periodic newsletter that is still in use today.[5]

The Steward of the Land Award

Peggy Rockefeller remained on the AFT board of directors for sixteen years, until her passing in March 1996.[6] To commemorate her contributions to the organization, AFT established the annual Steward of the Land Award.

Over the years that followed, AFT would take nominations for farmers nationwide who best epitomized the values of conservation stewardship, community responsibility, and protection of the land to which Peggy Rockefeller had committed much of her life. Each year a national Steward of the Land was named, and their laudable work was made known in their community and across the nation. There was also a $10,000 cash prize awarded to the winner. Between 1997 and 2008, twelve highly deserving farmers received this award.

The criteria for the award included environmental responsibility, community engagement, and protection of the land. Typically, the farmers who were selected were already quite well known and much admired in their local communities, so the award was often a matter of considerable local pride. For each recipient, AFT would hold a widely promoted local event at which to present the award, inviting the press.

The winners were also easy to like and a joy to talk and write about. These Steward of the Land Awards generated some great local and regional press for AFT as well as for the winning farmer.[7]

Building in a Structure for Outreach

Much of AFT's work was funded through foundation grants, money that was hard to come by—and every dime of which needed to be fully explained and justified. Grant funding typically didn't cover the full cost of the project work. By the time the basic work was done, the money had often run out, with nothing left for essential publicity.

Shortly before 2000, when the AFT regional expansion was under way, AFT adopted a policy: When writing the budget for almost any project, the program manager was expected to include funding for outreach. There would need to be money for a properly published project report, for proper distribution to the intended audience, for media, for publicity. What good were the lessons learned in almost any project if nobody knew about them? From that point forward, proper public outreach became a component of everything the organization undertook.

A Cooperative Message for a Collaborative Organization

Consistent with the collaborative, middle-of-the-road nature of the organization, a series of principles emerged in the day-to-day practice of AFT's communications work:[8]

Stay in the middle ground. Every communications staffer was fully conscious that credit for AFT's accomplishments needed to be understated and prudently shared with the organization's partners. Beyond that, however, they all also understood that AFT's credibility and success hung upon the respect it had assiduously won within *both* the agriculture industry and the environmental and land use community.

Take a long-term perspective. AFT had deep ties to agriculture as well as to the environmental community. For both farm and environmental groups, the legislative vote they needed to stay alive tomorrow could sometimes be the one they'd lose by focusing, instead, on a problem that might be important only five years down the road.

AFT, however, was focused on the future. It had the mixed luxury of caring about the agriculture and the environment of ten, twenty, or fifty years from now. Because it was able to do that, it could be respected by advocates on both sides of the issue. And when they accomplished one of those jointly supported objectives, the gains tended to endure because their achievement was supported by both sides in the debate.

Make no enemies. AFT didn't make enemies. Its public communications didn't demonize people. Whenever possible, the solutions it sought would be voluntary and based on incentives. Or they'd be painstakingly crafted and thoroughly negotiated so they met the needs of all the key participants. AFT's emphasis was always on enlisting partners. It focused on believable research. It valued the worldviews and perspectives of all players. It might seek to educate and inform those views. But it always did so with respect for the people who held them. AFT did not tell people what to do: it asked, convinced, and encouraged them to do what, hopefully, they would ultimately come to understand to be the right thing.

Take no sides. AFT didn't take sides favoring any particular type of farming (organic versus conventional, small versus large, family-run versus corporate, direct market versus wholesale, and so on). AFT supported a better future for society and for agriculture: all of agriculture. AFT believed that all farms and ranches—regardless of size and structure—have an important role to play in our future, both advancing environmental health and providing life-giving food.

There is a natural inclination to feel that one's chosen solution to a problem is the sole answer. There are often many answers to problems, however, including those facing agriculture. Organic farming can help address issues with pesticides, but so can integrated pest management. An agricultural easement can reduce farmland loss, but so can a thoughtfully designed zoning law. Small, direct-market farmers can bring fresh, local food to urban consumers, but the prices may be beyond what some customers can afford. Conservation management practices are needed to address critical environmental issues, but some measures are costly to implement: Do we prefer that the farm fail and the land fall to suburban or recreational housing?

AFT was about finding as many workable, effective, and broadly supportable solutions as possible.

Honor diversity. The future of agriculture may depend, in part, on people who today represent a minority of our farmers. AFT's communications needed to respect that future by including past and future farmers as well as those who inhabit the industry today.

The Communications Ace: People Love Farmers

People love farmers.[9] Our farm employment population may have diminished to only 2 percent of our numbers currently, but agriculture is still a major US industry,[10] and more important, our farmers and ranchers represent cultural roots that are deeply valued by the vast majority of Americans.[11]

Yes, people also love unspoiled landscapes and a clean, healthy environment. But AFT offers a long-term future in which a robust agriculture industry strengthens its own economic vitality by protecting those landscapes and preserving and enriching the environment. It is a future in which the public, by supporting agriculture, is also protecting the environment.

CHAPTER 20
Fertile Fields for Development

The involvement of the Rockefeller family and of an influential and deeply committed board gave American Farmland Trust a strong head start. It is not possible, however, to grow and sustain a successful non-profit organization on the charitable support of a few board members.

By the end of 1981, AFT had assembled fifteen thousand members, reaching fifty thousand by 2000.[1] As of 2021, membership stands at an all-time high of almost sixty thousand. That may sound like a lot. But these numbers are nominal compared to memberships for the larger national nonprofit environmental groups and farm industry trade groups.

Organizations have multiple motives for cultivating members. They can represent a political power base, for example. Here are committed individuals from across the country who are likely to respond to requests for political activism, local and national. But those members are also the organization's funding base. And significant major donors are often recruited from among an organization's previously more modest contributors.

But memberships also come at a cost. For the vast majority of members, the contributions they make just match the cost of acquiring and retaining them. Most nonprofits see a return on their investment in membership only after several years of cultivating members who later become major contributors.[2]

Taken together, individual contributions have made up roughly half of AFT's income with the balance consisting of foundation grants, corporate gifts, paid consulting services, and government contracts.[3]

But who are these people? Many of AFT's individual donors appear to be political moderates with roots in agriculture and, very often, a sense of nostalgia about its slow, tragic, but seemingly steady disappearance from many of our communities.[4] As a group, they are older and, thus, diminishing in numbers as our population's ties to agriculture grow ever more distant over time. They may also be people who lament the increasingly polemic nature of American public political discourse.

Foundations, Consulting, Government, Corporate

Cynthia Wilson, who was AFT's foundation and corporate development director for many years, refers to AFT's middle-ground position as "both a blessing and a curse" for development.[5]

Wilson came to AFT in 1995, bringing experience in nonprofit management, fund development, and government relations. According to Wilson, AFT's centrist mission did help with some of the more "establishment" funders. But there was a long history of environmental groups doing bitter battle with the Farm Bureau and other farm industry trade groups. Over the years, they'd fought over issues like DDT, the Clean Water Act, and the Endangered Species Act. Many environmental funders had come to view farmers as hopeless "bad actors." The idea that anything positive could be accomplished by working with agriculture fell outside their world view.

Wilson says there was another barrier as well: AFT's work was mostly accomplished on private land. An environmental funder with previous negative experience could find it difficult to appreciate how keeping a private farm in working agriculture or how relying on a private farm owner, no matter how well incentivized they might be, to voluntarily manage their land in a way that respected the environment could possibly be in the public's interest. What was to keep that easement-protected private farm from still being operated in a way that harmed the public interest? What if the farmer changed their mind about protecting the environment? What if they sold out to another, less well-intended farmer?

Getting past those prior years of antipathy and breaking through a funder's initial reluctance was a significant struggle both nationally and locally.

On the upside, AFT's centrist roots gave it grounding that appealed to more mainstream, contributors, people who would have been disconcerted by a more strident tone. As the years passed, those initial funders often moved on to new prospects. It soon became necessary to transition to seeking support from the more ardent environmental foundations and to hope that they would appreciate what could be accomplished through AFT's more collaborative approach.

Success varied from region to region. In California and the Pacific Northwest, funders tended to be more environmental in orientation than, for example, in the Midwest or the South. In areas like the Northeast, where there was an emerging policy tradition of local government PACE programs, it was easier to enlist support for farmland protection. In the West, funders often wanted to see more immediate environmental results.

Nationwide, it was also harder to raise money for farmland protection than for projects that focused on conservation practices that would produce a visible and more immediate environmental payoff. Corporate help was also difficult to come by, perhaps because the protection of farmland and opposition to sprawling development may have seemed anti-capitalist.

The principal institutional funding resource on which AFT's middle-ground, research-oriented work relied was government grants and contracts. There were sometimes state and local government resources available for "consulting" projects like conducting cost of community services studies, structuring new local PACE programs, taking public input on agriculture issues, or developing local farm economic development plans. There was often public money for these kinds of AFT services because AFT got things done without generating political fallout.

Some of those struggles continue; others have been successfully resolved. AFT has rebounded from financial declines in 2001–03 and then again in 2009–15. And, with time and persistence, it has gained the support of many mainstream and environmental funders alike as the connections between land ownership, farming, and good stewardship are realized. And as more people have come to appreciate the surprising power of the center field.

CHAPTER 21

New Leadership and New Ideas

It may be only a single long day's drive from Belfast, Maine, to the nation's capital, but the two places are a world apart. Belfast, with a population of about 6,500, is a classic, picturesque Maine coastal town. Maine Farmland Trust (MFT), wedged between Alexia's Pizza on one side and the Old Professor's Bookshop on the other, looks out through its storefront office windows onto a view down Main Street that could go straight onto a postcard.

In summer 2016, when John Piotti packed up a rented van and made a life-changing trip down I-95 to Washington, DC, to take on the job as American Farmland Trust's new president, he was leaving all that behind. He passed through the outskirts of Boston, through New York City, Newark, Philadelphia, and Baltimore—a journey through the oldest and most densely populated region in the country. It would be impossible for him to have made that drive without imagining how spectacular this countryside must have looked two or three hundred years earlier, in the days of our agrarian past and our nation's birth.

Piotti was a former Maine state legislator who'd served as that state's House majority leader and chair of its Agriculture Committee. He had deep professional roots in community development and sustainable agriculture. And he'd led Maine Farmland Trust—one of the state-based agricultural land trusts that had sprung up across the nation in the previous two decades with a little help from AFT.

In 1999, Piotti became one of MFT's first board members. Then in 2006, he was tapped to become its new president. In the ten years from 2006 to 2016, Piotti increased the number of staff members from three to over forty, quadrupled its supporters, and built the organization's net assets from about $125,000 to over $25 million. This new capacity enabled MFT to take on new programs that significantly ramped up the amount of Maine farmland being protected while simultaneously increasing agricultural viability—both by supporting existing farmers and by helping new farmers get started. Due in no small part to MFT's work, Maine experienced an agricultural renaissance during this period, with a growing number of farms and one of the highest percentages of new and beginning farmers in the nation.[1]

Piotti's success at MFT made it harder for him to leave. He knew what could still be done in Maine, especially now that he'd laid a firm foundation for further growth. When the job offer came, he initially turned AFT down.

What finally tipped the scale was the climate crisis.

Piotti understood the massive needs and challenges of farmland protection itself. And he was fully aware of AFT's role in protecting the environment. But for him, climate was the critical issue. He was convinced that agriculture both could and must be part of the solution to climate change—a conviction he had written about and shared with AFT's leadership during their months of recruiting.[2] In the end, AFT's board chair persuaded Piotti that at AFT, he would have a chance to make a real difference on a national stage on *the* issue of our time.

A Climate Crisis

With a new wave of interest in the interplay between agriculture and climate, AFT was well poised to share its research and policy solutions. But when Piotti arrived at AFT, there was no dedicated funding and no organized national AFT climate initiative. In early 2017, soon after Piotti had carefully reevaluated AFT's current position and programs with his staff and board, he made climate an organizational priority and turned to AFT staffer Jimmy Daukas to lead the effort.

Daukas is a long-term AFT career professional and a veteran of AFT's climate work—in particular through his role in the Waxman–Markey climate bill a decade earlier. He'd been thinking about the deeper farm–environmental issues, specifically those related to climate, for decades. Daukas would need to pull together the disparate array of climate work that AFT was doing and frame a new organization-wide initiative.

AFT called this effort Farmers Combat Climate Change, to highlight how farmers and ranchers could become part of our planet's climate solution. With a lot of hard work, leavened by early fundraising, Daukas and Piotti were able to fund some programming. This, in turn, led to some additional fundraising success that made it possible to leverage other AFT research, education, and policy work that was already accelerating conservation practices to combat climate change.

By mid-2019, just two and a half years later, AFT had created a national initiative engaging four newly added PhD-level scientists with expertise in soil science and field staff in several regions. As a result, AFT was selected by the United States Climate Alliance (USCA)—a collection of twenty-five states committed to realizing the goals of the Paris Agreement—as one of USCA's first Natural and Working Lands Impact Partners,[3] charged with helping states develop ways for agriculture to draw down atmospheric carbon and reduce greenhouse gas (GHG) emissions.

To understand the full story, one must first understand how climate is linked to agriculture.

Engaging Agriculture

By 2016, public discussion about agriculture and climate had begun to shift. Agriculture had been identified as a leading cause of climate change—contributing about a quarter of all greenhouse gases globally and about 10 percent domestically. At the same time, a small but growing number of people appreciated how atmospheric carbon could be captured in the soil through natural processes unleashed by better farming practices. This group initially comprised mostly scientists, farmers, and key people within companies and organizations that worked with farmers. But the group was expanding, spurred by 2015's designation as the International Year of Soils, by the 2015 UN Climate Change Conference,[4] by the work of some key researchers like Keith Paustian and Rattan Lal, as well as by some well-regarded publications, such as Eric Toensmeier's *Carbon Farming Solution.*[5]

The message in all this was clear: agriculture could affirmatively mitigate climate change. And with fully half the planet's habitable land surface managed by farmers, that was a very big deal.[6] There was every reason for the agriculture industry to actively participate in solving the planet's climate crisis:

First, agriculture, as an industry, would be hugely impacted and challenged by climate change—think drought, disappearing water resources, unprecedented storms, worsening flooding, shifting climate zones, and exposure to new pests and new invasive plant species.[7] These are changes for which most farmers are ill prepared.

Second, as the social struggle to address a worsening climate intensifies, agriculture could become a target of direct regulation—compelled to take actions the industry could ill afford and that could easily become counterproductive.

Third, and perhaps most critical: despite the regulatory cost of caps on GHG emissions, agriculture might well be a net economic winner in carbon and environmental markets because farms can reduce GHG and sequester carbon relatively inexpensively. With relatively modest public help, farmers could potentially afford to make huge greenhouse gas gains through improved grazing practices, reduced application of nitrogen fertilizer, and other regenerative practices. This could become a massive part of the climate solution, and farmers could be compensated for providing those environmental benefits while continuing in profitable agriculture.[8]

Farmers are practical people who pay close attention to the realities that drive their future. Back in 2009, when the Waxman–Markey bill was before the US Congress, for example, AFT's leadership in the "Gang of Five" (described in chapter 10) had helped get the bill passed through the House of Representatives by organizing substantial agriculture industry support for the measure. The bill ultimately died in the Senate. But without the farmers' help, Waxman–Markey would never have made it out of the House—a testament to the industry's clear self-interest in the highly practical carbon cap-and-trade solution.

AFT helped convince agriculture to come on board. But perhaps the greatest initial challenge was to get funders, policymakers, and more of the general public to conceive of farming as a climate *solution* and farmers as people helping to solve the problem rather than merely contributing to it.[9]

Climate and Farmland

In 2016, AFT's California state office completed a groundbreaking climate study and produced the California Greener Fields Study Report.[10]

Conducted with partners at the University of California, Davis, the study demonstrated the potential reduction in greenhouse gases that could be achieved by reducing farmland loss and keeping our cities compact and efficient. Compared to sprawl, constrained and efficient development stabilizes and reduces future emissions while still allowing the economy to flourish. Even without special management, farms sequester carbon and mitigate GHG emissions a great deal better than urban sprawl does.

The surprising findings of the study, included the following:

Lost farmland. If nothing was done, 1.4 million acres of California farmland were destined to be lost to development by mid-century.

Developed lands emit more GHG. An acre of developed urban land produces fifty-eight to seventy times the greenhouse gas emissions of an acre of working farmland.

Compact growth saves GHG. Comparing compact, efficient growth with the sprawl currently occurring, AFT projected that protecting farmland and growing cities in a compact manner would save thirty-three tons of GHG (per acre per year).

Huge GHG benefits from saving farmland. Cutting farmland loss by 75 percent by 2050, or by seven hundred thousand acres, would reduce our GHG emissions the equivalent of taking 1.9 million cars off the road each year.

That last calculation was especially significant: for western US states, automobile transportation represents the largest single source of greenhouse gases.[11] California had committed to fighting climate change by establishing a goal of reducing statewide GHG emissions by 80 percent by 2050. AFT's study offered the state a great opportunity to use farmland protection as a cost-efficient way to meet its goal.

Building upon this study's compelling results, AFT and its partners

then pushed California—the only state with a cap-and-trade program—
to earmark a portion of the program's revenue for farmland protection.
The first installment of funding provided over $100 million through a
new Sustainable Agricultural Land Conservation program;[12] by the end
of 2022, a full $500 million in funding is expected to flow to farmland
protection projects in California. This represented the first time the dots
between PACE funding and climate change had been connected.

In 2017, AFT replicated its *Greener Fields* study for New York, where
it demonstrated that farmland emits sixty-six times less in greenhouse
gases than developed land. If New York farmland loss was reduced by 80
percent by 2050, the gain would be the equivalent of removing a million
cars from the road.[13] Though New York does not have a cap-and-trade
program like California, the fact that protecting farmland is a highly
effective way to realize climate goals helped move New York to earmark
$14 million in new funding for purchasing agricultural easements.[14]

A Broader Climate Initiative

Keeping farmland from being developed is one way to combat climate
change; another critically important strategy—and one finally beginning to gain some public attention—is to farm in a manner that captures
atmospheric carbon in the soil. Carbon sequestration happens naturally
when plants grow. But by following certain farming practices—those
specifically designed to build soil health—the amount of carbon drawn
into the soil can be greatly increased.

AFT had been advancing soil-building farming practices since 1982.
Granted, the focus initially was on improving soil health as a way to
reduce erosion, decrease nutrients leaving the farm, retain moisture, and
increase crop yields. But the same practices that produce those outcomes
are also highly efficient at sequestering carbon. As early as the 1990s,
AFT was promoting this broader benefit among people who understood
soil science and were concerned about the threat of global warming.

By the next decade, AFT was actively promoting adoption of so-called regenerative or climate-smart practices among farmers.

After the Senate defeat of Waxman–Markey in 2009, many of the foundations that had supported AFT's climate work refocused on other opportunities—and AFT's climate work took a big hit. AFT continued to advance better farming practices after that, though often with a different stated purpose. As of 2016, most of AFT's work in this space was focused on reducing erosion and improving water quality.

In early 2017, Piotti and Daukas were deep in discussion on a strategy to rebuild AFT's climate portfolio. The California *Greener Fields* study and the similar study for New York would surely be one piece, as it tied climate to farmland protection and would generate significant new PACE funding. Another component was AFT's current soil health programming in the Midwest and around the Great Lakes. Even though much of that work was focused on improving water quality by planting cover crops and changing tillage practices, these were the same practices that sequestered carbon. AFT would now stress the multiple benefits of this work, thus creating more interest among funders and enabling AFT to expand its soil health programs and impact.

Beyond farmland protection and sequestering carbon in the soil, a third leg of the climate strategy would involve promoting renewable energy, in particular solar energy. As public concern about climate change had grown, and as the price of solar panels dropped, there had been a rush to locate new solar energy facilities that could, if poorly sited, affect high-quality farmland. AFT's objective was to increase solar energy development, but in a way that did not undermine farm operations or convert our best land. The challenge: to generate more electricity while *also* protecting the land on which we grew our food and which also provided numerous other environment benefits, including carbon capture.

Soon after Piotti came to AFT, he was approached by some concerned Maryland residents who told him that solar farms, not urban sprawl, were now the greatest threat to farmland in their communities. Similar concerns were being raised in parts of New York and New England.

Daukas began gathering information and assessing what AFT could do. He put together a partnership with several other nonprofit organizations involved in solar energy or conservation. Each came to the issue from their own perspective, but all were committed to smart solar siting—expanding solar while protecting our best agriculture and forestland. He then secured grant funding to launch this smart-solar siting partnership as part of AFT's climate work.

Informing the Public and Congress

The final piece of the puzzle involved public awareness. Although there was a growing awareness that agriculture could be a climate solution, most people—including most policymakers—knew very little about it. In 2017, agriculture was still generally viewed solely as a carbon contributor. Outside of a few circles, the term *regenerative agriculture* was unknown.

Thus AFT's climate initiative also needed to tell a story, to spread word about how farming could help. Piotti and Daukas began to talk about climate in every public presentation, in communications with AFT members, and via social media. It all began with reinforcing the positive message that farmers can be part of the solution. That message was included in the program's name: Farmers Combat Climate Change.[15]

They also targeted the United States Congress. Piotti and Daukas identified potential legislative partners, offering AFT as a resource to any member of Congress or congressional staffer. At the top of that list was Rep. Chellie Pingree of Maine.

Congresswoman Pingree served on the Agriculture Committee and, perhaps more important, on Agriculture Appropriations. Though a progressive Democrat, she worked closely and successfully with her

Republican colleagues on many issues. She gravitated toward practical common-ground solutions—as evidenced by her Local Foods Act, parts of which had been incorporated into the last farm bill.

A former state senator, Pingree had worked with Piotti on agricultural policy issues in Maine stretching back twenty years. She had also served with Piotti on the board of Maine Farmland Trust in the early years after its founding.

Beyond all this, Pingree was a farmer. She didn't need to be educated about regenerative farming practices or how farmers could combat climate change. But like most members of Congress who arrived after Waxman–Markey, she had little knowledge of AFT's experience and expertise on climate issues. She and her staff appreciated learning that history and reviewing AFT's data and analysis.

Pingree has since become a major voice in Congress on all issues linking agriculture and climate. And interest in Congress is now much stronger than when Piotti and Daukas first launched AFT's climate initiative.

Piotti gives most of the credit for that change in attitude to rising public awareness spurred by the United Nations Intergovernmental Panel on Climate Change (IPCC). In 2018, the IPCC released a report clearly stating that as essential as it is to reduce carbon emissions, such an effort on its own will never get us to the goals of the Paris Accords. To meet those goals, we must also actively pursue natural solutions that sequester carbon; regenerative farming practices top the list of effective, low-cost natural solutions. Unlike many other scientific studies—which land with a thump and then collect dust on shelves—the IPCC report resonated with influential members of the lay public, including lawmakers in Congress.

Another important change occurred within Congress itself. In the November 2018 elections, the House of Representatives flipped from Republican to Democratic control. While climate change should not be a partisan issue, the switch in House leadership brought far greater attention to the issue, especially after Speaker Pelosi created the House Select Committee on the Climate Crisis.[16]

That committee began hearings in mid-2019. Unlike most previous public discussions about climate, this one recognized agriculture as a critical part of the issue—and as one potential part of the solution. One positive force was the states themselves. Twenty-five governors had by then joined the USCA.[17] And AFT, as one of the alliance's Impact Partners, had been providing these state administrations with information about the power of regenerative farming practices and how they could be a part of state climate plans. For members of Congress who stayed in close touch with state efforts, this only reinforced the message of farming's promise.

Daukas was no longer operating alone. By late 2018, AFT had hired Dr. Jennifer Moore-Kucera, a widely respected soil scientist formerly with USDA, to lead the climate initiative. Her work plan included developing a powerful new analytical tool that draws on existing data to provide estimates and maps of the carbon reduction potential of agricultural practices, by county, on all the farmland in America—a tool that will help states develop policies and programs for healthy soils.

In fall 2019, when the House Select Committee on the Climate Crisis needed an expert witness on agriculture and climate, it turned to AFT, and AFT put forward Dr. Moore-Kucera. Her testimony captured the full breadth of the issue.[18] It also utilized data from AFT's new analytical tool to show what American agriculture could do: By combining practices such as conservation tillage, cover cropping, and nutrient management, US cropland has the potential to counter over 85 percent of agriculture's carbon emissions. And if grazing land is also managed with regenerative practices, US agriculture could sequester more carbon than it currently emits, becoming a net carbon sink and thus compensating for other economic sectors.

In other words, farming—done a little differently, yet utilizing proven practices—can be a game changer.

But just because this *can* happen doesn't mean that it *will* happen. We can't expect struggling farmers and ranchers to do more without added support. The income that farmers receive for the food they produce is often barely enough to cover their cost of production, let alone the environmental services they provide. The future demands a new model.

Further, regenerative practices realize their full potential only if sustained. The benefits of a well-managed farm that has been sequestering carbon evaporate if, ten years later, the property is developed and the captured soil carbon returns to the air. Moreover, the ability to sequester carbon at scale depends entirely on having sufficient land. With every lost acre of agricultural land, we lose the opportunity to apply better farming practices on that land.

In short, the answer is not regenerative practices alone. If agriculture is to fulfill its promise to combat climate change, we also need to retain our agricultural land and ensure that our farmers and ranchers can be financially successful while following planet-healing practices.

Farmland Loss and Farmland Protection

At the same time that AFT was reinvigorating its climate portfolio, the organization was also moving forward on two other fronts: in May 2018, AFT released the first report in its latest mapping study, *Farms Under Threat*,[19] which showed how the United States was losing irreplaceable farmland way too fast; and in December 2018, the farm bill passed with considerable new support for the federal Agricultural Conservation Easement Program (ACEP)—an additional $200 million a year over ten years, totaling an unprecedented $2 billion!

The first accomplishment represents a thorough documentation of a major public challenge, while on the surface, the second appears to offer a direct policy response to that challenge. Yet the two accomplishments, while interrelated, were not "cause and effect." Rather, AFT was traveling two parallel tracks.

The Right Study at the Right Time

Farms Under Threat: The State of America's Farmland was the latest iteration in a series of AFT's studies on farmland loss, stretching back to the organization's earliest years. Yet this study was more comprehensive than anything AFT had ever done. It would utilize the latest geographic information systems (GIS) technology and previously unavailable data sets. Recognizing the technical demands, AFT teamed up with Conservation Science Partners (CSP),[20] a nonprofit research group with expertise in spatial imagery. The involvement of CSP, a global leader in this field, increased the odds that the study would prove cutting edge. USDA's NRCS would be the third partner, providing financial support, technical guidance, and essential data.

There was a significant barrier, however. Much of the data critical to the study was housed in the NRCS National Resources Inventory. By act of Congress, NRCS is not allowed to share this data in a form that might reveal proprietary information about individual farms or ranches.[21] Under a special confidentiality agreement, NRCS can provide such data to carefully vetted non-advocacy research groups like CSP—but only for research purposes. And under the agreement, CSP would not be allowed to reveal proprietary information either. But it could aggregate this data and use it to ground-truth publicly available information.

AFT's partner, CSP, made the application. CSP, composed of scientists and academics, had no advocacy role, which made the NRCS decision easier. But its partnership with AFT, clearly an advocacy group, inevitably created questions. In the end, the project would not have been possible but for four decades of collaboration and trust between NRCS and AFT created by people like Ann Sorensen, Jennifer Dempsey, Julia Freedgood, and, of course, Ralph Grossi himself. And, obviously, by Norm Berg, the former NRCS chief who'd opened so many early doors for AFT.

But this time, AFT had yet another key player at work: John Larson, who had joined the organization only a year earlier. Larson had previously served as CEO for the National Association of Conservation Districts, an organization that works hand in hand with NRCS and is one of the agency's tightest nongovernmental associates in a deeply valued, nationwide "conservation partnership." Larson, an engaging, likable soul, had already built many years of close, trusting relationships with NRCS staff and other key players in conservation agriculture. His hand was essential in making the final agreement come together.

Farms Under Threat was a multiyear and multiphased project. The first phase, *The State of America's Farmland*, as released in May 2018, provided a national accounting of land use and farmland loss over the previous twenty years, and produced a new national land cover map. Getting to these results required building an entirely new and incredibly complex geospatial platform that incorporated boatloads of data—often conflicting data—from more than forty sources. In some ways, the real power of the first phase was in creating a new technological foundation for mapping and analysis. The second phase, released in May 2020, not only refined the earlier national analysis but offered a detailed state-by-state breakdown besides. It also provided a comprehensive look at six relevant state policies and programs, including PACE, land use planning, current use taxation, and agricultural district programs. The third phase, expected to be complete by 2022, will look into the future, assessing different scenarios based on development activity and climate change.

Farms Under Threat made a mark. Combined with the further detail and refinements of phase two, *The State of the States,* released in 2020, the study offers four remarkable contributions:

Increased accuracy and detail. It documented with more accuracy than ever before the extent, diversity, location, and quality of agricultural land in the continental United States—as well as the threats to this land from expanding development—showing that farmland loss remains alarming. (Between 2001 and 2016, eleven million acres of irreplaceable farmland and ranchland were paved over, built up, or otherwise lost to agriculture—that's equal to the total amount of US cropland devoted to fruit, nut, and vegetable production in 2017.)

New perspectives on landscape data. The study incorporated new ways of viewing the landscape and underlying data. This occurred in several ways, but two are particularly novel and important: AFT categorized "nationally significant" ag land based on its productivity, versatility and resilience; and it developed a way to document and track so-called low-density residential land use, the breaking up of rural farm acreage into five- or ten-acre house lots that prevents viable farming but had previously been unaccounted for in most statistics.

Linkage to local conditions. It linked what's happening on the ground back to state circumstances and showed how states were responding through the Agricultural Land Protection Scorecard, which evaluates state-level policies and programs.

Broader perspectives. The research raised broader issues—about food security, community resilience, and what we need to know to avert a future food and environmental crisis—and it provided a foundation to explore those issues further.

2018 Farm Bill

Sen. Pat Roberts and Rep. Mike Conaway, chairmen of the Ag Committees in their respective chambers, had forewarned that the 2018 Farm Bill would be "evolutionary, not revolutionary." In the end, there was little change in overall federal policy, even when viewed through an evolutionary lens. A more accurate description might be "business as usual."

One of the few exceptions, however, was the Agricultural Conservation Easement Program (ACEP).[22] Established by the 2014 Farm Bill,
ACEP combined existing programs that focused primarily on wetland
easements with the Farm and Ranchlands Protection Program (FRPP).
In the 2018 Farm Bill, ACEP funding increased from $250 million to
$450 million per year—and was authorized over a ten-year period.

Yet the success—though real—must be viewed in context: $450
million was actually a return to the same level of funding Congress
had provided in 2014 (though, at that time, it had been structured to
diminish each subsequent year). Still, it was a huge accomplishment
to restore funding to its previous level and to put in place a ten-year
authorization that, although not a guarantee of ongoing support,
increased the odds that Congress would stick with $450 million a year
over that period.

Of that amount, it was unclear how much would be used for easements on farmland and ranchland that would depend on future USDA
decisions. But AFT assumed that probably about half would flow to ag
easements. Sadly, that was still not nearly enough funding to address the
need. Even with the extra funding gained in the latest farm bill, less than
10 percent of the farmers and ranchers who applied would likely be
funded. And even that was an underrepresentation of demand, because
some landowners interested in the program never apply, because they
know the chances of success are slim.

Farms Under Threat documented the conversion of over eleven
million acres of irreplaceable farmland and ranchland in just fifteen
years—land that could have been available for both growing food
and providing beneficial environmental services. It was clearly in the
public interest to prevent the loss of our most important and vulnerable ag land. What would that cost? AFT estimates that if the United
States wanted to permanently protect just 50 percent of the nation's
absolutely best agricultural land (what *Farms Under Threat* classifies

as "nationally significant" land that scores high for productivity, versatility, and resilience), the price tag would likely top $533 billion.[23] If this investment occurred over a reasonable time horizon of, say, twenty years, the annual cost (ignoring inflation) would be $27.6 billion. Yet at present, total funding for purchasing ag easements from all government sources—not only ACEP but also state and local PACE programs—is under $500 million annually.

The level of ACEP funding secured through the 2018 Farm Bill is therefore not yet aligned with overall need—whether defined as the number of applicants interested in protecting their land, or the total amount of exceptional agricultural land vulnerable to conversion (and thus worthy of permanent protection).

The amount of ACEP funding was determined not by assessing the true threat and then providing funding sufficient to address that threat, but rather, through a political process that works very differently. For the 2018 Farm Bill, the general feeling throughout Congress, regardless of party, was that there would not be any major new expenditures. Congress might be open to a different balance of funding between programs within Title II (the Conservation title), for instance, but overall funding for the title would not grow.

This reality created complications for AFT. Not only had the organization been a primary force behind incorporating a Conservation title into the 1985 Farm Bill, but it actively worked to add new programs into the title ever since. Yet many of the Conservation title programs had become mainstream, with active support from multiple national organizations. With some programs, in fact, AFT now played a nominal role. Not so with ACEP.

Other national groups cared about ag easements, but none were anywhere near as connected to the issue of farmland itself as American Farmland Trust: AFT had shaped federal and state policy on this subject, crafted PACE programs across the nation, maintained the authoritative data on farmland protection and farmland loss, operated the national Farmland Information Center, helped create several state and regional land trusts, and provided key services to the full community of agricultural land trusts.

The Conservation Coalition that AFT had organized in advance of the 1985 Farm Bill was still active—and AFT still played a key role in it. But over the decades, the coalition's composition and tenor had changed. More groups had joined it, including several that were a bit less inclined to work from the political center.

The challenge for AFT in this farm bill cycle was that, given the enormous need, AFT felt compelled to work to restore ACEP funding to the 2014 level. But additional funding for ACEP would likely come at the expense of other Conservation title programs.

AFT's two-pronged strategy could be summarized as follows:

1. ACEP needs more money.
2. No Conservation title programs should be cut.

This message came across to most audiences as an honest opinion that both outcomes were essential. But not all groups in the Conservation Coalition viewed it that way. Some felt that AFT was giving lip service to the overall title, while secretly working to shift funding to ACEP.

Both chambers were then led by Republicans—and this added a twist. With each rumor that ACEP might receive more funding (and then when committee reports came out stating exactly that), AFT was accused of not just working against the rest of the Conservation title but also working with Republicans, which was a problem for a few of the more liberal groups in the coalition.

Indeed, AFT *was* working with Republicans and Democrats, closely and wherever possible, notwithstanding party affiliation. Otherwise, it is unlikely the 2018 Farm Bill would have turned out with as strong a Conservation title as it did.

In the end, ACEP got a big boost, while most other key conservation programs fared fairly well—with CRP, EQIP, and RCPP all seeing a modest increase during the next five years. Over the next ten years, overall conservation funding remained essentially level with the last farm bill, as expected. The new funding for ACEP and other programs was balanced by major reductions in the Conservation Stewardship Program (CSP). Had it not been for AFT's advocacy for ACEP, and good relations with Republican operatives, the final farm bill could easily have resulted in a net loss to conservation.

AFT did not do this work alone. Many of the groups in the Conservation Coalition actively supported ACEP, just as AFT supported conservation programs they championed. What's more, AFT advocated for ACEP with the Land Trust Alliance and an informal coalition of about twenty of the nation's top agricultural land trusts.

AFT had a long history of supporting ag land trusts and advocating for federal policy on their behalf. But whereas in the past, AFT may have contacted such groups and orchestrated a collaboration, now the land trusts were approaching AFT, with both clear goals and resources.

In addition to wanting more funding for ACEP, these land trusts wanted to make operational improvements to the program. This effort would require some new legislative language; but the real work would begin after the farm bill passed, in the rule-making process.

In 2020, AFT formalized its services to the farmland protection community, including its advocacy work, by creating the National Agricultural Land Network[24]—the very name harking back to the National Agricultural Land Study that started it all in the late 1970s. Within a month, membership in the network had swelled to over a hundred entities, primarily ag land trusts and state departments of agriculture.

Buy-Protect-Sell

When John Piotti was leading Maine Farmland Trust, he had developed one of the largest programs in the nation that pursued protection in a different way. Rather than purchasing agricultural easements from interested farmers and simply holding the easement for them so they could continue in business, more and more land trusts around the country were beginning to take another approach. When a key farm property was placed on the real estate market, the land trust would buy it outright, place an easement on it, and then resell it to another farmer at its new and lower price as protected land.

Piotti became a big advocate of this approach. Farms that were already on the market were obviously highly vulnerable to development, so protecting them was definitely timely. And protecting and then reselling them also made it immediately possible for other farmers—often new farmers—to acquire land at a much more affordable price. Piotti argued the advantages of this approach in public presentations he made throughout the land trust community. And, in doing so, he coined a term for it: *buy-protect-sell*. In his presentations, he often remarked that the name might be boring and unsophisticated, but at least it was "descriptive," accurately expressing what these projects did.

One of the priorities for the informal coalition of twenty or so agricultural trusts that approached AFT on the 2018 Farm Bill was making changes in federal law to help facilitate agricultural easements. Such projects were becoming increasingly common in some regions. Typically, they were secured with state or local PACE program funding. Unfortunately, federal money was off-limits in these direct acquisitions because ACEP could compensate only private landowners, not land trusts. That was what this coalition of land trusts wanted to change in the 2018 Farm Bill.

Some months into the process, Piotti realized that this coalition was using his term, *buy-protect-sell,* in arguing its case before Congress. And that terminology ended up being baked into the proposed legislation.

America's Farmers and Ranchers

In some circles, AFT may be best known for its iconic NO FARMS NO FOOD bumper sticker. But for years, AFT also circulated another bumper sticker: IT'S NOT FARMLAND WITHOUT FARMERS.

Our farmers and ranchers are key to both saving America's farmland and managing it wisely. After all, farmland can be protected with a permanent easement only if that is what the landowner (usually a farmer or rancher) wants; conversely, unprotected farmland can in most cases be sold for development if *that* is what the landowner wants. (The exception is where zoning forbids it—and that is quite rare nationally.) Programs like PACE and current use taxation may make it financially possible for a farmer to consider an easement or to avoid selling to developers—and thus they are essential tools in helping save farmland. But ultimately, the only way to ensure that we retain enough farmland is if enough farmers and ranchers are determined to keep their land in agriculture because they see a business future in doing so.

Likewise, we rely on our farmers and ranchers to steward the land, both to produce our food and provide a great many environmental services. If we want to eat, and if we want our farms and ranches to be actively managed for benefits to wildlife, water resources, and air quality, then we need to help farmers and ranchers remain in business and on the land.

AFT sees multiple connections between the land itself, the practices occurring on that land, and the farmers and ranchers who steward it. It's a three-legged stool—and all three legs are necessary. Or to put it another way: it's an *interdependent* system.

A sustainable agricultural system that both grows our food and provides essential environmental services is possible only if farmers can do both those things while still affording to stay in business. And if would-be farmers can afford to enter the business of agriculture. The stool won't stand if agriculture is not economically viable. But if it is viable, then the environment is a big winner.

Piotti understood this. While at Maine Farmland Trust, he moved an organization that had previously focused narrowly on donated easements to one that increasingly purchased easements to support farmers financially, and later crafted new programs to help farmers expand markets and run more successful operations. He also understood how protecting farmland would fall short of its full promise unless Maine could recruit enough new farmers. That's why he led MFT to develop a robust FarmLink program, helping would-be farmers find land, while utilizing easement projects strategically to make farmland more affordable for incoming farmers.

AFT staffer Julia Freedgood understood the value of systems thinking and how agricultural viability was key. When Piotti arrived in 2016, she was overseeing AFT's work on community food systems and the next generation of farmers—two topics that she accurately views as being interconnected, linked to each other and to this larger issue of agricultural viability.

As discussed in chapter 16, Freedgood articulates a broad and sophisticated definition of *agricultural viability*. It may come down to the ability of individual farmers and ranchers to make a living, but their survival is dependent on so such more, including local agricultural infrastructure (that is, the presence of grain suppliers, equipment dealers, veterinarians, food processors, and the like); the adequacy of roads, rail, and broadband; local land use planning and zoning; local attitudes toward farming; whether farmland owners who are not themselves farming are open to leasing their land to others—and under what terms; whether local farmers and farmland owners are aware of and benefiting from USDA conservation programs that provide cost-share; and the presence (or absence) of various services that are often necessary to help would-be farmers access land and then operate successfully.

The challenge was determining where and how a small NGO like AFT might make a difference in this immense space that covers so much ground.

Strategic Choices

AFT had in the past addressed this issue not so much by supporting farmers directly but by advancing public policy that supported those farmers. For instance, AFT's efforts to develop state-based current use taxation programs led to the enrollment of 290 million acres of agriculture land in such programs by 2016—providing a financial benefit to a half million farmers and ranchers. And AFT's role developing and then expanding federal cost-share programs in the farm bill's Conservation title had since 1985 provided over $110 billion to help farmers do what's right by the land. By and large, AFT's work in this space had involved operating wholesale, not retail.

As much as Piotti, Freedgood, and others at AFT might want to provide more direct services to farmers, within an organization of AFT's size, the opportunities to do so would be limited.[25] But at the same time, they needed to be thoughtful and strategic with broader, higher-level wholesale programs. The resulting package involves a blend of wholesale and retail activities designed to reinforce one another wherever possible.

Helping Other Organizations Do More

The world had changed since AFT was founded in 1980. By 2016, there was a whole community of organizations that recognized the connections between agriculture and the environment. This included major environmental organizations that had learned to count farmers as key partners, and several national farm groups that now appreciated both the value and necessity of conservation practices. It also included a large and growing number of land trusts, community organizations, and state departments of agriculture.

AFT had over the years provided a range of services to these entities, from helping new land trusts get started to helping states develop PACE programs to helping individual communities better understand farming. In addition, AFT's research and case studies had aided entities all across the nation to establish or refine their programs and communicate more effectively with their constituencies.

It made sense to build upon this proven approach and provide more services and support to the ever-expanding community of players in this space.

One example was AFT's new Land Access Network. Not long before Piotti came to AFT, Freedgood had secured a major grant from USDA to develop a curriculum to teach service providers who wish to support beginning farmers. By 2017, AFT had begun to train interested parties at other organizations around the country. As the program evolved, it became clear that the most impactful strategy would be for AFT to "train the trainer," using its curriculum to enhance knowledge and standards at other organizations, so that those groups throughout the country could better serve beginning farmers. In 2019, AFT began to "certify" the professionals trained through the program, in an effort to elevate the field of practice. All the people who have been trained, as well as all the groups involved in this work, have now been organized into a Land Access Network overseen by AFT.

Another example was AFT's creation of the National Agriculture Land Network, intended to formalize AFT's relationship with private agricultural land trusts and public PACE programs (state, county, and local). Creating the network was critical because the field was—and is—still evolving; as that happens, the full power of what can be accomplished through smart easement projects becomes ever clearer. The more forward-looking land trusts and government programs had already begun to realize that farmland protection strategies are also strategies for getting new farmers on the land and for enhancing agricultural viability generally—and maybe even for advancing better farming practices. Yet not all land trusts and PACE programs were in the same place. Many got the concept but had yet to take any steps to realize the potential for broader benefits. Others had been experimenting, but with mixed success. Here was both a real need and a real opportunity for AFT to organize a network that could inform these entities about what approaches worked and help them learn from each other.

A third example of AFT's renewed efforts to help other organizations do more involves AFT's dissemination of its research findings.

Farms Under Threat, AFT's comprehensive land use study, provided a unique opportunity to share information with community planners, state officials, land trusts, and a wide range of agricultural groups. Since the release of the first *Farms Under Threat* report in 2018, AFT staff shared maps and data to support other groups. In fact, after the release of the second report in 2020, which focused on state data and actions, AFT conducted (through the National Agricultural Land Network) thirty-five separate webinars, each focused on a different state or multistate region.

In a separate project, AFT began working with Farm Credit East in 2018 to build upon *Farms Under Threat*'s foundational data to incorporate new information about agricultural viability. This project included creation of an index that assesses the level of ag viability by county throughout the Northeast—an extremely useful new tool.

When it comes to farming practices, AFT created and widely disseminated a series of farmer case studies during Piotti's tenure, documenting both the economic and environmental benefits of building soil health. And in 2020, AFT went public with its powerful analytical tool, CaRPE,[26] which assesses the carbon reduction potential of various regenerative farming practices by county for the entire nation: for the first time, government entities as well as farm and environmental groups have the data they need to quantify where and how farmers in their region can combat climate change.

Freedgood refers to this work as AFT's "extension function,"[27] issuing research findings and underlying data and conducting outreach and education to share the findings in a manner that helps other organizations understand what's happening on the land, enabling them to support farmers and ranchers more effectively and efficiently.

Staying Grounded

Where possible, AFT combines its high-level work supporting other groups and sharing relevant research (described earlier as wholesale programming) with on-the-ground services it provides directly to farmers and ranchers (that is, retail programming). Thus, at the same time AFT might be sharing broad information about how farmers can, say, combat climate change, it would—in select locations—be conducting hands-on soil health workshops with farmers. This grounds AFT in the realities of the work, helping to ensure that its wholesale programming, as well as its policy advocacy, does not get ahead of what's practical on the farm. But it also works the other way. What AFT does on the farm benefits from a "big picture" view and a national context.

An example of this two-way flow involves how AFT works with beginning farmers. In New York, AFT operates a statewide farmland-finder program that helped over two hundred new farmers get on the land in a four-year period. Farmland for a New Generation New York goes far beyond simple matchmaking. AFT engages dozens of other organizations across the state to help beginning farmers assess their needs and to provide them with essential technical assistance, including business planning. AFT's experience running this New York program informed

AFT's national efforts to support next generation farmers, including development of its Land Access Network. At the same time, AFT's national efforts, especially its work developing curriculum to train service providers, helped inform the initial design and later evolution of the New York program.

Piotti was intent to do more of this wherever practical, believing that AFT was not only well suited to this approach but must pursue this approach to operate efficiently.

Piotti says his strong views on the subject stem from advice he received from a mentor over twenty-five years ago, when he worked at a Maine community development organization that successfully combined programming with advocacy. The president of that organization made the point that their success advancing public policy was due in no small measure to the fact that they were also active practitioners. Piotti carried this nugget of wisdom forward to MFT, and then to AFT, where he felt that this approach fit with efforts to not only advance policy but inform and support other organizations as well. AFT may be a thought leader, but it is not afraid to get its hands dirty. This was one of the reasons Piotti was so supportive of AFT rebuilding its land trust function, as described in chapter 17. If AFT was to continue to play a meaningful role assisting other agricultural land trusts, then it was essential that AFT itself experiment with those strategies and techniques through projects of its own.

Filling in the Gaps

This is not to say that every program AFT undertakes has both a wholesale and retail component, or that AFT always develops programs with that possibility in mind. Sometimes, AFT has pursued programs simply to fill gaps within a region or with a given population—and the program then develops organically. One example of this is AFT's Women for the Land[28] initiative. Launched in 2017, it was initially designed to target Midwest women who own farmland but who do not themselves farm it—a growing population that has traditionally received little support from USDA and is often unaware of the conservation practices that could be employed on their land.

So-called nonoperating landowners are becoming more common, particularly in the Midwest, where farm consolidation has been occurring for decades. That often means that someone who once farmed, say, 160 acres, may now farm 3,000 acres—made possible by larger machinery and at times required to keep the farm in business. In many cases, the farmer leases the bulk of that land from neighbors, sometimes several of them, who used to farm it—or increasingly, as time has passed, from their heirs. In part because women generally outlive men, the proportion of nonoperating landowners who are women continues to grow.

Midwest Regional Director Jen Filipiak conceived the Women for the Land program in response to what she was seeing on the ground. Though some other organizations were undertaking modest programming to support Midwestern women farmers, none were focusing on the untapped potential of the nonoperating landowners among them, and none were making the direct link back to conservation practices. With more and more land being farmed by people who do not own it, there was a huge need—and enormous upside potential—to encourage leasing farmers to invest in conservation practices that will bring long-term benefit to both farmer and landowner. Yet doing so requires an up-front investment that often prevents action. Filipiak saw a gap and filled it, created new programming that utilized learning circles to inform women nonoperating landowners of the potential benefits of conservation practices, alert them to federal cost-share programs, and advise them how to work with leasing farmers to effect change.

The program soon grew into a national initiative, expanding to other regions and adding women farmers into the mix. A 2019 study concluded that 71 percent of program participants had taken steps to bring about a significant conservation outcome on their farm.

Spurred by the needs and opportunities highlighted by this initiative, AFT on a parallel track undertook new research to identify the broader needs of nonoperating landowners—both female and male. It is remarkable that so little is known about this group, given that it's now estimated that approximately 40 percent of US agricultural land is in the hands of nonoperating landowners.

Diversity in Farm Ownership

By 2016, the face of agriculture was changing. To begin with, farmers were getting older; the average age of an American farmer was over fifty-nine, up from fifty in 1978 on the eve of AFT's birth.[29] That increasing average age accelerated farm ownership transfers in the years ahead. Many of those transfers would inevitably expose those farms to development.

When those farmers did need to sell, if their land was to stay in farming, there needed to be buyers interested in farming it. But the demographics of those who would be most likely to want to do that were changing. While older farmers would be selling, their kids had often long gone to the city. And even though some established farmers were looking to buy more land, they alone couldn't handle all the supply.

Others were interested, however: new and younger farmers, women, immigrants, people of color—as well as people interested in starting second careers, including veterans. Sadly, few of them were in a position to afford to buy the land, especially at its "fair market value."

Part of the reason the average age of farmland owners is so high is likely that these very groups—the ones now most interested in farm ownership—are also largely populations that may have the least access to land, given how land values are being driven up by development pressure and sprawl. All too often, the only people who can afford to compete in the market for farmland are those who are prepared to develop it or who have independent means, perhaps acquired through success in some other profession.

When Piotti began at AFT, there were a million female farm operators in America, and the numbers were growing. A half a million more women owned farms and leased them out.[30] Women farmers faced gender barriers that could be addressed through research, support networks, and technical assistance. New and young farmers often needed assistance with farm credit, land acquisition, and assembling the knowledge and experience needed to succeed. And, just as in other walks of life, farmers of color faced racial, cultural, language, economic, and historical barriers that would require new public policy, education, and technical assistance.[31]

AFT has since worked hard to begin to address some of these needs, through initiatives that specifically target new farmers as well as women farmers and nonoperating landowners. And given that more and more people of color are farming or trying to farm, AFT has also worked to better serve this population, including specific projects supporting underserved communities and a new partnership with the Black Family Land Trust.[32] Yet it's clear to Piotti and his team that AFT is not yet doing nearly enough.

One of the most profound changes at AFT in the last few years has been a recognition that if the organization is serious about the third leg of its mission—keeping farmers on the land—then it must do more to bring new people into farming and ranching, and that means it must do far more to support people of color, immigrants, and others who do not currently own much of our nation's farmland or control much of American agriculture. This is a challenging endeavor, as it is connected to complex issues of discrimination, injustice, and historic land takings. Yet it is in a direction that AFT needs to go—the future of farming demands it.

The Bottom Line

There's been a growing appreciation in recent years that farmers are not always paid adequately for the food they produce, that much of the financial benefit flows to agricultural suppliers and food companies. There's also been a growing understanding that government policies at times keep consumer food prices artificially low—and that this also negatively impacts farmers. (In one ag sector, dairy, federal policy goes even further, as it sets the price paid to farmers for their milk[33]—and that price is often less than what it costs farmers to produce it.)

At the same time, the American public sees the large subsides that flow to many farmers. Billions of dollars flow year after year through the Commodity title of the farm bill. Then during the Trump administration, even more funding flowed through supplemental payments to counter trade imbalances caused by new tariffs and market disruptions caused by the COVID-19 pandemic. Some may think that farmers are getting rich, or at least that some of them are. But in truth, these subsidies are seldom adequate. More often than not, the vast majority of farms and ranches—whether big or small, conventional or organic, growing commodities or specialty crops—are struggling financially.

We can talk about how we need farmers and ranchers to grow our food and heal our planet, but we can't count on them to do any of that if they can't make a living. We will need a better system for compensating farmers and ranchers if we expect to retain a sufficient number of them to serve us in the future.

By 2016, it was becoming clearer and clearer that what we needed were not incremental improvements but transformational change. As Piotti sees it, we ultimately need a system that fairly compensates farmers and ranchers for not only the food they produce but *all* the environmental services they provide. This is a huge and critical issue—perhaps the overarching issue that will determine the future of agriculture, and in turn, the future of our planet. To address it will require both major policy advances and new environmental service market mechanisms.

Such market mechanisms come in two forms:

First, there are tradable credits, through which farmers can be directly compensated for the environmental benefits they produce through a credit marketplace made possible with funding provided by one or more entities needing to offset emissions—this might include airlines, manufacturers, public utilities, motivated individuals, or possibly government. (Such strategies are being pursued by a few forward-looking companies, including Nori and IndigoAg.[34])

Second, there are marketplace systems, where food companies—in tandem with consumer interest—source their ingredients from farmers and ranchers who follow regenerative practices. The goal is that the consumer be willing to pay a premium for these products and that at least some of that premium flows back to the participating farmers and ranchers. (Such strategies are being pursued by a wide range of food companies, including General Mills and Kellogg.[35])

Since 2016, AFT has begun to help select food companies think through strategies to advance regenerative practices and has taken its own next steps with water quality credits and engaged with others on carbon credits. This work is important, but not without challenges. Though many food companies want to do what's right, they also have to make the numbers work—and they can only go where the consumer is willing. And when it comes to credits, it is extremely difficult to provide precise results, especially with carbon sequestration. Indeed, the amount of carbon captured on two similar farms following identical practices can vary greatly, owing to unavoidable circumstances, such as variations in the day's weather. (That's one reason part of the answer may lie with CaRPE, AFT's tool that quantifies the sequestration potential of a collection of farms in a region—as this is a case where an average of what's possible from many farms may prove more accurate than knowing what will happen on any given specific farm.)

The challenges in quantification suggest the need for new public policy. If we *know* that certain regenerative practices provide value but cannot *quantify* that value in a manner that satisfies credit markets, that may be an appropriate place for government involvement. Farm bill programs could provide incentives to ensure that regenerative practices are followed at some threshold level by most farms and ranches.

The ultimate system might involve multiple tools: tradable credits playing a role on the more easily quantifiable activities; marketplace systems playing a role with certain consumer products; and public policy filling in the gaps of the market mechanisms—and in this way, ensuring that all farmers and ranchers can afford to provide essential environmental services upon which, along with food and fiber, our very survival depends.

There are some who think that the market alone can solve these challenges; and others who think that only government intervention can do so. Piotti believes that both are necessary. They are two sides to the same coin—each a part of the whole.

CHAPTER 22
A New Vision for the Future

John Piotti's AFT is quite different today from the organization first imagined by Peggy Rockefeller. Back when AFT opened its doors, in August of 1980, federal agencies were indirectly encouraging farmland loss. The IRS did not yet recognize conservation easements as a publicly worthwhile charitable contribution—let alone agricultural conservation easements. The farm bill was almost entirely an industry vehicle for delivering farm subsidies; public incentives for on-farm environmental practices were mostly unknown. Nationwide, there was but a sprinkling of those interesting new nonprofits they called land trusts, their legal status was sometimes unclear, and most of them had little interest in protecting agriculture. The recent Clean Water Act was focused almost entirely on large institutional polluters; there was limited concern about or effort to control nonpoint pollution. Climate change was a largely academic topic rarely discussed in public.

AFT's early laser focus on farmland protection necessarily and inexorably broadened. What good was preserving farmland without also preserving its agricultural soils and water? To do both would call for new public policy—policy that would also need to deal with farm impacts on the wider environment and therefore necessitate broad public engagement. Thus environmentalists needed to be brought on board. New, previously unheard-of coalitions were required to bridge vast political and cultural divides—coalitions that needed a grounding in deeply shared community values.

American Farmland Trust's role in building these coalitions may not have been planned, but it did happen for a reason. The explanation lies in a common, simple truth: beneath all the political chaos and conflict, most people want genuine solutions to real problems. And when they're treated with respect, they'll usually reciprocate.

There is an appropriate role for both mandatory regulations and voluntary, publicly funded incentives in addressing agriculture's environmental and land use issues: a role that lies somewhere between, for example, a law mandating farm management practices and a program of purely voluntary conservation practice cost-share incentives. The regulatory options place the cost of the fix predominantly on the people regulated. Voluntary incentives and easement programs spread the cost across society. Which approach should be chosen, in any given circumstance, is a matter of what is *fair*—to the farmers and to the rest of us.[1]

That balance between regulations and incentives is typically struck in the public policy arena. After all, only government can enforce needed regulations. And usually, it is only from government-mandated taxes or government-defined environmental markets that the money can be made available to protect farmland with voluntary PACE programs, to fund environmental performance "incentives," or to provide added economic development support for a robust, successful farm business.

Despite some progress, farmer–environmentalist confrontations over land use and environmental quality continue in Congress, in statehouses, before local county councils, and wherever— government environmental policy is made. Yet there have always been individual farmers who are willing to step forward everywhere and participate in admirable efforts to protect the environment. Likewise, there have always been environmentalists willing to work with them.

AFT is by no means the only organization that brings farmers and environmentalists together to improve farming and the environment.[2] But AFT has demonstrated a capacity to enlist diverse and often fractured farm, environmental, and other interested constituencies in collaborations in the policy arena. That capacity will become ever more critically important in the years to come. AFT's founders may not have had a road map.[3] But they did set forth on this journey with honest respect for the people on both edges of the farm–environmental divide. And that genuine respect may have been the one truly critical guiding principle that led to this organization's success.

A Tolerance for Risk

Along with building coalitions, AFT can trace its most significant accomplishments to taking studied risks. In the lead-up to the 1985 Farm Bill, AFT took on a risky role as intermediary between a cluster of robustly activist environmental groups and an array of long-established agricultural trade associations. AFT helped all of them rethink a deeply entrenched but antiquated farm policy that had been in place for generations. The result was a newly transformed legal and policy relationship between the nation's agriculture industry and its natural environment offered up in the first Conservation title in farm bill history.

In another bold move, AFT's Jerry Cosgrove argued to the City of New York that if it would just help Catskill region farmers protect their land and pay the cost of adopting conservation management practices on their farms, they could clean up the city's drinking water. And he assured them that it could all be done for a fraction of what they'd pay for a new multibillion-dollar treatment plant. He then helped convince those Catskill farmers that the whole thing would be to their long-term advantage. It was risky, but it worked.

The 2015 AFT board pulled from AFT's diminished financial reserves to invest heavily in a multiyear research project that might be natural given AFT's historic role as the go-to player on farmland data, but which required a true leap of faith. No one knew what the research would reveal or whether it would even prove relevant. Yet the resulting initiative—*Farms Under Threat*—has not only resulted in the most comprehensive study of US land use ever conducted but also identified and documented key threats to farmland—such as low-density rural development—that have never before been systematically analyzed.

John Piotti, a new and untested AFT president, made the case to his struggling organization that growth was essential; then he encouraged AFT's board and staff to think anew about where and how AFT could once again play an outsized role on some of the most pressing and controversial issues confronting agriculture—issues so big that they will determine our planet's very livability in the years to come. The resulting initiatives are currently advancing regenerative farming practices, linking those practices to farmland protection, and nurturing a new generation of farmers and ranchers who will be essential to combating the changing climate, which could be our planet's greatest threat.

In every case, AFT took a risk and put its credibility and limited resources on the line.

Future Challenges

Today's AFT is taking on challenges that could never have been dreamed of forty years ago. To succeed, it needs to transform the long-term future of agriculture itself. In this twenty-first century, the three legs of the AFT mission—the land itself, the farming practices utilized on that land, and the people who do the work—can be secured only if agriculture has the support of a deeply committed American public, a public that respects and values services that only agriculture can provide. What farmers need, in short, is not just a sustainable land base, sustainable farming practices, and a sustainable farm business. The agriculture industry itself needs to achieve a yet larger goal. It needs to become socially and politically sustainable as well—to become truly integral to the broader community it serves.

What is finally becoming clear as American Farmland Trust enters its fifth decade is that there is real hope. There is a genuine prospect that agriculture may actually achieve its full promise. There is the very real possibility that agriculture, while continuing to provide the food and fiber that sustain us, could one day in the foreseeable future also become the deeply appreciated answer for some of our nation's most difficult, most existential economic, social, and environmental challenges.

Acknowledgments

Special appreciation is owed to the several American Farmland Trust founders and early supporters mentioned in the text, including Doug Wheeler, Fred Winthrop, Bill Dietel, Ralph Grossi, Patrick Noonan, Bill Reilly, and Rich Rominger. (Rich tragically passed away shortly before the book was published. He will be missed.) Nearly all these founders gave of their time for personal interviews at the outset of the writing of this book. Also, a huge thank-you is owed to the current and former AFT staff members who provided both content and incredibly helpful direction. Sadly, only a fraction of their amazing work could be described here. They deserve our deep gratitude for their commitment, creativity, and diligence.

Particular thanks to AFT's president and CEO, John Piotti, who suggested I write this book, and then actively supported its completion and publication. John provided much valued detail regarding AFT's more recent programming, challenges, and direction. He also offered extensive editorial assistance throughout.

I very much wish it had been possible to include a great many more of the amazing stories that could be told by AFT board members and staff who continue their efforts every day. We are beneficiaries of their remarkable and deeply influential work.

Finally, but most important of all, thank you to the thousands of AFT members, supporters, and partners whose willingness to see beyond heated rhetoric and draw upon the amazing but often overlooked power of collaboration makes these miracles happen daily.

APPENDIX A
AFT Board Members and Tenures

Lillian Ebonie Alexander	North Carolina	2019–
Steve Adams	Oklahoma	1986–92
Arthur Aleshire	Maine	2010–11
Helen Alexander	Kentucky	1996–99
Robert Anderson	New Mexico	1987–95
Dwayne Andreas	Illinois	1984–96
Tom Barron	Colorado	1992–95
Elizabeth Beck	Maryland & DC	2010–18
Lou Benzak	New York	1988–97
Bill Boehm	Wisconsin	2013–
Emily Broad Leib	Massachusetts	2020–
Bill Brown	Iowa	1982–84
Robert Chinn	Louisiana	1980–91
Lynn Clarkson	Indiana	2018–
Anne S. Close	South Carolina	2000–2001
Bill Cohan	New York	2011–18
David Cole	Virginia	2001–3
Mel Coleman	Colorado	2007–16
Dennis Collins	California	1991–2001
Doyle Conner	Florida	1984–93
Sam Cooke	Hawaii	1993–96
Joan Davidson	New York	1991–93
Carolyn Davis	Maryland	1996–98
Bill DeLauder	Delaware	2005–13
Philip DeNormandie	Massachusetts	1999–2009

Bill Dietel	Virginia	1987–90, 1996–2005 (chair 1999–2001)
Otto Doering	Illinois	2019–
Jean W. Douglas	DC	1988–98
Dan Esty	Connecticut	1998–2007
Betsy Fink	Connecticut	2000–2009
Sandra Fraizer	Kentucky	2010–11
Iris Freeman	South Carolina	2002–11
Bob Gallo	California	1994–2005
Gina Gallo	California	2015–
Tom Gallo	California	2005–15
Miley Gonzalez	New Mexico	2010–12
Ralph Grossi	California	1980–85, 2019–
Gil Grosvenor	DC	1987–98
Eileen Growald	Vermont	1996–2000
John Hardin	Indiana	2009– (chair 2018–)
Ed Harte	Texas	1985–2007
Will Harte	Texas	2010–19
Patricia Hewitt	Illinois & Pennsylvania	1980–86
Nancy Hirshberg	New Hampshire	2008–17
Libby Jones	Kentucky	2010–19
Miranda Kaiser	New York	2000–2014 (chair 2010–14)
A. G. Kawamura	California	2011–19
Garrison Keillor	New York	1988–91
John Kluge	New York	1995–97
Ann Korologos	DC	1989
Laurie Landeau	New York	2011–21
Tony Lapham	DC	1995–2005
Amy Longsworth	DC	2000–2009
Tom Lyon	Wisconsin	1985–93
Nan Tucker McEvoy	California	1996–2000
Rev. A. J. McKnight	Louisiana	1980–81
Craig McNamara	California	2010–15
Mas Masumoto	California	2011
Cannon Michael	California	2019–
Elin Miller	Oregon	2002–4
Ralph Morris	Minnesota	1991–2000

Jim Moseley	Indiana	2015–
Peter C. Myers	DC	1989–90
Pat Noonan	Maryland	1985–96
		(chair 1987–94)
Gil Ordway	Wyoming & California	1995–97
Eamon O'Toole	Wyoming	2014–
Betty Peacock	Illinois	1991–96
Jean Mari Peltier	California	2014–18
Bill Reilly	DC & California	1980–89, 1993–99
		(chair 1996–99)
Peggy Rockefeller	New York	1980–96
Rich Rominger	California	1986–93, 2001–10
Manya Rubinstein	Rhode Island	2016–
Gus Schumacher	DC	2004–12
Truman Semans	North Carolina	2010–19
Daniel Shaw	Colorado	2004–13
Carla Skodinski	New York	2000–2011
Morgan Smith	Colorado	1983–90
Obie Snider	Pennsylvania	1991–2001
Steve Stranahan	Colorado	2004–11, 2013–14
Ted Taylor	Massachusetts	1988–99
		(chair 1994–96)
Buzz Thompson	California	2004–13, 2014–20
(chair 2014–18)		
Dick Walden	Arizona	2002–11
Nan Walden	Arizona	2017–18
Mason Walsh	Pennsylvania	1986–95
Greg Watson	Massachusetts	2015–17
Douglas Wheeler	DC & California	1999–2009
		(chair 2001–6)
Julia H. Widdowson	New York	2001–10
Fred Winthrop	Massachusetts	1980–90
		(chair 1980–87)
Grant Winthrop	New York	2012–
Jay Winthrop	New York	2001–10
		(chair 2006–10)
John Winthrop Sr.	South Carolina	1991–2000
Dennis Wolff	Pennsylvania	2010–16

Public Service Engagement by AFT Board and Staff

Examples among AFT Board members:

- A. G. Kawamura was California's Secretary of Food and Agriculture.

- Jim Mosely was US Deputy Secretary of Agriculture under President George W. Bush.

- Bill Reilly was Administrator for the US Environmental Protection Agency under President George H. W. Bush.

- Rich Rominger was US Deputy Secretary of Agriculture under President Clinton, and prior to that, he was California's Secretary of Food and Agriculture.

- Gus Schumacher was US Undersecretary of Agriculture under President Clinton, and prior to that, he was Massachusetts's Commissioner of Agriculture.

- Greg Watson was Massachusetts's Commissioner of Agriculture.

- Fred Winthrop was Massachusetts's Commissioner of Agriculture and Chairman of the National Association of Secretaries of Agriculture.

- Doug Wheeler was California's Secretary of Natural Resources.

- Dennis Wolff was Pennsylvania's Secretary of Agriculture.

Examples among AFT's professional staff:

- Norm Berg was Chief of the Soil Conservation Service (later renamed the Natural Resources Conservation Service) under President Carter.

- Cris Coffin was staff to the US Senate Committee on Agriculture, Nutrition, and Forestry and later served as Chief of Staff to Senator Herb Kohl.

- Jerry Cosgrove left AFT to become New York's Deputy Commissioner for Agriculture; he later returned to AFT.

- Bob Gray was staff to Representative Jim Jeffords and later led the National Agricultural Lands Study (NALS), conducted jointly by USDA and the President's Council on Environmental Quality.
- Nathan L'Etoile was Massachusetts's Assistant Commissioner of Agriculture.
- Andrew McElwaine was staff to Senator John Heinz.
- John Piotti served in the Maine Legislature, where he chaired the Committee on Agriculture, Conservation, and Forestry and was later elected House Majority Leader.
- Jon Scholl was Counselor to the Administrator for Agricultural Policy at the US Environmental Protection Agency.
- Bob Wagner was staff to Representative Jim Jeffords.

AFT Presidents and CEOs

AFT is privileged to have had a series of remarkable leaders who served as president and CEO over the past forty-two years.

Douglas Wheeler, 1980–85

Doug Wheeler is currently senior counsel with the Washington, DC, law firm of Hogan Lovells. He is widely known for his public service and major contributions to national environmental policy, including pioneering work on habitat conservation, mitigation banking, and transfer of development rights.

Prior to becoming AFT's first president, Wheeler served as executive director of the National Trust for Historic Preservation, and prior to that, as deputy assistant secretary for fish and wildlife and parks in the US Department of Interior. After leaving AFT in 1985, he become executive director of the Sierra Club. He later served as vice president of the World Wildlife Fund (WWF) and then as secretary for resources for the State of California.

Wheeler has contributed to multiple boards, including valued roles with the Chesapeake Conservancy and Duke University's Nicholas Institute for Environmental Policy Solutions. Wheeler began a decade of volunteer service on AFT's board in 1999, serving as board chair for five of those years. He currently serves on AFT's President's Council.

Wheeler graduated from Hamilton College and received a law degree from Duke University School of Law.

Ralph Grossi, 1985–2008 (and interim 2015–16)

Ralph Grossi is a third-generation farmer from Marin County, California, where he continues to farm on family land protected with an agricultural conservation easement. Since retiring as AFT's president, he has added viniculture to what had been a dairy and beef operation.

In 1980, Grossi helped found the Marin Agricultural Land Trust, one of the first organizations of its kind in the nation. He was soon recruited to join AFT's board. He became AFT president and CEO in 1985, a position he held for the next twenty-three years. In addition, he later served as interim president. Grossi returned to AFT's board in 2019.

Recognized as the 1976 Outstanding Young Farmer and Rancher of the California Farm Bureau Federation and the 2002 Progressive Farmer Man of the Year in Service to Agriculture, Grossi also received the 1985 Feinstone Environmental Award.

Grossi chaired the executive committee of Smart Growth America and served on the boards of directors of the Charles Valentine Riley Memorial Foundation, the Natural Resources Council of America, and the California Holstein Association. He also served on advisory boards for the Yale School of Forestry and Environmental Studies, University of California system, and the Wallace Institute for Alternative Agriculture.

Grossi graduated from California Polytechnic State University.

Jon Scholl, 2008–13

Jon Scholl is currently an instructor of agricultural policy at the University of Illinois Urbana-Champaign. He also manages his family's corn and soybean farm in McLean County, Illinois.

Prior to becoming AFT's third president in 2008, Scholl served as counselor to the administrator for agricultural policy at the US EPA, where he led the development of the first National Agricultural Strategy. Prior to EPA, Scholl served over twenty-five years with the Illinois Farm Bureau in a series of positions, including executive assistant to the president, director of public policy, director of national legislation, and director of natural resources. He worked closely with the Illinois congressional delegation and coordinated several legislative initiatives at state and local levels. Scholl previously worked at the Illinois Department of Agriculture.

Scholl served as chair of the Illinois FFA Foundation Board of Trustees. In 2008, he received the University of Illinois College of Agricultural, Consumer, and Environmental Sciences Award of Merit.

Scholl graduated from the University of Illinois Urbana-Champaign with a degree in agricultural science.

Andrew McElwaine, 2013–15

Andrew McElwaine is vice president for sustainability with the Heinz Endowments in Pittsburgh, a position he took when he left AFT in 2015. McElwaine joined AFT in 2013, after seven years as president and CEO of the Conservancy of Southwest Florida. At the conservancy, he significantly advanced local efforts to protect farmland, supported a successful campaign for a state constitutional amendment to reduce property taxes on eased farmland, and sought solutions to Florida's long-term water and growth management problems.

Prior to that, McElwaine served as president and CEO of the Pennsylvania Environmental Council. Previous positions include director of environmental programs at the Heinz Endowments, staff member on President George H. W. Bush's Commission on Environmental Quality, and senior legislative assistant to Sen. John Heinz.

McElwaine earned a bachelor's degree in political science from Duke University, and advanced degrees in policy and history from Carnegie Mellon University and in history from George Mason University.

John Piotti, 2016–present

AFT's current president, John Piotti, has worked at the forefront of sustainable agriculture since the early 1990s. He focused initially on economic development projects that supported farmers in his home state of Maine. In 1999, he helped establish Maine Farmland Trust, and then in 2006, he became its president and CEO.

Piotti has served on multiple boards and commissions dealing with agriculture, food insecurity, community development, land use planning, and smart growth—in Maine and beyond. This includes his past role as chair of the Northeast Sustainable Agriculture Working Group.

Piotti also served in the Maine State Legislature, where he chaired the

Committee on Agriculture, Conservation, and Forestry and was elected House Majority Leader.

Piotti has been recognized for his contributions to agriculture and conservation by the Maine Dairy Industry Association, Maine Conservation Voters, and other groups. He was named to *Maine* magazine's inaugural list of the fifty people who have done the most for the state of Maine. In 2005, Piotti was awarded a prestigious Eisenhower Fellowship, which he used to study agricultural policy in Europe.

Piotti holds three degrees from the Massachusetts Institute of Technology, in engineering, public policy, and systems management.

APPENDIX D
A Forty-Year Timeline

A selection of activities and achievements from 1980 to 2020, compiled by AFT's Kirsten Ferguson from past annual reports, newsletters, and other sources.

1980

- Concerned about the loss of the nation's farmland and rising tension between farmers and environmentalists, the American Farmland Trust is established by Peggy Rockefeller and a team that includes Bill Dietel, Patrick Noonan, Bill Reilly, and Doug Wheeler.
- Seed money is provided by the Rockefeller Brothers Fund.
- Doug Wheeler is named AFT's first president.

1981

- USDA and the President's Council on Environmental Quality release the National Agricultural Lands Study, which raises the alarm about the amount of American farmland being converted to highways, subdivisions, and strip malls.
- With assistance from AFT, Congress passes the 1981 Farm Bill, including the Farmland Protection Policy Act, which, for the first time, requires federal agencies to consider their own conversion of agricultural land.
- AFT completes its first farmland protection project by placing an agricultural conservation easement on a Pennsylvania farm.

1982

- Prominent conservationist Norm Berg joins AFT as a senior advisor after retiring as chief of USDA's Soil Conservation Service.
- AFT launches the Pennsylvania Farmland Project and works with Kentucky and Missouri to devise agricultural districting programs.
- AFT works with local coalitions to pass ballot referendums in Rhode Island and

New Jersey, which become the fifth and sixth states to adopt farmland protection programs.

- AFT expands the number of acres it has permanently protected through conservation easements to 10,000, completing projects in Oregon, Connecticut, Colorado, and Georgia.

1983

- AFT launches its Ohio Farmland Project with the Ohio Farm Bureau to promote land conservation and the state's agricultural district program.

- After a 390-acre dairy farm is donated to AFT in Vermont, AFT protects it with an easement and sells it to local farmers, catalyzing other farmland protection projects in the area.

- AFT permanently protects scenic grazing land on the California coast, a 6,000-acre Montana ranch, and critical farmland in Pennsylvania and Connecticut.

1984

- Members of Congress hail AFT's Soil Conservation in America report, which lays the groundwork for creating the Conservation Reserve Program (CRP) in the upcoming farm bill.

- The 600-acre Wolfe's Neck Farm in Maine is donated to AFT. AFT protects the property with an easement and then helps create a new nonprofit to operate the farm for public education and research.

- AFT helps save a 1,200-acre cattle ranch in the scenic Blue River Valley of Summit County, Colorado, and a 440-acre model dairy farm in Sauk County, Wisconsin.

1985

- Ralph Grossi is named AFT's second president.

- Congress enacts the 1985 farm bill, which includes the first-ever Conservation title—as championed by AFT. It advances CRP, conservation compliance, and innovative Sodbuster and Swampbuster provisions.

- A 1,100-acre ranch in Monterey County, California, heads the list of prime farm properties protected by AFT.

- An AFT study in Michigan finds that agriculture contributes almost as much to that state's economy as the auto industry—$11 billion compared to the auto industry's $14 billion.

- AFT celebrates its fifth anniversary at a reception at USDA attended by 200 people, with congratulatory remarks by Secretary Block.

1986

- AFT conducts its first Cost of Community Services study, demonstrating that farmland benefits a community fiscally, since residential development requires costly public services.

- AFT successfully promotes executive orders in Michigan and Ohio that limit the conversion of farmland and helps create a farmland protection program in Mecklenburg County, North Carolina.

- AFT helps protect farms in New York and three New England states—including nine farms in Massachusetts.

- AFT publishes *Small Is Bountiful*, highlighting the often-overlooked economic significance of the nation's small farms.

1987

- AFT publishes its first *Farming on the Edge* report, which demonstrates that much of the nation's most threatened and productive farmland lies in the shadows of cities.

- For the first time, Congress allocates significant funding ($4.5 million) to study sustainable agriculture, a victory for AFT and other groups that worked to secure the appropriation.

- Pennsylvania voters approve $100 million for a new farmland protection program that AFT helped design and promote.

1988

- California voters approve $63 million in bond funding for farmland protection and AFT helps several counties establish programs with the new funding.

- AFT staff takes Vermont legislators on a tour of protected farms in Massachusetts and Connecticut, which inspires them to establish Vermont's farmland protection program.

- AFT and a conservation-minded landowner work together to protect a 1,245-acre farm in New York, one of several AFT projects in the Hudson Valley.

- AFT's video production, *Growing Concerns: The Future of America's Farmland*, filmed in seven states, brings the plight of American farms to screens across the country.

1989

- AFT rescues 507 acres of cherry orchard land on Michigan's Old Mission Peninsula, helping turn the tide on development in this critical fruit-growing area.

- AFT begins its Central Valley Project to protect and enhance California's most significant agricultural region.

- AFT helps farmers adopt new conservation practices through on-farm demonstration projects with farmers in Illinois (later expanded to Indiana and Missouri).

- AFT holds agricultural policy workshops across the country, giving farmers, conservationists, and state officials an opportunity to voice their opinions on federal farm policy.

1990

- AFT secures key victories in the 1990 farm bill, including creation of the Wetlands Reserve Act and the Farms for the Future Act (which leads to the establishment in 1996 of the Federal Farm and Ranchlands Protection Program).

- A historic 3,500-acre Colorado ranch is protected with AFT's assistance. AFT also helps protect key farms in Maine, North Carolina, and Maryland.

- AFT designs a farmland protection program for California's Santa Cruz County.

- AFT releases *Agriculture and the Environment: A Study of Farmer Practices and Perceptions*, a landmark study based on personal interviews with nearly 500 farmers.

1991

- AFT receives the President's Environmental and Conservation Challenge Award, in recognition of exemplary efforts to save farmland and promote better farming practices.

- AFT holds the first national farmland protection conference, Saving the Land that Feeds America: Conservation in the Nineties.

- AFT helps enact new state farmland protection programs in Delaware and Wisconsin, and secure dedicated funding for Pennsylvania's program through an increase in the state's cigarette tax.

- AFT publishes its first guide to estate planning for farmers and ranchers: *Your Land Is Your Legacy*.

1992

- AFT opens its Center for Agriculture in the Environment at Northern Illinois University to undertake research on land use and the environment.

- AFT helps craft New York's Agriculture Preservation Act, the most sweeping legislation to date to address the state's farmland issues.

- Peggy and David Rockefeller donate easements protecting more than 2,000 acres on five working farms in the Hudson Valley.

- AFT publishes *Florida's Growth Management Plans: Will Agriculture Survive?*—a report targeting the problems facing Florida agriculture.

1993

- AFT's latest *Farming on the Edge* study names the twelve most threatened agricultural regions in the nation—from California's Central Valley to New York's Hudson Valley.
- Gov. Brereton Jones asks AFT to lead a task force to strengthen Kentucky agriculture, which leads to a comprehensive agricultural program for the state.
- The California Legislature passes a major farmland protection bill championed by AFT.
- AFT begins an outreach program intended to seek farmer input on how to improve conservation programs in the next farm bill.

1994

- AFT creates its Farmland Information Center in partnership with USDA to provide access to information about agricultural land and resources.
- AFT begins working with New York City's Watershed Agricultural Council to protect the city's drinking water supply by protecting farms in the Catskill Mountains.
- AFT protects the nation's oldest continuously farmed agricultural site along Virginia's James River, and works with ranchers to protect thousands of acres in Colorado's Upper Elk River Valley.
- With AFT's help, Peninsula Township, Michigan, creates the first publicly funded farmland protection program in the Midwest.

1995

- AFT helps launch the Colorado Cattlemen's Agricultural Land Trust.
- Gov. Pete Wilson of California signs an AFT-sponsored bill creating a statewide farmland protection program.
- AFT helps to protect the scenic 3,500-acre UX Ranch near Elko, Nevada, the historic Last Dollar Ranch near the Telluride ski resort in Colorado, and 1,000 acres once slated for a nuclear power plant opposite New York's Saratoga Battlefield.

1996

- AFT achieves its top priority for the 1996 Farm Bill with creation of the federal Farmland Protection Program (now the Agricultural Conservation Easement Program). This farm bill also enhances CRP and creates the Environmental Quality Incentives Program (EQIP)—changes championed by AFT.
- AFT founder Peggy McGrath Rockefeller passes away, and AFT announces the creation of its Steward of the Land Award in her memory.

- AFT protects the 450-acre Tall Grass Farm in Mercer County, Kentucky, and an 880-acre cattle ranch in Colorado's Upper Elk River Valley.

1997

- AFT launches FreshFarm Market, which opens the Dupont Circle Farmers Market in Washington, DC.

- AFT's updated *Farming on the Edge* report documents continued sprawl around the country. Press coverage reaches more than 110 million people.

- AFT begins a partnership with the US EPA to help farmers reduce use of pesticides. The partnership ultimately helps more than 5,500 farmers adopt integrated pest management on 750,000 acres.

- AFT works with the Maryland agricultural community and state officials to create the Rural Legacy Program to protect large undeveloped tracts, including farmland.

1998

- Eddie Albert, star of 1960s television show *Green Acres*, records a public service announcement promoting AFT.

- AFT issues a series reports on the fiscal impacts of sprawl around Chicago, generating major news coverage and leading to the formation of the Illinois Smart Growth Task Force.

- AFT's new report, *Investing in the Future of Agriculture: The Massachusetts Farmland Protection Program and the Permanence Syndrome*, finds that the state's program helps farmers purchase land, transfer farms, and improve agricultural operations.

1999

- The US Conference of Mayors and AFT announce a partnership to save farmland and help rejuvenate cities.

- AFT acquires the Agricultural Conservation Innovation Center, which explores what can be done to make it easier for farmers to adopt new conservation practices.

- In a project hailed as a model, AFT protects a 660-acre farm in the Connecticut River Valley and then sells the land to a trio of young vegetable farmers who plan to farm in partnership.

- An AFT survey finds that Vermont's statewide farmland program is succeeding in both protecting productive farmland and keeping farmers in business.

2000

- After years of work, an AFT–Farm Bureau partnership persuades Virginia's legislature to pass a Virginia farmland protection program. AFT helps shape the program and leads the charge to secure funding.

- AFT successfully fosters a landowner partnership in Colorado's San Luis Valley that ultimately protects 15,000 acres.

- To advance the idea that farmland protection is a key element of healthy communities, AFT helps launch Smart Growth America, a coalition of more than fifty influential advocacy groups.

2001

- AFT releases the first-ever public opinion poll on federal agricultural policies, finding that 85 percent of respondents agree that farmers and ranchers should be compensated for providing environmental benefits.

- AFT's holds a national conference in Illinois: Farming on the Edge: Conservation, Community & Commerce.

- AFT is instrumental in securing the first-ever federal farmland protection program dollars for Texas.

- AFT promotes local farmland protection programs in Wayne County, Ohio; Tompkins County, New York; San Luis Obispo County, California; and Kane County, Illinois.

2002

- AFT wins an unprecedented $1 billion for farmland protection in the 2002 Farm Bill. This farm bill also nearly doubles the amount of funding available to help farmers and ranchers improve soil health, protect water quality, and promote biodiversity.

- After five years of successfully operating multiple farmers markets in and around Washington, DC, AFT's FreshFarm Market is spun off as a separate nonprofit.

- AFT's *Rocky Mountain West, Strategic Ranchland in the Rocky Mountain West* report reveals that more than 24 million acres of ranchland in seven western states are under threat.

- AFT helps Washington become the twentieth state to create a farmland protection program, while securing additional funding for existing programs in California, Massachusetts, New York, and Ohio.

2003

- AFT releases *Going, Going, Gone?*, an influential study documenting the impacts of land fragmentation on Texas agriculture and wildlife.

- In the most in-depth analysis of agricultural easement programs ever undertaken, AFT documents the progress of 46 programs in 15 states through its *National Assessment of Agricultural Easement Programs*.

- Years of work in the Connecticut River Valley of Massachusetts result in *Growing Together*, a strategic plan for integrating agriculture and growth management.

2004

- Acclaimed author and farmer Wendell Berry addresses AFT's national conference in Kentucky: Farming on the Edge: Meeting the Challenge.
- Through the California Sustainable Winegrowing Alliance, AFT partners with over 600 vineyards to reduce pesticide use in the production of world-class wines.
- AFT expands its Best Management Practices (BMP) Challenge—a pioneering risk insurance tool that guarantees that participating farmers will not suffer financial losses if they follow environmentally forward practices.

2005

- After years of effort, an AFT-led campaign results in the passage of a statewide farmland protection program in Texas.
- AFT's work also leads to a new farmland protection program in Hawaii; increased easement funding in Maryland, Maine, New York, and Connecticut; an agricultural district program in North Carolina; and a tax abatement program for farmers in Ohio.
- Working with the group Shared Strategy for Puget Sound, AFT launches a new grant program to help Washington farmers stay viable while protecting salmon habitat.

2006

- AFT helps create the Texas Agricultural Land Trust.
- Years after AFT organized Connecticut's Working Lands Alliance to increase the state's commitment to farming, the Alliance becomes an official AFT project.
- AFT's *The Future Is Now: Central Valley Farmland at the Tipping Point?* report calls for California to guide growth away from the most productive farmland.
- AFT and the US Department of Defense issue a joint publication, *Working to Preserve Farm, Forest and Ranch Lands: A Guide for Military Installations.*

2007

- AFT helps craft legislation to create the new Virginia Office of Farmland Preservation and a new Office of Farmland Preservation in Washington State.
- Along with more than 100 sustainability experts, AFT helps draft *The Presidential Climate Action Plan*, with recommendations to combat climate change.
- AFT begins a series of listening sessions around the country with farmers and ranchers about emerging markets for environmental services.
- Soil conservation icon and longtime AFT advisor Norm Berg passes away. In his honor, AFT launches the Berg Special Collection, an online archive of speeches and articles.

2008

- Jon Scholl is named AFT's third president.

- Congress passes the 2008 farm bill with many improvements championed by AFT, including more than $4 billion in new funding for conservation practices and new support for farmers who grow for local markets.

- AFT launches the Mid-Atlantic Clean Water Initiative to reduce the run-off of fertilizer to Chesapeake Bay.

- AFT explores innovative water quality trading systems to reduce runoff and strengthen agriculture in the Ohio River Basin and Minnesota's Sauk River watershed.

- California passes the AFT-backed Senate Bill 375, which fundamentally changes the rules for land development to reduce greenhouse gas emissions and farmland loss.

2009

- The AFT-led Campaign for Wisconsin's Farm and Forest Lands leads to the passage of the Working Lands Initiative, which advances farmland protection and an agricultural enterprise program.

- AFT holds the first national Farmers Market Celebration to raise awareness about the importance of locally grown food.

- AFT's *Texas Land Trends Study*, co-released with Texas A&M University, sheds light on the rapid pace of land development and fragmentation in that state.

- AFT leads a groundbreaking agricultural coalition to support the Waxman–Markey climate bill (which passes the House, but ultimately fails in the Senate).

2010

- AFT directs the California Agricultural Vision project, which brings together agricultural leaders to address challenges faced by California's farmers and ranchers.

- AFT leads the New England Farm & Food Security Initiative to strengthen food and farming in the region.

- AFT launches a multiyear project in Illinois to help farmers reduce fertilizer use and to monitor resulting water quality improvements.

- AFT advances the dialogue on climate change by publishing several studies— including one in partnership with the National Association of Wheat Growers.

2011

- When Wisconsin's governor calls for eliminating the state's farmland protection program, AFT mobilizes farmers, activists, and citizens to convince the state legislature to keep the program intact.

- AFT releases *A Vision for Rhode Island Agriculture*, a strategic plan for building a stronger and more resilient farm and food system.
- AFT releases *Cultivating Maine's Agricultural Future* in partnership with Maine Farmland Trust, a guide for supporting local farms.
- AFT further expands its BMP Challenge program, helping more farmers adopt environmentally forward farming practices.

2012

- AFT helps secure over $20 million for farmland protection in Pennsylvania through the Save Our Farms campaign.
- Together with the Electric Power Research Institute, AFT launches the first-in-the-nation Water Quality Trading Program to reduce runoff into the Ohio River Basin.
- In California's San Joaquin Valley, AFT utilizes a Greenprint strategy to advance sustainable management of land and water resources.
- Key policies from AFT's *Agenda 2012: Transforming U.S. Farm Policy for the 21st Century* are included in the Senate and House marker bills.

2013

- Andrew McElwaine is named AFT's fourth president.
- AFT launches Farm to Institution New York State—a partnership to expand the amount of local food served at schools, hospitals, and prisons.
- AFT creates a seven-state Farmland Advisors program to train professionals in facilitating farm transfers and increasing farmland access.
- AFT launches a pilot *Women & the Future of Agriculture* campaign to give women landowners better access to information on conservation options.

2014

- Congress passes the 2014 Farm Bill with landmark reforms advocated by AFT, including a requirement that farmers who receive crop insurance assistance adopt a conservation plan that protects soil and wetlands.
- In Kentucky, AFT holds the Farmland, Food, and Livable Communities Conference, with a focus on farmland protection, food system planning, and next-generation farmers.
- In Massachusetts, AFT helps secure passage of the largest environmental bond bill in state history, including $20 million for farmland protection.

2015

- Ralph Grossi returns to AFT as interim president.

- The Ohio River Basin water quality trading program launched by AFT and partners wins the prestigious United States Water Prize.
- AFT's Growing Food Connections initiative helps a diverse selection of communities around the nation strengthen local food systems by supporting family farmers and underserved residents.
- AFT and other groups convince Congress to reauthorize the Land and Water Conservation Fund and to provide enhanced tax incentives for donations of conservation easements.

2016

- John Piotti is named AFT's fifth president.
- AFT is asked to join a new soil health initiative by President Obama's White House Office of Science and Technology Policy.
- Building off its "Greener Fields study," which documented how compact development and open farmland reduce greenhouse gas emissions, AFT convinces California to earmark over $100 million for farmland protection.
- AFT and partners fight to pass Maryland's Open Space Trust Fund Act, which establishes a dedicated source of funding to protect farmland.
- AFT launches an innovative Farmland Protection Pollinator Program, which supports farmers who provide habitat for bees and other wild pollinators on protected land.

2017

- AFT scales up its ongoing efforts to help women landowners adopt conservation practices by launching a new national initiative, Women for the Land.
- In Great Lakes states, AFT launches a major new project to reduce the amount of sediment and nutrients entering streams and rivers.
- AFT refocuses its Farms for the Next Generation initiative by expanding farmland-finder services and launching a nationwide training program for professionals who help farmers secure suitable land.
- In the ramp-up to the next farm bill, John Piotti is asked to testify before Congress about the urgent need to save farmland and support conservation programs.

2018

- AFT achieves a major victory in the 2018 Farm Bill, increasing federal funding for the Agricultural Conservation Easement Program by $2 billion.
- AFT releases the first phase of *Farms Under Threat*, the most comprehensive assessment of US agricultural land ever undertaken.

- AFT launches a new national initiative, Farmers Combat Climate Change, to accelerate regenerative farming practices that build soil health and capture carbon.
- To provide farmers with new decision-making tools, AFT studies the environmental and economic benefits of adopting soil health practices on farms in five states.

2019

- AFT becomes the first "impact partner" of the US Climate Alliance, a coalition of governors committed to meeting the goals of the Paris Climate Accord in the absence of federal action.
- AFT's work encouraging states to take action on climate change pays off in New York with passage of the Climate Leadership and Community Protection Act.
- AFT's Dr. Jennifer Moore provides expert testimony before the US House of Representatives' new Special Select Committee on the Climate Crisis.
- AFT launches an initiative in California that provides hands-on training to underserved populations—including veterans, socially and economically disadvantaged farmers, and farmers whose primary language is not English.

2020

- AFT creates the National Agricultural Land Network to support both public agencies and private organizations working to protect farmland.
- AFT launches a Farmer Relief Fund, which raises over $1.7 million to support direct-to-market farmers severely affected by the COVID pandemic after the closure of restaurants, schools, and farmers markets.
- AFT releases *Farms Under Threat: The State of the States*, the second phase of an ongoing study that documents farmland loss and how well state policies have responded.
- AFT creates a New England Farmer Microgrants program to help farmers access farmland, expand production, and stay viable.
- Across the nation in 2020, AFT trains over 16,000 farmers, landowners, and professionals on farmland protection and regenerative farming practices—including nearly 700 traditionally underserved farmers and more than 300 women landowners.

Notes

1. A Quiet Revolutionary

1. Georgia McIntyre, "What Percentage of Small Businesses Fail? (And Other Need-to-Know Stats)," *Fundera*, last modified November 20, 2020, https://www.fundera.com/blog/what-percentage-of-small-businesses-fail.

2. Daniel Fisher, "The Real Patent Crisis Is Stifling Innovation," *Forbes*, June 18, 2014, https://www.forbes.com/sites/danielfisher/2014/06/18/13633/#596713e96f1c.

3. Chip MacGregor, "Ask the Agent: What Are My Odds of Getting Published?" MacGregor & Luedeke (blog), April 11, 2016, http://www.macgregorandluedeke.com/blog/ask-agent-odds-getting-published/; Leigh Shine, "Calculating the Odds of Getting a Traditional Publisher," *Publishizer* (blog), Medium, December 22, 2016, https://medium.com/publishizer/calculating-the-odds-of-getting-a-traditional-publisher-798b1c7b94b0.

     There are, at best, only educated estimates about this. But it appears that about 1 in 100 manuscripts submitted to a commercial publisher ends up published. And only 1 in 10 queries results in a request to see the manuscript. Given that many publishers accept queries solely from agents, and agents are extraordinarily difficult to get, the overall odds may actually be much worse than stated.

4. Sunlight Foundation, "Only Four Percent of Bills Become Law," Huffington Post, last modified December 6, 2017, https://www.huffpost.com/entry/the-vast-majority-of-bill_n_268630.

5. Wolfgang Bielefeld, "The Challenges of New Nonprofits," *Nonprofit Quarterly*,

December 31, 2014, https://nonprofitquarterly.org/the-challenges-of-new
-nonprofits/.

6. Women in World History: A Biographical Encyclopedia, Encyclopedia.com,
s.v. "Rockefeller, Margaret (1915–1996)," accessed December 27, 2020,
https://www.encyclopedia.com/women/encyclopedias-almanacs-transcripts
-and-maps/rockefeller-margaret-1915-1996.

7. Ralph Grossi, in discussion with the author, May 4, 2019, Chesapeake Bay,
MD.

8. Note that, at the time, such a donation was not tax deductible. That rule
change would not happen until a good deal of AFT effort and several years
later. The Soil Conservation Service was later renamed the Natural Resources
Conservation Service.

9. Hence the emergence of the new property rights movement. (See "Emergency
Land Use and Property Rights Movements" in chapter 2.)

10. Debbie Weingarten, "Why Are America's Farmers Killing Themselves?"
Guardian, December 11, 2018, https://www.theguardian.com/us-news/2017
/dec/06/why-are-americas-farmers-killing-themselves-in-record-numbers.

2. A Changing Landscape

1. The Environmental Protection Agency was created in 1970; the Wilder-
ness Act was passed in 1964; Wild and Scenic Rivers Act, 1968; Clean Air
Act (expansion), 1970; National Environmental Policy Act, 1970; Marine
Mammal Protection Act, 1972; Nuclear Waste Policy Act, 1972; Coastal
Zone Management Act, 1972; Marine Protection, Research, and Sanctuaries
Act, 1972; Ocean Dumping Act, 1972; Endangered Species Act, 1973; Safe
Drinking Water Act, 1974; Federal Land Policy and Management Act, 1976;
Fisheries Conservation and Management Act, 1976; Resource Conservation
and Recovery Act, 1976; Toxic Substances Control Act, 1976; Clean Water
Act, 1972 and 1977; Surface Mining Control and Reclamation Act, 1977.

2. Edward G. Goetz, "The Big Tent of Growth Management: Smart Growth as a
Movement," in *Policies for Managing Urban Growth and Landscape Change:
A Key to Conservation in the 21st Century*, Proceedings of a Symposium at the
Society for Conservation Biology 2004 Annual Meeting, tech ed. David N.
Bengston (Saint Paul: USDA Forest Service, North Central Research Station,
2005), 45–51, https://www.nrs.fs.fed.us/pubs/gtr/gtr_nc265/gtr_nc265_045
.pdf. Much of the modern smart growth movement emerged in the 1970s
and 1980s but was not formalized under that name until the 1990s.

3. Technically, farm lending is extended based on the capacity of the farm
business to repay, not on the broader market value of the farmland offered as

security. But, in practice, a well-secured business loan application can be hard for a lender to resist and lenders can differ in their respect for the principles of business lending. In any case, this *is* how farmers perceived the situation.

4. Again, technically a farm business loan is extended based on *farm* business value. A great many farm landowners, however, do not make (or truly believe that lenders make) that distinction.

5. "Property Rights Movement," Pollution Issues, accessed December 24, 2020, http://www.pollutionissues.com/Pl-Re/Property-Rights-Movement.html.

6. Federico Cheever and Nancy A. McLaughlin, "An Introduction to Conservation Easements in the United States: A Simple Concept and a Complicated Mosaic of Law," *Journal of Law, Property, and Society* 1 (May 1, 2015): 107–84, https://digitalcommons.du.edu/cgi/viewcontent.cgi?article=1033 &context=law_facpub.

7. Cheever and McLaughlin, "Conservation Easements," 107–84.

8. "Uniform Law Commission Conservation Easement Act," Uniform Law Commission accessed December 24, 2020, https://www.uniformlaws.org /HigherLogic/System/DownloadDocumentFile.ashx?DocumentFileKey=95 e58042-e8d2-2051-1868-617b5d89a7f9&forceDialog=0.

9. An Act to Extend Certain Temporary Tax Provisions, and for Other Purposes, Pub. L. No. 96-541, § 6, 94 Stat. 3204 (1980); Daniel Halperin, "Incentives for Conservation Easements: the Charitable Deduction or a Better Way," *Law and Contemporary Problems* 74, no. 29 (Fall 2011): 20–50, https:// scholarship.law.duke.edu/cgi/viewcontent.cgi?article=1644&context=lcp.

10. Cheever and McLaughlin, "Conservation Easements," 107–84.

11. "2015 National Land Trust Census at a Glance," Land Trust Alliance, accessed December 24, 2020, http://s3.amazonaws.com/landtrustalliance .org/2015NationalLandTrustCensusReportGlance.pdf.

12. Bradford L. Miner, "Mass. Celebrates 40 Years of Keeping Farmland Open," *Telegram & Gazette* (Worcester, MA), October 25, 2017, https://www.tele gram.com/news/20171025/mass-celebrates-40-years-of-keeping-farmland -open. Massachusetts Agricultural Preservation Restriction (APR) Program (1977). "Welcome to MALPF," Maryland Agricultural Land Preservation Foundation, https://mda.maryland.gov/malpf/Pages/default.aspx. MALPF (1977). Paul Frisman, "Genesis of the Connecticut Farmland Preservation Program," *OLR Research Report,* September 9, 2005, https://cga.ct.gov/2005 /rpt/2005-R-0684.htm. Connecticut (1978). "Agriculture Preserve Board," Lancaster County Government Center, https://co.lancaster.pa.us/126 /Agricultural-Preserve-Board. Lancaster County Agriculture Preserve Board

(1980). "Farmland Preservation Program," King County, WA, accessed December 24, 2020, https://www.kingcounty.gov/depts/dnrp/wlr/sections -programs/rural-regional-services-section/agriculture-program/farmland -preservation-program.aspx. King County Farmland Preservation Program (1980).

13. Barbara Krasner-Khait, "The Impact of Refrigeration," *History Magazine*, accessed December 24, 2020, https://www.history-magazine.com/refrig.html.

14. "History of Containerization," World Shipping Council, accessed December 24, 2020, http://www.worldshipping.org/about-the-industry/history-of -containerization.

15. "Shipping Container History: Boxes to Buildings," Discover Containers, last modified May 11, 2020, https://www.discovercontainers.com/a-complete -history-of-the-shipping-container/.

16. "Why Have Containers Boosted Trade so Much?" *Economist*, May 22, 2013, https://www.economist.com/the-economist-explains/2013/05/21/why-have -containers-boosted-trade-so-much.

17. Wikipedia, s.v. "Post–World War II economic expansion," last modified December 9, 2020, https://en.wikipedia.org/wiki/Post–World_War_II_eco nomic_expansion; *Encyclopaedia Britannica Online*, eds, s.v., "General Agree-ment on Tariffs and Trade (GATT)," accessed December 24, 2020, https:// www.britannica.com/topic/General-Agreement-on-Tariffs-and-Trade.

18. "Fast Facts about American Agriculture," American Farm Bureau Federation, accessed December 24, 2020, https://www.fb.org/newsroom/fast-facts.

19. SPEX CertiPrep Group, "The Evolution of Chemical Pesticides," *Lab Reporter*, no. 4 (2016), https://www.fishersci.com/us/en/scientific-products /publications/lab-reporter/2016/issue-4/the-evolution-chemical-pesticides .html.

20. "Farming and Farm Income," USDA Economic Research Service, last modi-fied December 2, 2020, https://www.ers.usda.gov/data-products/ag-and -food-statistics-charting-the-essentials/farming-and-farm-income/.

21. "A Brief History of the Highway Transportation System in the U.S.," Supply Chain Resource Cooperative, NC State University July 5, 2006, https://scm .ncsu.edu/scm-articles/article/a-brief-history-of-the-highway-transportation -system-in-the-u-s.

22. Jerome M. Stam and Bruce L. Dixon, *Farmer Bankruptcies and Farm Exits in the United States, 1899–2002*, USDA Economic Research Service, Agriculture Information Bulletin No. 788, 2004, https://www.ers.usda.gov/webdocs /publications/42532/17750_aib788_1_.pdf?v=4.

23. Stam and Dixon, *Farmer Bankruptcies.*

24. Jayson Lusk, "The Evolution of American Agriculture," *Jayson Lusk: Food and Agricultural Economist* (blog), June 27, 2016, http://jaysonlusk.com/blog /2016/6/26/the-evolution-of-american-agriculture.

25. "The U.S. 1979 Farm Population Was 6.24 Million Or . . . ," UPI, October 8, 1980, https://www.upi.com/Archives/1980/10/08/The-US-1979-farm -population-was-624-million-or/2247339825600/.

26. "1979 Farm Population," UPI; "Farming and Farm Income," USDA Economic Research Service, last modified December 2, 2020, https://www .ers.usda.gov/data-products/ag-and-food-statistics-charting-the-essentials /farming-and-farm-income/.

27. Ralph Grossi, in discussion with the author, May 4, 2019, Chesapeake Bay, MD. Ralph Grossi recalls this term coming into use, at the time, in connection with the formation of the Marin Agricultural Land Trust.

3. An Idea Whose Time Had Come

1. Paul Kane, "How Jim Jeffords Single-Handedly Bent the Arc of Politics," *Washington Post*, August 8, 2014, https://www.washingtonpost.com/news /the-fix/wp/2014/08/18/how-jim-jeffords-single-handedly-bent-the-arc-of -politics/. Jeffords later joined the US Senate, from which he retired in 2007. He was succeeded by Sen. Bernie Sanders. In 1991, Jeffords left the Republican Party to become an Independent and caucus with the Democrats—a historic move that transferred control of the US Senate to the Democrats.

2. A purchase of development rights or PDR program is one that pays fair market value to farmers in exchange for their placing an agricultural conservation easement on their land restricting its future development. AFT has adopted the convention of referring to these as purchase of agricultural easement or PACE programs.

3. Kimberly Amadeo, "OPEC Oil Embargo, Its Causes, and the Effects of the Crisis: The Truth about the 1973 Arab Oil Crisis," The Balance, January, 30, 2020, https://www.thebalance.com/opec-oil-embargo-causes-and-effects -of-the-crisis-3305806.

4. Wendell Fletcher, *The American Cropland Crisis: Why U.S. Farmland Is Being Lost and How Citizens and Governments Are Trying to Save What Is Left* (Washington, DC: American Land Forum, 1982), https://www.amazon.com /American-cropland-crisis-farmland-governments/dp/0960789804. There was a flurry of scholarly writing on this topic in the late 1970s and early 1980s.

5. "Farmland Preservation," Suffolk County Government, accessed December 25,

2020, https://www.suffolkcountyny.gov/Departments/Economic-Develop ment-and-Planning/Planning-and-Environment/Open-Space-and-Farmland /Farmland-Preservation.

6. "Agricultural Preserve Board," Lancaster County Government Center, accessed December 25, 2020, https://co.lancaster.pa.us/126/Agricultural-Preserve -Board.

7. "Farmland Preservation Program," King County, WA, accessed December 25, 2020, https://www.kingcounty.gov/depts/dnrp/wlr/sections-programs/rural -regional-services-section/agriculture-program/farmland-preservation-program .aspx.

8. "Mission & History," Marin Agricultural Land Trust, accessed December 25, 2020, https://malt.org/mission-history/.

9. Frederic Winthrop, in discussion with the author, May, 4, 2019, Chesapeake Bay, MD.

10. Edward Thompson, email message to author, April 24, 2020. It seems likely that Wahman and Jeffords knew each other and had discussed this idea directly.

11. Ed Thompson later went on to join AFT staff, where he served in various roles, as policy director, research director, and ultimately California state office director, from which he retired in 2017.

12. Bob Gray is a principal in the national public affairs firm of Gray & Oscar.

13. "Executive Summary," *National Agricultural Lands Study: Final Report* (Washington, DC: USDA and the President's Council on Environmental Quality, January 1981), 8–20, https://s30428.pcdn.co/wp-content/uploads /sites/2/2019/09/Final_Report_1.pdf. In the words of the study, farmland losses raised concerns about the "adequacy of America's agricultural land base to provide a continued supply of essential goods and services at reasonable cost." The study pointed out that these concerns were "bipartisan and shared by both the executive and legislative branches of the federal government." "National Resources Inventory," USDA Natural Resources Conservation Service, accessed December 25, 2020, https://www.nrcs.usda.gov/wps/portal /nrcs/main/national/technical/nra/nri/. The National Resources Inventory (NRI) was a new nationwide statistical and research framework created by President Carter's Soil Conservation Service chief, Norm Berg. The NRI would later provide important foundations for AFT's work. In 1979–80, it supplied the scientific, statistical basis without which the NALS would never have been possible. Norm Berg would later join AFT's staff.

4. The Big Ask

1. "Patrick Noonan," Chesapeake Conservancy, June 4, 2020, https://chesapeake conservancy.org/teams/patrick-f-noonan/.

2. Mrs. Rockefeller was on TNC's board at some point during this time period; the exact dates are unclear.

5. Beginning the Journey

1. Edward Thompson, email message to author, April 24, 2020.

2. This would be consistent with the view that AFT would become a "Nature Conservancy for agriculture."

3. Douglas Wheeler (presentation, AFT Board Meeting, Chesapeake Bay, MD, May 4, 2019); Douglas Wheeler, in discussion with the author, Cheseapeake Bay, MD, May 4, 2019.

4. Current use taxation appraises land for property tax purposes based upon its current use (e.g., farming) rather than upon its potential future use (e.g., development).

5. MGL chap. 184, §§ 31–33. The Massachusetts Agricultural Preservation Restriction (APR) program was adopted in 1977.

6. MALT formed in 1979.

7. Ralph Grossi was one of the very first dairy farmers in America to install an anaerobic digester, which converted livestock waste into energy and environ-mentally responsible fertilizer rather than emitting methane, a highly potent greenhouse gas.

8. Frederic Winthrop, in discussion with the author, Chesapeake Bay, MD, May 4, 2019.

9. "Farms for a New Generation in California," American Farmland Trust, accessed December 25, 2020, https://farmland.org/project/farms-for-a-new -generation-in-california/. AFT has recently implemented an Underserved Farmer Outreach Program and other new work in this arena. The leadership of Lillian "Ebonie" Alexander, executive director of the Black Family Land Trust of Durham, North Carolina, and a 2019 appointment to the AFT board, may, among other things, also herald a strong future AFT role in this arena.

10. Mr. Reilly later served as AFT board chair (1996–99) and provided the thoughtful foreword for this book.

11. S. 100, Oregon Legislative Assembly (1973), https://www.oregon.gov/lcd/OP /Documents/sb100.pdf. Oregon Senate Bill 100 created the state's land use management law.

6. A New Voice in American Farm Policy

1. At least initially. Rockefeller doubtless also saw a national leadership role for the organization in the land trust community, as well as possibilities in federal policy. But the land trust role seems to have been paramount.

2. The Conservation Reserve Program.

3. Julia Freedgood, *Saving American Farmland: What Works* (Northampton, MA: American Farmland Trust, 1997), https://farmlandinfo.org/publications /saving-american-farmland-what-works/. The complete AFT Farmland Protection Toolkit is much more extensive and detailed than this list.

4. It is easy to overestimate the cost of this approach. It can be done quite strategically, over time, and in conjunction with other efforts. It is also permanent. And it offers assorted beneficial environmental side benefits that can make it well worth the investment.

5. The Nature Conservancy had also, not long before, come to the same conclusion. Douglas Wheeler, email message to John Piotti, November 11, 2020.

6. Don Stuart, "Why a Farmer Might Be Interested in Participating in a PACE (PDR) Program," American Farmland Trust and DonStuart.net, accessed December 25, 2020, http://donstuart.net/wp-content/uploads/2012/01/21 -Why-a-farmer-would-be-interested-in-PDR.pdf.

7. The 1981 Farm Bill: An Early Policy Victory

1. AFT's first offices were at 1717 Massachusetts Avenue in a space sublet, thanks to Bill Reilly, from the Conservation Foundation.

2. Jeff Stein, "Congress Just Passed an $867 Billion Farm Bill. Here's What's in It," *Washington Post*, December 12, 2018, https://www.washingtonpost.com /business/2018/12/11/congresss-billion-farm-bill-is-out-heres-whats-it/.

3. "2017 U.S. Census of Agriculture, Table 3. Economic Class of Farms by Market Value of Agricultural Products Sold and Government Payments 2017 and 2012," *2017 Census of Agriculture* (Washington, DC: USDA, 2017), https:// www.nass.usda.gov/Publications/AgCensus/2017/Full_Report/Volume_1, _Chapter_1_US/st99_1_0003_0003.pdf; "Ag and Food Sectors and the Economy," USDA Economic Research Service, last modified December 16, 2020, https://www.ers.usda.gov/data-products/ag-and-food-statistics-charting -the-essentials/ag-and-food-sectors-and-the-economy.aspx.

4. Federal Farm Loan Act (1916); Agricultural Adjustment Act (1933, 1938); Agricultural Adjustment Act Amendment (1935); Soil Conservation and Domestic Allotment Act (1936); Agricultural Act (1948, 1949, 1954, 1956, 1961, 1970, 2014); Food and Agriculture Act (1965); Agriculture and

Consumer Protection Act (1973); Food and Agriculture Act (1977); Agriculture and Food Act (1981); Food Security Act (1985); Food, Agriculture, Conservation, and Trade Act (1990); Federal Agriculture Improvement and Reform Act (1996); Farm Security and Rural Investment Act (2002); Food, Conservation, and Energy Act (2008); Agriculture Improvement Act (2018).

5. "2018 Farm Bill Primer: What Is the Farm Bill?," *In Focus*, Congressional Research Service, March 8, 2019, https://crsreports.congress.gov/product /pdf/IF/IF11126.

6. "Public policy has a great deal of impact on land ownership so it may be that the evolution [of AFT's work] in the direction of public policy was inevitable, but I don't think we really anticipated that fully at the very start." Frederic Winthrop, in discussion with the author, Chesapeake Bay, MD, May 4, 2019.

7. Federal Farmland Protection Policy Act, Pub. L. No. 97–98, 95 Stat. 1341, 7 U.S.C. § 4201 ff (1981).

8. Edward Thompson, in discussion with the author, August 8, 2019.

9. Thompson, discussion. Later, under Ronald Reagan's attorney general, Ed Meese, the Justice Department issued a subsequently withdrawn opinion to the effect that the FPPA couldn't be enforced at all, because it contained language (inserted by Farm Bureau legislators) saying it was not to be interpreted in a way that would affect private property. The Meese Justice Department claimed this would, for example, prevent the FPPA's application to siting a federal highway project because the value of the land through which the new project would pass would be affected. FPPA also included, of course, another provision to the effect that private citizens could not sue to enforce it. So there was nothing to be done to overcome this new Meese official interpretation.

10. As was documented in the National Agricultural Lands Study.

8. The 1985 Farm Bill: A Transformation in American Farm Policy

1. J. Douglas Helms, "Leveraging Farm Policy for Conservation: Passage of the 1985 Farm Bill" (lecture, Policy History Conference, University of Virginia, Charlottesville, June 2, 2006), https://www.nrcs.usda.gov/Internet/FSE _DOCUMENTS/stelprdb1044129.pdf.

2. Food Security Act of 1985, P.L. 99–198; Zachary Cain and Stephen Lovejoy, "History and Outlook for Farm Conservation Programs," *Choices*, Quarter 4 (2004): 37–42, http://www.choicesmagazine.org/2004-4/policy/2004-4-09. htm.

3. Jonathan Coppess, "Historical Background on the Conservation Reserve

Program," *Farmdoc Daily* 7, no. 82 (May 4, 2017): table 1, https://farmdoc daily.illinois.edu/2017/05/historical-background-on-the-crp.html.

4. Cain and Lovejoy, "Farm Conservation Programs," 37–42. Among the studies assembled by Bob Gray was an economic study that demonstrated that going to ten-year leases under CRP—rather than one-year leases, as in previous programs—would result in much reduced cost and the ability to protect much more land.

5. The irony of these programs' names no doubt reflects the political struggle required to pass them.

6. Edward Thompson, in discussion with the author, August 8, 2019.

7. Linda A. Malone, "Swampbuster, Sodbuster, and Conservation Compliance Programs," *Agricultural Law Update* 5 (January 1988): 4–6, https://scholar ship.law.wm.edu/popular_media/103/.

8. Helms, "Leveraging Farm Policy."

9. Tim Lehman, *Public Values, Private Lands: Farmland Preservation Policy 1933– 1985* (Chapel Hill: University of North Carolina Press, 1995), 162–63.

10. Helms, "Leveraging Farm Policy."

11. No doubt Sierra Club's new executive director, Doug Wheeler, played a part in its involvement.

12. Charles Calomiris, Glenn Hubbard, and James Stock, "The Farm Debt Crisis and Public Policy," *Brookings Papers on Economic Activity* 2 (1986): 441–85, https://www.brookings.edu/wp-content/uploads/1986/06/1986b_bpea_calo miris_hubbard_stock_friedman.pdf.

13. TRCP Staff, "Celebrating the Greatest Private Lands Conservation Initiative in Modern History," Theodore Roosevelt Conservation Partnership, December 3, 2015, http://www.trcp.org/2015/12/03/celebrating-the-greatest -private-lands-conservation-initiative-in-modern-history/.

9. The IRS Finally Acts, and a Land Trust Phenomenon

1. 26 C.F.R. § 170(b)(1)(E)(iv); Fed. Reg. 1499 (Jan. 14, 1986).

2. Edward Thompson, in discussion with the author, August 8, 2019.

3. When I became AFT's Pacific Northwest regional director in 2000, one of my first events was attending and presenting at the LTA Rally to educate and encourage their embrace of agricultural easements.

4. Douglas Wheeler (presentation, AFT Board Meeting, Chesapeake Bay, MD, May 4, 2019); Douglas Wheeler, in discussion with the author, Chesapeake Bay, MD, May 4, 2019.

5. Wheeler, discussion.

6. Robert Wagner, in discussion with the author, August 5, 2019. In both these cases, AFT was closing a regional office and did what it could to transfer its continuing project work to these new local agricultural land trust organizations.

7. Protecting agricultural lands is currently one of the top three priorities for land trusts across the nation. "2015 National Land Trust Census at a Glance," Land Trust Alliance, http://s3.amazonaws.com/landtrustalliance.org/2015 NationalLandTrustCensusReportGlance.pdf.

8. Wagner, discussion.

9. Although AFT is again accepting easements, it does so only in locations where there is no agricultural land trust or for innovative or complex projects that a local land trust would not want to undertake.

10. Wheeler, presentation.

11. *Saving American Farmland: 2017 Nationwide Survey of Land Trusts that Protect Farm and Ranch Land,* American Farmland Trust, 2018, 1–4, https:// s30428.pcdn.co/wp-content/uploads/sites/2/2019/09/AFT_FIC_Land_Trust _Survey_lo-res_01.03.2019.pdf.

10. Power at the Center

1. Ralph Grossi, in discussion with the author, Chesapeake Bay, MD, May 4, 2019; Douglas Wheeler (presentation, AFT Board Meeting, Chesapeake Bay, MD, May 4, 2019); Douglas Wheeler, in discussion with the author, Chesapeake Bay, MD, May 4, 2019. The organization knew early on that some of its greatest leverage was going to be in the policy arena.

2. As an AFT staffer, I had occasion to see Ralph Grossi do exactly this on multiple occasions. He was amazing at it.

3. Don Stuart, *Barnyards and Birkenstocks: Why Farmers and Environmentalists Need Each Other* (Pullman: Washington State University Press, 2014).

4. Perhaps the best-known example taken from US foreign policy is in the Middle East dispute. Kenneth J. Bialkin, "The Prerequisite for Peace in the Middle East: Arab Recognition of the Legitimacy of Israel," BESA Center Perspectives Paper no. 100, March 4, 2010, https://besacenter.org/perspec tives-papers/the-prerequisite-for-peace-in-the-middle-eastarab-recognition -of-the-legitimacy-of-israel/.

5. The Oregon State Farm Bureau vigorously supports the Oregon Statewide Growth Management Law, originally passed back in the 1970s. That law is also strongly supported by the state's smart growth community.

6. David A. Hoffman, "Ten Principles of Mediation Ethics," Boston Law Collaborative, accessed December 25, 2020, https://blc.law/wp-content/uploads/2016/12/2005-07-mediation-ethics-branchmainlanguagedefault.pdf.

7. American Farmland Trust, *Alternatives for Future Urban Growth in California's Central Valley: The Bottom Line for Agriculture and Taxpayers* (Washington, DC: American Farmland Trust, October 1995), https://s30428.pcdn.co/wp-content/uploads/sites/2/2019/09/FUTURE_URBAN_GROWTH_IN_CALIFORNIAS_CENTRAL_VALLEY_2ND_PRINTING_1.pdf.

8. "Oregon Property Land Use, Measure 37 (2004)," Ballotpedia, accessed December 25, 2020, https://ballotpedia.org/Oregon_Property_Land_Use,_Measure_37_(2004). *Ballot Measures 37 (2004) and 49 (2007) Outcomes and Effects*, Oregon Department of Land Conservation and Development, accessed December 25, 2020, https://www.oregon.gov/lcd/Measure49/Documents/M49_BallotMeasures37_and_49_OutcomesEffects_2011.pdf.pdf. AFT also supported Oregon Ballot Measure 49 in 2007, which remedied much of the damage done by Measure 37.

9. Jennifer Langston, "Property-Rights Initiative Being Explored," *Seattle PI*, February 24, 2005, https://www.seattlepi.com/local/article/Property-rights-initiative-being-explored-1167248.php; Eric Pryne, "Your Guide to the Property Rights Initiative 933," *Seattle Times*, October 2006, https://www.seattletimes.com/seattle-news/your-guide-to-the-property-rights-initiative-933/.

10. Grossi, discussion. Amanda Reilly and Kevin Bogardus, "Climate: 7 Years Later, Failed Waxman-Markey Bill Still Makes Waves," *E&E News*, June 27, 2016, https://www.eenews.net/stories/1060039422.

11. American Farmland Trust, "American Farmland Trust Joins Nation's Mayors in Historic Partnership to Protect Farmland and Revitalize Cities," news release, June 18, 1999, http://web.archive.org/web/20000309125822/http://www.farmland.org/news/061899.htm; "Smart Growth Network," US Environmental Protection Agency, last modified May 18, 2018, https://www.epa.gov/smartgrowth/smart-growth-network.

12. Edward Thompson, "Hybrid Farmland Protection Programs: A New Paradigm for Growth Management?," *William & Mary Environmental Law and Policy Review* 23, no. 3 (Fall 1999): 831–55.

13. Grossi, discussion.

14. Grossi, discussion. Grossi emphasized AFT's importance in administrative rule-making.

15. Grossi, discussion.

16. Jimmy Daukas, email message to author, December 29, 2020.

17. The American Farm Bureau Federation's current policy on carbon markets today is considerably more supportive. "Sustainability in Agriculture: Carbon Markets" accessed September 15, 2021, https://www.fb.org/land/sustainability -in-ag.

18. Reilly and Bogardus, "Failed Waxman-Markey Bill."

11. Helping Farmers Protect the Environment: An Emerging AFT Mission

1. An anaerobic digester is a sealed, oxygen-free system that uses microorganisms to convert livestock waste into energy and other more carbon-stable products, such as fertilizers, livestock bedding, and compost.

2. Sam Parry, "Reagan's Road to Climate Perdition," *Consortium News*, January 29, 2012, https://consortiumnews.com/2012/01/29/reagans-road-to-climate -perdition/.

3. American Farmland Trust, "President's Message," *1987 Annual Report, 1989 Annual Report, 1993 Annual Report, 1995 Annual Report.*

4. Conservation districts are small, local governments operating in communities throughout the country with the mission to preserve agricultural soils and water and protect the environment. See the website of the National Association of Conservation Districts, https://www.nacdnet.org/, for general information.

5. Francis S. Zaworski Jr., "Maintaining Agriculture's Public Image: An Opinion Survey of Agricultural Communications Leaders," *Journal of Applied Communications* 63, no. 4 (1980): 9–15, https://newprairiepress.org/cgi/viewcontent .cgi?article=1829&context=jac.

12. Launching a New Farm Policy Vision

1. J. Douglas Helms, "Leveraging Farm Policy for Conservation: Passage of the 1985 Farm Bill," *Historical Insights*, No. 6 (June 2, 2006) (USDA/Natural Resources Conservation Service, https://www.nrcs.usda.gov/Internet/FSE _DOCUMENTS/stelprdb1044129.pdf.

2. Today this agency is called the Natural Resources Conservation Service.

3. The 1990 Congress also expanded lands eligible for CRP and identified certain critical locations in the country to be prioritized. It also limited enrollment to no more than 25 percent of the cropland in any given county out of concern for potentially damaging local farm economies.

4. Doug O'Brien, "Summary and Evolution of U. S. Farm Bill Conservation Titles—Expanded Discussions," National Agricultural Law Center, accessed December 25, 2020, https://nationalaglawcenter.org/farmbills/conservation /expanded-discussions/#sodbuster-90.

5. "Agricultural Conservation Easement Program," USDA Natural Resources Conservation Service, accessed December 25, 2020, https://www.nrcs.usda .gov/wps/portal/nrcs/main/national/programs/easements/acep/; Mark A. McMinimy, *The 2018 Farm Bill: Summary and Side-by-Side Comparison*, Congressional Research Service Report, February 22, 2019, https://crsreports .congress.gov/product/pdf/R/R45525.

6. "New Public Opinion Polls Shows Strong Support for Farmers and Farm Policy," Farm Policy Facts, accessed September 16, 2021, https://www.farmpolicy facts.org/new-public-opinion-polls-shows-strong-support-farmers-farm -policy/.

7. Steven Kull, "What Americans Think about Farm Subsidies," *Globalist*, March 3, 2004, https://www.theglobalist.com/what-americans-think-about-farm -subsidies/.

8. Roman Keeney, "The End of the Direct Payments Era in U.S. Farm Policy," *APEX—Ag Policy Explained*, December 2013, https://www.extension.purdue .edu/extmedia/EC/EC-774-W.pdf.

9. Ralph M. Chite, *The 2014 Farm Bill (P.L. 113-79): Summary and Side-by-Side*, Congressional Research Service Report, February 12, 2014, http://national aglawcenter.org/wp-content/uploads/2014/02/R43076.pdf.

13. The 2008 Farm Bill: Strategic Research

1. In 2000, the Joyce Foundation in Chicago invested $400,000 for CAE to survey public opinion in advance of the 2002 Farm Bill, which demonstrated that both the voting public and farmers strongly supported more conservation funding.

2. "Average Crop Revenue Election (ACRE) Program Backgrounder," USDA FSA, last modified April 24, 2009, https://www.fsa.usda.gov/Assets/USDA -FSA-Public/usdafiles/dccp/acrebkgrd.pdf.

3. Renée Johnson, Coordinator, et al., *The 2008 Farm Bill: Major Provisions and Legislative Action*, Congressional Research Service Report for Congress, last modified November 6, 2008, https://nationalaglawcenter.org/wp-content /uploads/assets/crs/RL34696.pdf.

4. *2019 Status of State Purchase of Agricultural Conservation Easement Programs*, (Northampton, MA: American Farmland Trust, September 3, 2019), https:// farmlandinfo.org/publications/2019-status-of-state-purchase-of-agricultural -conservation-easement-programs/.

5. *2014 Farm Bill Fact Sheet: Base Acre Reallocation, Yield Updates, Agriculture Risk Coverage (ARC) & Price Loss Coverage (PLC)* (Washington, DC: USDA

FSA, September 2014), https://www.fsa.usda.gov/Internet/FSA_File/base
_acre_reallocate_arc_plc.pdf.

14. The Power of Research

1. Farmland Information Center, https://farmlandinfo.org. Center for Agriculture in the Environment, https://www.aftresearch.org.

2. Norm Berg and Robert Gray, *Soil Conservation in America: What Do We Have to Lose?* (Washington, DC: American Farmland Trust, 1984), https://farmlandinfo.org/publications/soil-conservation-in-america-what-do-we-have-to-

3. Farmland Information Center, "Cost of Community Services Studies," American Farmland Trust, September 2016, https://s30428.pcdn.co/wp-content/uploads/sites/2/2019/09/Cost_of_Community_Services_Studies_AFT_FIC_201609.pdf.

4. Timothy R. Mahoney, "The Small City in American History," *Indiana Magazine of History* 99 (December 2003): 311–30, https://history.unl.edu/docs/Faculty/pdfs/IMH2.pdf.

5. Only in those locations without a current use taxation system.

6. Farmland Information Center, "Community Services Studies."

7. Julia Freedgood, *Cost of Community Services Studies: Making the Case for Conservation* (Northampton, MA: American Farmland Trust, 2002), https://farmlandinfo.org/publications/cost-of-community-services-studies-making-the-case-for-conservation/.

8. Farmland Information Center, "Community Services Studies."

9. It can actually be much higher. The $0.16 deficit is an average for all residential properties, including those within the highly service-efficient urban core. Residential properties in sprawling suburbia tend to have a much higher service cost to tax deficit.

10. American Farmland Trust, *Farming on the Edge: Sprawling Development Threatens America's Best Farmland* (Washington, DC: American Farmland Trust, 2002), https://farmlandinfo.org/publications/farming-on-the-edge-sprawling-development-threatens-americas-best-farmland/.

11. American Farmland Trust, *Farms Under Threat: The State of America's Farmland* (Washington, DC: American Farmland Trust, 2018), https://s30428.pcdn.co/wp-content/uploads/sites/2/2019/09/AFT_Farms_Under_Threat_ExecSum-min.pdf.

12. Edward Thompson Jr., *Alternatives for Future Urban Growth in California's Central Valley: The Bottom Line for Agriculture and Taxpayers* (Davis, CA: American Farmland Trust, 1995), https://farmlandinfo.org/publications

/alternatives-for-future-urban-growth-in-californias-central-valley-the-bottom-line-for-agriculture-and-taxpayers/.

13. For a description of the California Farmland Conservancy Program, see https://www.conservation.ca.gov/dlrp/grant-programs/cfcp. The study left open the possibility of regulatory approaches such as were used in Oregon. See Oregon ballot measures 37 (2004) and 49 (2007) for example. In general, see the Wikipedia pages on this topic: https://en.wikipedia.org/wiki/Oregon_Ballot_Measures_37_and_49.

14. In Oregon, for example, the State Farm Bureau and most of the state's commercial agriculture industry strongly support the State's growth management law—believed to be the most rigorous statewide growth management law in the country. AFT has also joined the Oregon State Farm Bureau in supporting the growth management program in various statewide ballot measures over the years. "Oregon Property Land Use, Measure 37 2004," Ballotpedia, accessed December 25, 2020, https://ballotpedia.org/Oregon_Property_Land_Use,_Measure_37_(2004). AFT also supported Oregon Ballot Measure 49 in 2007, which remedied much of the damage done by Measure 37. "Ballot Measures 37 (2004) and 49 (2007) Outcomes and Effects," Oregon Department of Land Conservation and Development, accessed December 25, 2020, https://www.oregon.gov/lcd/Measure49/Documents/M49_BallotMeasures37_and_49_OutcomesEffects_2011.pdf.pdf.

15. For a sample of the substantial work done by AFT's Center for Agriculture and the Environment, see the search results for *CAE* at the Farmland Information Center website: https://www.farmlandinfo.org/search?search_api_views_fulltext=CAE.

16. Bill Ganzel, "The Chemical Age Dawns in Agriculture," Wessels Living History Farm, accessed December 25, 2020, https://livinghistoryfarm.org/farminginthe40s/pests_01.html.

17. "Summary of the Food Quality Protection Act," US Environmental Protection Agency, accessed December 25, 2020, https://www.epa.gov/laws-regulations/summary-food-quality-protection-act.

18. "Average Age of U.S. Farmer Climbs to 57.5 Years," *Farm Progress*, April 11, 2019, https://www.farmprogress.com/farm-life/average-age-us-farmer-climbs-575-years.

19. Robin Sherman, Suzanne Milshaw, and Robert C. Wagner, *Investing in the Future of Agriculture: The Massachusetts Farmland Protection Program and the Permanence Syndrome* (Northampton, MA, American Farmland Trust, Deerfield Land Trust, Franklin Land Trust, 1998), https://farmlandinfo.org

/publications/investing-in-the-future-of-agriculture-the-massachusetts-farm
land-protection-program-and-the-permanence-syndrome/.

20. Alvin Sokolow and Anita Zurbrugg, *A National View of Agricultural Easement Programs* (DeKalb, IL, American Farmland Trust, 2003, 2006), https://farm
landinfo.org/publications/the-national-assessment-of-agricultural-easement
-programs/. These programs were first enacted in local jurisdictions like Lancaster County, Pennsylvania, and King County, Washington, and in states like Massachusetts, Vermont, and Maryland.

15. Institutional Efforts

1. See the substantial Norm Berg collection at AFT's Farmland Information Center, https://farmlandinfo.org/the-norm-berg-collection/.

2. With additional funding from the Gaylord and Dorothy Donnelly Founda-tions. "Norm Berg: A Calling for Conservation," American Farmland Trust, September 1, 2007, https://s30428.pcdn.co/wp-content/uploads/sites/2
/2019/09/norm_berg_profile_1.pdf.

3. The only real way to get a feel for the value and importance of these mate-rials is to browse them yourself. I invite the reader to spend some minutes (or hours) getting lost in the FIC's amazing body of research, advocacy, and public information materials.

4. Ed Thompson, in discussion with the author, August 9, 2019.

5. This was, itself, a sign of the politically centrist promise of AFT and of the power it can leverage.

6. Julia Freedgood, *Saving American Farmland: What Works* (Washington, D. C., American Farmland Trust, 1997), American Farmland Trust, Farmland Infor-mation Center, https://farmlandinfo.org/publications/saving-american-farm
land-what-works/.

7. American Farmland Trust, news release, June 25, 1997, http://web.archive.org
/web/19971021034057/http://www.farmland.org/Farmland/files/media
/marketus.html.

8. "History of Organic Farming in the United States," USDA/SARE, October 2003, https://www.sare.org/Learning-Center/Bulletins/Transitioning-to
-Organic-Production/Text-Version/History-of-Organic-Farming-in-the
-United-States.

9. "10 Certification Agencies Creating a More Sustainable Food System," Food Tank: The Think Tank for Food, October 2015, https://foodtank.com/news
/2015/10/ten-certification-agencies-creating-a-more-sustainable-food-system/.

10. Cynthia Wilson, in discussion with the author, July 31, 2019. Wilson had in

her files a copy of the July 2, 1997, Certificate of Occupancy issued by the City of Washington, DC. It is not known whether the ambassador relented or whether City officials simply bypassed his concerns.

11. Becky Krystal, "FreshFarm Markets Founders to Retire This Year," *Washington Post*, January 7, 2015, https://www.washingtonpost.com/lifestyle/food/fresh farm-markets-founders-to-retire-this-year/2015/01/06/da71d1de-8b9b-11e4 -a085-34e9b9f09a58_story.html.

16. Local Food, Local Farms, and Local Farm Communities

1. Julia Freedgood, *Saving American Farmland: What Works* (Washington, DC: American Farmland Trust, 1997), 6–8, https://s30428.pcdn.co/wp-content /uploads/sites/2/2020/02/2_SavingAmericanFarmland-WhatWorks_Intro duction.pdf.

2. "Farm to Institution in New York State," American Farmland Trust, https:// farmland.org/project/farm-to-institution-new-york-state/; Ed Thompson, Alethea Marie Harper, and Sibella Kraus, "San Francisco Foodshed Assess- ment," (Washington, DC: American Farmland Trust, 2018), https://www .sagecenter.org/wp-content/uploads/2015/11/San-Francisco-Foodshed-Assess ment.pdf; Kimberly Libman, Amanda Li, and Christina Grace, "The Public Plate in New York State: Growing Health, Farms and Jobs with Local Food," New York Academy of Medicine, Dash NY, Farm to Institution for New York State, American Farmland Trust, November 2017, https://s30428.pcdn.co /wp-content/uploads/sites/2/2019/09/POL_PublicPlateFINAL11_1_17.pdf.

3. Julia Freedgood, in discussion with the author, October 2, 2019. This think- ing is particularly relevant given our nation's unfortunate current "red–blue" rural–urban political divide.

4. Just consider the annual profitability, market value, or rental value per square foot of vertical retail shelf space or of floor space in a manufacturing facility, an apartment building, or even a private single-family residence and compare that with what the most efficient farmer could ever hope to earn growing a crop on that same square foot of bare land.

5. Mark W. Rosegrant et al., "Climate Change and Agriculture: Threats and Opportunities," PreventionWeb (Eschborn, Germany: Federal Ministry for Economic Cooperation and Development, November, 2008), https://www .preventionweb.net/publications/view/11890; "Challenges and Opportunities for the Global Food System," Organisation for Economic Co-operation and Development, accessed December 25, 2020, https://www.oecd.org/agricul ture/understanding-the-global-food-system/opportunities-and-threats-for -agriculture/; Don Stuart, *Barnyards and Birkenstocks: Why Farmers and*

Environmentalists Need Each Other (Pullman: Washington State University Press, 2014).

6. "Nutrient Pollution: The Sources and Solutions—Agriculture," US Environmental Protection Agency, accessed December 25, 2020, https://www.epa .gov/nutrientpollution/sources-and-solutions-agriculture; Nigel Dudley and Sasha Alexander, "Agriculture and Biodiversity: A Review," *Biodiversity* 18, no. 2–3 (July 28, 2017), https://www.tandfonline.com/doi/full/10.1080/148 88386.2017.1351892; "How California Farmers Can Help Salmon Survive, and What's in It for Them," Environmental Incentives, March 4, 2016, https://enviroincentives.com/blog/how-california-farmers-can-help-salmon -survive-and-whats-in-it-for-them/; "Farmers Combat Climate Change," American Farmland Trust, accessed December 25, 2020, https://farmland .org/project/farmers-combat-climate-change/.

7. "Quantifying Economic and Environmental Benefits of Soil Health—Soil Health Case Studies," American Farmland Trust, accessed December 25, 2020, https://farmland.org/project/quantifying-economic-and-environmen tal-benefits-of-soil-health/.

8. "Risk in Agriculture," USDA, Economic Research Service, last updated June 30, 2020, https://www.ers.usda.gov/topics/farm-practices-management/risk -management/risk-in-agriculture/.

9. Jesse Colombo, "Here's Why More American Farms Are Going Bankrupt," *Forbes*, November 29, 2018, https://www.forbes.com/sites/jessecolombo /2018/11/29/heres-why-more-american-farms-are-going-bankrupt/#4cf3337 165a7; George Jared, "CDC: 'Farm Stress,' Suicides a Rising Rural Health Concern," TB&P, May 14, 2019, https://talkbusiness.net/2019/05/cdc-farm -stress-suicides-a-rising-rural-health-concern/.

10. Ann Sorensen et al., *Farms Under Threat: The State of America's Farmland* (Washington, DC: American Farmland Trust, May 9, 2018), https://s30428 .pcdn.co/wp-content/uploads/sites/2/2020/05/AFT_FUT_SAF_2020final .pdf.

17. A New Regional Presence

1. Robert Wagner, in discussion with the author, August 5, 2019. Ralph Grossi is said to have commented that what was needed, in all these regions, was a "mini-Ralph" who could adapt to local needs.

2. Wagner, discussion.

3. "Status of State Purchase of Agricultural Easement Programs—2020," American Farmland Trust, accessed December 25, 2020, State_Purchase_of_Agri cultural_Conservation_Easement_Programs_2020_AFT_FIC_.pdf.

4. "Pioneers in Conservation: Stories From the Field," American Farmland Trust, accessed September 21, 2021, http://blog.farmland.org/tag/pioneers-in-con servation/; "Advocating for Farmland Forever in the Pacific Northwest: An Interview with Dennis Canty, Pacific Northwest Director," American Farmland Trust, December 20, 2012, http://blog.farmland.org/tag/pioneers-in -conservation/.

5. AFT's Southeast regional director, Gerry Cohn, was on the founding board. "Around the Country—the Southeast Region" American Farmland Trust, December 17, 2004, http://web.archive.org/web/20041217095712/http:// farmland.org/southeast/index.htm.

6. 88 Stat. 1660 (1974), 42 U.S.C. 300 ff.

7. "New York City 2017 Drinking Water Supply and Quality Report," NYC Environmental Protection, 2017, https://www1.nyc.gov/assets/nyw/down loads/pdf/nyw-2017-dep-water-report.pdf.

8. "Watershed Agricultural Council," accessed December 25, 2020, https://www .nycwatershed.org/.

9. "San Joaquin Land and Water Strategy," American Farmland Trust, accessed December 25, 2020, https://farmland.org/project/san-joaquin-land-and -water-strategy/.

10. Kara Heckert, in discussion with the author, August 3, 2019.

11. "San Joaquin Valley Agriculture," University of California Cooperative Exten- sion: Vegetable Research and Information Center, January 3, 2017, https:// vric.ucdavis.edu/virtual_tour/sanjoq.htm.

12. Tad Brown, *Special Report: The Success of Oconee County and the Challenges of Implementing USDA Agricultural Land Easements in Georgia*, Food First, December 14, 2017, https://foodfirst.org/special-report-the-success-of -oconee-county-and-the-challenges-of-implementing-usda-agricultural-land -easements-in-georgia/.

13. Neal Wilkins et al., *Texas Rural Lands: Trends and Conservation Implications for the 21st Century* (College Station: Texas A&M University System and American Farmland Trust, March 2003), https://www.texas-wildlife.org /images/uploads/Texas_Rural_Lands_study_by_IRNR.pdf.

14. *The Washington Post* ran a three-part series on the matter in 2003, which received widespread national press coverage. David B. Ottaway and Joe Ste- phens, "The Nature Conservancy: Nonprofit Land Bank Amasses Billions," *Washington Post*, May 4, 2003, https://www.washingtonpost.com/archive /politics/2003/05/04/nonprofit-land-bank-amasses-billions/10fdb070-d956 -40e7-a508-b03483c21899/.

15. I recall that there were nearly one hundred such visits, meetings, and presentations.

16. "History of Legislative Amendments to WWRP (1990–2016)," Washington Wildlife and Recreation Coalition, January 2017, https://wildliferecreation .org/wp-content/uploads/2017/01/HistoryOfLegislativeAmendmentsto WWRP-1990-2016.pdf.

17. "Ohio River Basin Water Quality Trading Project Case Study," Electric Power Research Institute, December 2017, https://www.acwa-us.org/wp-content /uploads/2017/12/Ohio-River-Basin-WQT-Case-Study.pdf; "Ohio River Basin Water Quality Trading Project," Electric Power Research Institute, accessed December 25, 2020, https://wqt.epri.com/overview.html.

18. "Polluted Runoff: Nonpoint Source (NPS) Pollution—Nonpoint Source: Agriculture," US Environmental Protection Agency, accessed December 25, 2020, https://www.epa.gov/nps/nonpoint-source-agriculture.

19. Ann Sorenson, *Involving Agriculture in Water Quality Trading Markets* (DeKalb, IL: American Farmland Trust Center for Agriculture in the Environment, August 31, 2013), https://farmlandinfo.org/publications/involv ing-agriculture-in-water-quality-trading-markets/.

20. "Water Quality Case Study," Electric Power Research Institute, December 2017, https://www.acwa-us.org/wp-content/uploads/2017/12/Ohio-River -Basin-WQT-Case-Study.pdf; "Ohio River Basin Water Quality Trading Project," Electric Power Research Institute, accessed December 25, 2020, https:// wqt.epri.com/overview.html.

21. "Upper Scioto River Watershed—Farming for Cleaner Water," American Farmland Trust, accessed December 25, 2020, https://farmland.org/project /farming-for-cleaner-water-in-ohio/.

22. Don Stuart and Dennis Canty, *Guide to Environmental Markets for Farmers and Ranchers* (Washington, DC: American Farmland Trust, October 2010), https://www.yumpu.com/en/document/read/31679116/guide-to-environ mental-markets-for-farmers-and-ranchers; "Farmers Combat Climate Change," American Farmland Trust, accessed September 18, 2021, https:// farmland.org/project/farmers-combat-climate-change/; "Involving Agriculture in Water Quality Trading Markets," American Farmland Trust, August 31, 2013, https://farmlandinfo.org/publications/involving-agriculture-in -water-quality-trading-markets/.

23. Don Stuart, *Barnyards and Birkenstocks: Why Farmers and Environmentalists Need Each Other* (Pullman: Washington State University Press, 2014), 136 ff. For a comprehensive list of benefits to the environment and to agriculture,

see Don Stuart, "How Ecosystem Markets Can Transform Agriculture and Protect the Environment, American Farmland Trust," donstuart.net, January 2012, http://donstuart.net/wp-content/uploads/2012/01/3-How-Ecosystem -Markets-Can-Transform-Agriculture-and-Protect-the-Environment.pdf.

24. Amanda Reilly and Kevin Bogardus, "Climate: 7 Years Later, Failed Wax-man-Markey Bill Still Makes Waves," *E&E News*, June 27, 2016.

25. Alvin Sokolow, *A National Assessment of Agricultural Easement Programs* (Davis: University of California, Davis and American Farmland Trust, 2002–2005), https://www.farmlandinfo.org/national-assessment-agricultural -easement-programs.

26. *Farming on the Edge 2002* map, American Farmland Trust, 2002, https:// s30428.pcdn.co/wp-content/uploads/sites/2/2019/09/map_national.pdf.

27. Wagner, discussion.

18. Individual Land Projects: Getting the Job Done, One Farm at a Time

1. Dennis Bidwell, in discussion with the author, August 12, 2019. Bidwell credits his predecessor with having made considerable strides toward making acquisitions more strategic. But more still needed to be done.

2. National Agricultural Land Network, American Farmland Trust, accessed December 25, 2020, https://farmland.org/project/national-agricultural-land -network/.

3. Jill Schwartz, "Twenty Years of Farmland Protection," American Farmland Trust, 2000, https://farmlandinfo.org/publications/twenty-years-of-farm land-protection/.

4. American Farmland Trust, *1981 Annual Report*. (For annual reports, please contact AFT: www.farmland.org.) One of AFT's first acquisitions, the Trask Farm in Vermont, illustrates how easement acquisitions require and depend on trust. Fred Trask, a retired insurance executive, had confidence in AFT primarily because of Peggy Rockefeller's involvement, and he deeded his dairy farm to AFT, which then reconveyed it to a young tenant farmer subject to a conservation easement—an early example of buy-protect-sell.

5. *1981 Annual Report*.

6. See Dan Flores, *Coyote America: A Natural and Supernatural History* (New York: Basic Books, 2016).

7. Judy Anderson and Jerry Cosgrove, "Examples of Agricultural Easement Language," Columbia Land Conservancy, 1993, https://farmlandinfo.org/publi cations/examples-of-agricultural-easement-language/.

8. "Stephen Stranahan, 1934–2019," Blade, January 14, 2019, 2020, https://

www.legacy.com/obituaries/toledoblade/obituary.aspx?n=stephen-stranahan &pid=191242742&fhid=16222.

9. "The Upper Elk River Valley Community Plan," Routt County Planning Commission, August 4, 2005, http://www.co.routt.co.us/DocumentCenter /View/279/Upper-Elk-River-Valley-Community-Plan.

10. Right to farm laws help limit the use of nuisance and other lawsuits against neighboring properties based upon activities common to their agricultural business.

11. Colorado Cattlemen's Agricultural Land Trust, accessed December 25, 2020, https://ccalt.org/.

12. Adam Burke, "Cattlemen Make Use of a Conservation Tool," *High Country News*, June 21, 1999, https://www.hcn.org/issues/157/5083.

13. Dennis Bidwell et al., "The Case Study Area: Peninsula Township," chap. 2 in *Forging New Protections: Purchasing Development Rights to Protect Farmland* (Washington, DC: American Farmland Trust, 1996), https://s30428.pcdn.co /wp-content/uploads/sites/2/2019/09/FORGING_NEW_PROTECTIONS _1.pdf.

14. Keith Schneider, "Town Finds Rare Way To Protect Farms: Tax," *New York Times*, September 11, 1994, https://www.nytimes.com/1994/09/11/us/town -finds-rare-way-to-protect-farms-tax.html.

15. Schneider, "Protect Farms."

16. Rene Sanchez, "Farmers Make a Stand to Preserve Their Fields," *Washington Post*, May 18, 2003, https://www.washingtonpost.com/archive/politics/2003 /05/18/farmers-make-a-stand-to-preserve-their-fields/2addc98e-5e31-4a65 -9478-2d5192629776/.

17. For a complete description of Cove Mountain Farm, see the material retained in the Internet Archives for American Farmland Trust's website, accessed December 26, 2020, http://web.archive.org/web/20020206233231/http:// grassfarmer.com/cmf/welco1.html.

18. Jim Dickrell, "Licensed Dairy Farm Numbers Drop Nearly 4% in 2017," *Dairy Herd Management*, February 21, 2018, https://www.dairyherd.com /news/licensed-dairy-farm-numbers-drop-nearly-4-2017.

19. "The Love Fund," American Farmland Trust, accessed December 26, 2020, https://farmland.org/project/the-love-fund/.

20. Bidwell, discussion.

21. The Land Trust Alliance now has an insurance pool fund with Terrafirma Risk Retention Group (https://terrafirma.org/about), to which smaller local

land trusts can contribute; it covers some of the larger litigation costs that can arise.

22. Ben Kurtzman, in discussion with the author, August 14, 2019.

23. Robert Wagner, in discussion with the author, August 5, 2019.

24. Policy for Agricultural Conservation Easement Acquisitions, American Farmland Trust, adopted October 1, 2017. These criteria included the following: agricultural productivity, location in a geographic area not adequately served by another public or private program, proximity to other AFT easement properties or to an existing AFT local office, partnership with other local organization building capacity, enhancement of AFT's profile in areas with high interest in farmland protection or for other reasons, inclusion of an innovative solution to working land conservation, advancement of other AFT program work, contribution to a critical mass of surrounding agriculture or other natural resources, vulnerability to conversion, capacity to property monitor and enforce, educational or public communications potential, anticipated project cost.

25. See Ed Thompson Jr., "Hybrid Farmland Protection Programs: A New Paradigm for Growth Management," *William & Mary Environmental Law and Policy Review* 23, no. 3 (Fall 1999): 831–55, https://scholarship.law.wm.edu/cgi/viewcontent.cgi?article=1254&context=wmelpr.

19. Communicating the Message

1. In my interviews with AFT's founders, Doug Wheeler, Fred Winthrop, Ralph Grossi, Rich Rominger, Bill Dietel, and others, none of them mentioned media and publicity as a priority; all were clearly focused on how their new organization could protect the land.

2. See Doug Wheeler's comments in AFT's *1982 Annual Report*.

3. Ralph Grossi recalls having to occasionally "rein in" AFT's communications and membership professionals when they naturally tended to claim accomplishments that needed to be more carefully shared. Ralph Grossi, in discussion with the author, Chesapeake Bay, MD, May 4, 2019.

4. *Farming on the Edge* (Washington, DC: American Farmland Trust, January 1, 2002), https://farmlandinfo.org/publications/farming-on-the-edge-sprawling-development-threatens-americas-best-farmland/.

5. Ferguson was also a huge help in the writing of this book and produced the amazing timeline of AFT events included in appendix D.

6. Enid Nemy, "Margaret Rockefeller, 80, Backer of Farm and Conservation Causes," *New York Times*, March 27, 1996, https://www.nytimes.com/1996

/03/27/nyregion/margaret-rockefeller-80-backer-of-farm-and-conservation
-causes.html.

7. The last Steward of the Land Award winner was Nash Huber, a farmer from
Sequim, Washington, who won the award in 2008. Huber was also the first
Steward of the Land whose extensive organic mixed produce and livestock
products were sold mostly in direct-market venues.

8. Kirsten Ferguson, in discussion with the author, July 25, 2019. Much of the
content of this chapter was supplied by Ferguson, who is a longtime AFT
communications professional.

9. "New Public Opinion Polls Shows Strong Support for Farmers and Farm Policy," Farm Policy Facts, accessed September 19, 2021, https://www.farmpol
icyfacts.org/new-public-opinion-polls-shows-strong-support-farmers-farm
-policy/.

10. Benjamin Elisha Sawe, "The Biggest Industries in the United States," World
Atlas, August 1, 2017, https://www.worldatlas.com/articles/which-are-the
-biggest-industries-in-the-united-states.html. Agriculture ranks nineteenth
among major industries in the United States.

11. Paul Harvey, "So God Made a Farmer," convention speech, Future Farmers
of America, November 7, 1978, Kansas City, MO, YouTube video, 2:35,
https://www.youtube.com/watch?v=7UBj4Rbq3ZI.

20. Fertile Fields for Development

1. American Farmland Trust, *1981 Annual Report*, *2000 Annual Report*; John
Piotti, email message to Douglas Wheeler, November 11, 2020. Early on,
there was internal debate about how to solicit memberships. The organization
ended up hiring a consultant by the name of Dave Dawson. Despite a good
deal of staff skepticism, the initial direct mail effort resulted in thousands of
responses. There were mailbags piled up on the floors of the offices. In some
cases, generous new members would return the survey questionnaire with a
donation. One of these, an unbidden check for $30,000, prompted a quick
thank-you trip by Doug Wheeler and Will Shafroth to the donor's home on
Kauai—tough duty that resulted in a useful subsequent survey of farmland
loss in Hawaii.

2. "The Smart Guide to Donor Acquisition Campaigns for Small Nonprofits,"
Smart Annual Giving, August 2013, https://smartannualgiving.com/wp
-content/uploads/2013/08/Donor-Acquisition-for-Small-Nonprofits.pdf.

3. This was calculated using representative AFT annual reports taken at approximately five-year intervals.

4. Ralph Grossi, in discussion with the author, Chesapeake Bay, MD, May 4, 2019.

5. Cynthia Wilson, in discussion with the author, July 31, 2019. Much of the material in this section was informed by this interview

21. New Leadership and New Ideas

1. Markie Hageman, "2017 Census of Agriculture: Beginning Farmers See a Rebound," *AG Daily Insights News*, April 12, 2019, https://www.agdaily.com /insights/2017-census-agriculture-beginning-farmers/.

2. See John Piotti, "One Man's Meat," Maine Farmland Trust, June 10, 2015, https://www.mainefarmlandtrust.org/one-mans-meat/.

3. "US Climate Alliance Impact Partnership," accessed December 27, 2020, http://www.usclimatealliance.org/uscaimpactpartnership.

4. "2015 International Year of Soils," United Nations Food and Agriculture Organization, accessed December 27, 2020, http://www.fao.org/soils-2015 /about/en/.

5. Eric Toensmeier, *The Carbon Farming Solution: A Global Toolkit of Perennial Crops and Regenerative Agriculture Practices for Climate Change Mitigation and Food Security* (White River Junction, VT: Chelsea Green, 2016).

6. Hannah Ritchie, "Half of the world's habitable land is used for agriculture," Our World in Data, November 11, 2019, https://ourworldindata.org/global -land-for-agriculture.

7. "Climate Change Impacts on Agriculture and Food Supply," US Environmental Protection Agency, January 29, 2017, https://19january2017snapshot.epa .gov/climate-impacts/climate-impacts-agriculture-and-food-supply_.html.

8. "Agriculture's Role in Addressing Climate Change," Center for Climate and Energy Solutions, October, 2001, https://www.c2es.org/document/agricul tures-role-in-addressing-climate-change/.

9. For a hopeful look at the agriculture industry's current perspective on climate, see: "Sustainability in Agriculture: Climate Smart Farming: Carbon Markets: Renewable Energy," American Farm Bureau Federation, accessed September 20, 2021, https://www.fb.org/land/sustainability-in-ag.

10. "Greener Fields: California Communities Combatting Climate Change," Executive Summary, American Farmland Trust, August 22, 2018, https:// farmlandinfo.org/publications/greener-fields-california-communities-com bating-climate-change/#:~:text=American%20Farmland%20Trust%27s%20 California%20Greener,by%2080%20percent%20by%202050.

11. "Sources of Greenhouse Gas Emissions," US Environmental Protection Agency, accessed December 27, 2020, https://www.epa.gov/ghgemissions /sources-greenhouse-gas-emissions.

12. "Sustainable Agricultural Lands Conservation Program," California Strategic Growth Council, accessed December 27, 2020, https://sgc.ca.gov/programs /salc/.

13. Sanaz Arjomand and David Haight, *Greener Fields: Combating Climate Change by Keeping Land in Farming in New York* (Saratoga Springs, NY: American Farmland Trust, May 18, 2017), https://farmlandinfo.org/publica tions/greener-fields-combating-climate-change-by-keeping-land-in-farming -in-new-york/.

14. "Farmland Protection Grants Available," *Sullivan County News*, December 31, 2019, https://www.sullivanny.us/news/farmland-protection-grants-available.

15. "Farmers Combat Climate Change," American Farmland Trust, accessed December 27, 2020, https://farmland.org/project/farmers-combat-climate -change/.

16. "Solving the Climate Crisis," House Select Committee on the Climate Crisis, accessed September 21, 2021, https://climatecrisis.house.gov/.

17. "States United for Climate Action." United States Climate Alliance, accessed September 21, 2021, http://www.usclimatealliance.org/.

18. "Testimony of Dr. Jennifer Moore Climate Initiative Director of American Farmland Trust before House Select Committee on the Climate Crisis," October 30, 2019, https://docs.house.gov/meetings/CN/CN00/20191030 /110162/HHRG-116-CN00-Wstate-Moore-KuceraJ-20191030.pdf.

19. Julia Freedgood et al., *Farms Under Threat: The State of the States*, (Northamp- ton, MA: American Farmland Trust, May 13, 2020), https://farmlandinfo .org/publications/farms-under-threat-the-state-of-the-states/21. This is for the privacy protection of the hundreds of thousands of farmers who receive conservation management assistance from USDA.

20. "Analysis and Web Maps by CSP Help to Launch New Agricultural Land Protection Initiative for the U.S.," Conservation Science Partners, May 20, 2020, https://www.csp-inc.org/analyses-and-web-maps-by-csp-help-to -launch-new-agricultural-land-protection-initiative-for-the-u-s/.

21. This is for the privacy protection of the hundreds of thousands of farmers who receive conservation management assistance from USDA.

22. "Agricultural Conservation Easement Program—Agricultural Land Ease- ments." USDA/Natural Resources Conservation Service, accessed September 21. 2021, https://www.nrcs.usda.gov/wps/portal/nrcs/main/national/pro grams/easements/acep/.

23. Based upon an average easement value of $3,200 per acre and 346 million

areas of nationally significant land. From *Farms Under Threat: The State of the States*.

24. "National Agricultural Land Network," American Farmland Trust, accessed December 27, 2020, https://farmland.org/project/national-agricultural-land -network/.

25. American agriculture is a $133 billion industry (about 1 percent of US GDP). It is a part of a larger food industry worth some $1.1 trillion annually. The scale of this industry reaches far beyond what a single small nonprofit can hope to do economically at a retail level. Agriculture and related services account for some 11 percent of total US employment. See "Ag and Food Sectors and the Economy," USDA Economic Research Service, updated June 2, 2021, https://www.ers.usda.gov/data-products/ag-and-food-statistics -charting-the-essentials/ag-and-food-sectors-and-the-economy/.

26. "The Carbon Reduction Potential Evaluation Tool," American Farmland Trust, accessed September 21, 2021, https://farmland.org/project/the-carpe -tool/

27. This is a reference to the Cooperative Extension technical education role played by the nation's land-grant universities.

28. "Empowering Women Farmers and Landowners to Protect their Land and Embrace Conservation," American Farmland Trust, Women for the Land initiative, accessed September 21, 2021, https://farmland.org/project /women-for-the-land/.

29. Chuck Abbott, "On Average, US Farmers Are Aging, But a Quarter of Them Are Newcomers," *Food and Environment Reporting Network—FERN*, April 11, 2019, https://thefern.org/ag_insider/on-average-u-s-farmers-are-aging -but-a-quarter-of-them-are-newcomers/.

30. "Empowering Women Landowners to Protect Their Land and Embrace Conservation," Women for the Land, American Farmland Trust, accessed September 21. 2021, https://farmland.org/project/women-for-the-land/.

31. Jess Gilbert, Spencer D. Wood, and Gwen Sharp, "*Who Owns the Land? Agricultural Land Ownership by Race/Ethnicity*" (Washington, DC: USDA Economic Research Service, December 1, 2002), https://farmlandinfo.org /publications/who-owns-the-land-agricultural-land-ownership-by-race -ethnicity/; Leah Douglas, "African Americans Have Lost Untold Acres of Land Over the Last Century: An Obscure Legal Loophole Is Often to Blame," *Nation*, June 26, 2017, https://www.thenation.com/article/african-americans -have-lost-acres/.

32. See the Black Family Land Trust website, http://www.bflt.org/.

33. See the description of USDA dairy price support programs at "Dairy," USDA Economic Research Service, updated July 30, 2021, https://www.ers.usda .gov/topics/animal-products/dairy/policy.aspx.

34. "The NORI Carbon Removal Marketplace," NORI, accessed December 27, 2020, https://nori.com/; "Catalyze Agriculture as a Climate Change Solution," IndigoAg Marketplace, accessed September 21, 2021, https://www .indigoag.com/carbon-supporters.

35. "Regenerative Agriculture," General Mills, accessed September 21, 2021, https://www.generalmills.com/en/Responsibility/Sustainability/Regenerative -agriculture; Andrew Winston, "How General Mills and Kellogg Are Tackling Greenhouse Gas Emissions," *Harvard Business Review*, June 1, 2016, https:// hbr.org/2016/06/how-general-mills-and-kellogg-are-tackling-greenhouse-gas -emissions.

22. A New Vision for the Future

1. Don Stuart, "Voluntary Incentives—Pro and Con," "Regulations—Pro and Con," "Choosing Between Incentives and Regulations," chap. 5–7 in *Barnyards and Birkenstocks: Why Farmers and Environmentalists Need Each Other* (Pullman: Washington State University Press, 2014).

2. Evidence for this abounds. Consider the hundreds of integrated pest management projects completed over the years by American Farmland Trust's Center for Agriculture in the Environment (see "CAE's Work with EPA on Integrated Pest Management Grants," in chapter 14). Consider the farmer-friendly salmon habitat restoration projects completed through AFT's Pioneers in Conservation grants through the Pacific Northwest office, mentioned in chapter 17. Consider the numerous farmers who have secured certifications in the many environmental responsibility certification programs around the county: "10 Certification Agencies Creating a More Sustainable Food System," Food Tank: The Think Tank for Food, October 2015, https:// foodtank.com/news/2015/10/ten-certification-agencies-creating-a-more-sus tainable-food-system/; Ana Paula Tavares and Andre de Freitas, "Are Sustainable Farming Certifications Making a Difference?" *GreenBiz*, April 28, 2016, https://www.greenbiz.com/article/are-sustainable-farming-certifications -making-difference.

3. A term used fondly among AFT board and staff members to refer to the occasionally idiosyncratic nature of AFT's operating approach.

About the Author

Don Stuart is a former director for AFT's Pacific Northwest regional office (2000–2011). Before that, he was executive director for the Washington Association of Conservation Districts (1997–2000) and executive director for Salmon for Washington, a nonprofit trade association of Washington commercial salmon fishers and fish processing firms (1990–96).

Stuart graduated from the University of Washington School of Law in 1968, served as a lieutenant in the US Navy JAG Corps (1968–72), and was a trial attorney in Seattle, Washington, before leaving the practice in 1979 to personally build and then skipper a forty-seven-foot commercial salmon troller, FV *Nightwings*, which he and his wife, Charlotte, fished in Southeast Alaska (1981–89). He also served as spokesman and campaign manager in the successful defense of a Washington statewide ballot measure (Initiative 640, 1995), and was a candidate for United States Congress (WA, First Congressional District, 1996).

Stuart is the author of *Barnyards and Birkenstocks: Why Farmers and Environmentalists Need Each Other* (Washington State University Press, 2014). He has authored two mystery novels, which focus on environmental and natural resource public policy issues, in the Washington

Statehouse Mystery series: *Final Adjournment* (Epicenter Press, 2017) and *Suspension of the Rules* (Northwest Corner Books, 2021). He also authored *Small Claims Court Guide for Washington: How to Win Your Case!* (Self-Counsel Press, 1979 and 1989). And he wrote and self-published a legal research guide for attorneys: *CLEDEX: The Index to Continuing Legal Education in Washington* (1986–91).

For a collection of other research and written materials on environmental policy and land protection issues in agriculture, fisheries, and natural resources, see Stuart's website: www.donstuart.net.

Index